W9-DHL-690

The Spiral of
Capitalism and Socialism

POWER AND SOCIAL CHANGE: STUDIES IN POLITICAL SOCIOLOGY

Series Editor
J. Craig Jenkins,
Department of Sociology and
the Mershon Center for International Security,
Ohio State University

The Spiral of Capitalism and Socialism

TOWARD GLOBAL DEMOCRACY

Terry Boswell
Christopher Chase-Dunn

LYNNE
RIENNER
PUBLISHERS

BOULDER
LONDON

Published in the United States of America in 2000 by
Lynne Rienner Publishers, Inc.
1800 30th Street, Boulder, Colorado 80301

and in the United Kingdom by
Lynne Rienner Publishers, Inc.
3 Henrietta Street, Covent Garden, London WC2E 8LU

Library of Congress Cataloging-in-Publication Data
Boswell, Terry.
    The spiral of capitalism and socialism: Toward global democracy
    Terry Boswell, Christopher Chase-Dunn.
        (Power and social change—studies in political sociology)
    Includes bibliographical references and index.
    ISBN 1-55587-824-5 (alk. paper).
    ISBN 1-55587-849-0 (pbk.   : alk. paper)
        1. Economic history—1990–   2. Economic forecasting.
    3. Socialism.   4. Capitalism.   I. Chase-Dunn, Christopher K.
    II. Title.   III. Series.
    HC59.15.B67   1999
    330.9—dc21   99-16269
                                                              CIP

British Cataloguing in Publication Data
A Cataloguing in Publication record for this book
is available from the British Library.

Printed and bound in the United States of America

        The paper used in this publication meets the requirements
 ∞ of the American National Standard for Permanence of
        Paper for Printed Library Materials Z39.48-1984.

5 4 3 2 1

For Kate and Nick,
and for Cori, Mae, Frances, Daniel, and Adam

Contents

Tables and Figures

Preface

We gazed upon the chimes of freedom flashing.
—*Bob Dylan*

This book is about the decline of state socialism and the future of the world-system. Our main point is that, though the word "socialism" is widely held in disdain in the current discourse about the world's past and its future, the idea of socialism as collective rationality and popular democracy is far from dead. Indeed, we argue that this idea is necessary if the human species is to survive and progress. It may emerge under a new name and surely will take on new forms. We contend that the new form must be global, and call it "global democracy."

We see the history of the modern world-system as a history of struggles. The struggles have been class struggles between capital and labor and political struggles between core and periphery—the so-called developed and underdeveloped countries. Our point is that the evolution of the modern system has been shaped both by the techniques of power constructed by dominant states and classes *and* by peoples, classes, and nations that have constructed organized forms of resistance to domination and exploitation. The interaction of these conflicts has produced a sequence of well-known major wars and a less recognized but equally important tandem of world revolutions. War and revolution periodically reset the rules of international politics and global exchange. This set of rules forms a "world order." States, corporations, and others break these rules quite frequently, as is true of any order, but they do so at the cost of sanctions, conflict, and loss of trust. Since the world revolution of 1848, "antisystemic" social and labor movements have been strong enough to rule out some of the worst forms of domination (such as slavery and colonialism) and to set minimum limits of humane conditions that rise with the level of development. The result is a spiral of economic expansion and social progress by which the modern world-system has expanded and intensified to become the global political economy of today.

For the last 150 years, antisystemic movements have coalesced around the vision and principles of socialism. The spiral of capitalism and socialism has produced the world in which we live. We contend that it may also produce a better world in the future if the peoples of the Earth understand the structures and processes of the modern world-system and act to transform the current system into a collectively rational and democratic global commonwealth. We present a model of how the world-system has worked in the past. In addition, we present an interpretation of the history of antisystemic movements, including the socialist states, that contains lessons for the present and the future of progressive politics.

Our theory of the modern world-system is based on the scientific comparative method. We reject teleological claims about the inevitability of progress or anything else. In social relations, nothing important is inevitable. But, some things are more likely than others. We employ a structuralist and materialist theory to explain social change, but we also recognize the importance of cultural factors and theories of individual decisionmaking. Our analysis and program are not intended as some final word, even from us. We want to start a conversation that uses social science and political sensibility to formulate a response to the current ideological hegemony of neoliberalism. We are not Old Leftists recycling their vision of the working class as the sole agent of history, nor are we willing to simply jettison all the ideas of the socialist past. Our considered splicing of the ideals and organizational strategies of popular movements of the distant and recent past is presented as a proposal to be discussed.

To the charge that socialism is part of the Eurocentric ideology that has been used to oppress the peoples of the world we say this: The ideas of the Enlightenment were used to legitimate European domination, but they were not the cause of this domination. The main cause was rather the powerful military and economic techniques that the Europeans deployed. People with superior power will find justifications for expansion and domination. In order for these justifications to resonate with influence beyond the powerful, they have to be expressed in universalistic terms about the way the world works or about the content of human nature. In so doing, they sometimes ironically provide ideological arguments against domination. This was the case with the notions of equality and justice that were part of the European Enlightenment.

To abandon the Enlightenment because of the evils of its progenitor would be like forgoing one's pay because the boss is a capitalist. The notions of social justice, democracy, and freedom that are contained in the idea of socialism do not derive exclusively from the European experience, just as institutional democracy was not invented only by Greeks. Many stateless societies had institutional mechanisms for producing equality and consensual decisionmaking. People all over the world have long resisted hierarchy and sought autonomy. The problem for human societies is how to have large-scale social organization without great inequalities. The political theories of democracy and socialism have drawn on the cultural heritages of peoples from all regions of the Earth for ideas about how to structure an egalitarian human society. It would be folly to exclude the traditions of the European Enlightenment from the corpus of democratic ideas because the Europeans temporarily dominated the world.

We are sociologists who regularly trespass on the disciplines of others. In the case of this book, we are trodding on the turf of philosophers, political scientists, anthropologists, geographers, and historians. Both of us have a predilection for quantitative methods for analyzing large-scale, long-run institutional structures, but this does not prevent us from addressing questions that are not easily quantifiable. We are also persons of the left, but we realize that it is necessary to know what is true before we decide what to do about it. Thus, we value the effort to be objective even though this is fraught with difficulty. Our social science and our politics have been influenced by many friends, colleagues, and comrades. Among these, we need to mention especially the following: Giovanni Arrighi, Al Bergesen, Fred Block, John Boli, Patrick Bond, Volker Bornschier, Randy Collins, Bill Dixon, April Eaton, Michael Elliot, Andre Gunder Frank, Jonathan Friedman, Barry Gills, Wally Goldfrank, Peter Grimes, Tom Hall, Alex Hicks, Susanne Jonas, Edgar Kiser, Barb Larcom, Bruce Lerro, Kelly Mann, Kristin Marsh, Phil McMichael, John Meyer, Joya Misra, Val Moghadam, Craig Murphy, Ralph Peters, Bob Ross, Nikolai Rozov, Rick Rubinson, Stephen Sanderson, Roberta Schulte, Beverly Silver, Dimitris Stevis, Tieting Su, Peter Taylor, William Thompson, Warren Wagar, Immanuel Wallerstein, Katherine Ward, and David Wilkinson.

Terry Boswell
Christopher Chase-Dunn

Introduction: Global Democracy

The Myth of Sisyphus Is a Myth

Among the punishments in hell, the most famous belongs to Sisyphus. He is condemned to roll a boulder up a hill, only to have it roll down again just before the summit. Sisyphus perpetually struggles and is always defeated. Such is the fate of humanity, says Albert Camus in *The Myth of Sisyphus* (1991 [1942]). Camus proclaims that humanity's struggle itself gives meaning to life even if we know that the summit, or heaven, or socialism, is unreachable.

Over fifty years after publication of *The Myth of Sisyphus*, we are not only still pushing the rock but the summit is now obscured from view. Contemporary theories of the modern world, including world-systems theory as well as Marxist, feminist, and ecological perspectives, much less liberal or realist ones, appear to offer no solution to Camus's condemnation. To be sure, we now know much more about the operations of modern capitalism, especially about its history and dynamics at the global level. Decades of research on capitalist development have substantiated the reality of a world-system with steady structures, repeating cycles, and one-way trends. To change the cycles or structures would be to alter the fundamental dynamics of capitalist accumulation and interstate competition. Yet every national state is involved in accumulation and competition; every state that tried to exit the system has failed. No matter how "revolutionary," no state or bloc of states has ever had the leverage to fundamentally alter the system or to escape from it. The impression we are left with is one of the impermeability of the global capitalist system to the actions of individual states, much less of social movements or revolutions from below.

The collapse of the Soviets' self-proclaimed "second world" of state socialism reinforces the seeming impossibility of changing the capitalist

1

world-system. While Stalin soon betrayed the socialist principles of the Russian Revolution, there was always Trotsky's hope, and Dulles's fear, that genuine democratization could restore it to a viable alternative. Trotskyites and other anti-Stalinist communists supported political revolution to overthrow the Soviet dictatorship, but opposed the destruction of the Soviet Union itself. It had to be defended because the USSR proved that socialism was possible, if only it could be made democratic. The CIA under Dulles and his successors sought to destroy any democratic socialist states, the latest being the Sandinistas, as their success would prove that democratizing socialism was possible. Regardless of whether those hopes and fears were reasonable possibilities in the past, they simply no longer exist. The "second world," which never existed in reality, is now also gone as myth.

Disillusionment with the possibility of fundamental change can be found in the following tragicomic definitions of socialism:

"Socialism is the path from capitalism to capitalism."

"Lenin defined socialism as all power to the Soviets and a program of electrification—the Soviets had all the power, but the people were still waiting for the damn electricity."

"Capitalism is the exploitation of humans by humans; socialism is exactly the opposite."

These definitions of socialism were popular jokes in Eastern Europe prior to the revolutions of 1989.[1] Given the widespread antipathy toward Communist Party rule, along with the deterioration of economic conditions, the derision of the "actually existing" state socialism as experienced in Eastern Europe is not unexpected. The initial, perhaps less expected, response was an embrace of unfettered market capitalism, including fondness for the likes of Margaret Thatcher, Milton Friedman, and even Augusto Pinochet in some circles. As the capitalist market worked its miracle of creative destruction and capital concentration, revulsion against growing poverty, crime, and inequality has tempered the amour. Former Communists are now winning the elections that they formerly opposed. Nevertheless, most of the former Communists coming back into power are nationalists first, closer to Pat Buchanan than to Karl Marx.

By "state socialist," we refer to countries with a sustained sole rule by a Communist Party (CP) whose "party/state" (Bunce 1989) held most productive property (and we will use the term "communist states" interchangeably). This includes the former Soviet bloc, which along with Yugoslavia and Albania discarded the "party/state" in 1989–1992. Of the remaining state-socialist countries, China, Vietnam, and to a lesser extent Cuba have become market-driven export promoters. The Communist Party remains in control, but it is also the spearhead of the market reforms. China seems bent on becoming the next Taiwan, a fast-growing one-party state led by bureaucratic entrepreneurs with egalitarian rhetoric. Vietnam has also taken this path. Cuba has similar aspirations, although more egalitarian, but also less successful economically (in no small part due to the U.S. embargo). All three retain CP rule, but court foreign investors and encourage internal entrepreneurs. Only North Korea, perhaps best described as a communist monarchy, remains true to its Stalinist heritage. As such, it illustrates plainly that state socialism has become an imperiled and isolated residue of a failed past rather than a glimpse of the unfolding future.

Since the fall of the regimes in Eastern Europe, there has been a great deal of shouting about the triumph of liberalism, as well as a heavy dose of talk about the "end of ideology." How different this is from the demands for "real socialism" found in the uprisings of Eastern European workers in 1956, 1968, and as late as *Solidarinosc*'s demands in 1980. Nor is the antipathy confined to the former Soviet bloc. Eurocommunist parties have changed their names and endorsed social democracy. Communists in Africa are also disappearing everywhere except South Africa, where they too are becoming social democrats. Gorbachev, to his credit, tried to steer a similar path to social democracy in Russia. He failed. Yeltsin failed to offer an alternative and the destruction of the Russian economy has yet to yield to creativity, except that offered by criminals. Perhaps a social-democratic path is still possible, but only if the former Communists abandon their imperialist ambitions to rebuild the Soviet Union.

Social democracy has not reaped a windfall from the disappearance of its erstwhile competitor on the left. Without the Communist alternative, social democrats have lost much of their hold on moderates seeking a party of reasonable compromise. The "third way," which once referred to democratic routes to socialism, is now the label for British Labour's move away from socialism orchestrated by Tony Blair and Tony Giddens. Socialist rhetoric has become suspect and social democrats endure derision and despair by association, despite the long-ago break with the Stalinist path and critique of Soviet tyranny. "Socialism is dead," shout even the likes of a Ralf Dahrendorf.[2]

Against this backdrop, it may seem foolhardy to write a book about global democracy and world socialism. We are not so foolish as to ignore the tragedies of the communist states or to advocate any sort of command economy, no matter how "new and improved." The purpose of this book is to begin to develop a global politics from a *world-systems perspective*. A world-systems perspective (i.e., Wallerstein 1974, 1984a; Chase-Dunn 1998; Arrighi 1994) starts with viewing the world economy as the unit of analysis, with its own systemic trends and cycles that are discernible only over the long term, and whose major inequality is between an industrial core and an underdeveloped periphery of former colonies.

How does the world-systems conceptualization of socialism differ from the socialism that has heretofore been understood as the transformation of national societies? We hold that none of the efforts to construct socialism at the level of national societies were successful in building a self-sustaining socialist mode of production. Given the strength of larger forces in the capitalist world economy, this was never feasible in practice. Is it necessary to rethink the basic idea of socialism in order to envision it at the world-system level? This is a question we will address below.

Revolutionaries of all stripes have long faced the conundrum of seeking to overthrow a particular state when the politico-economic system as a whole is global. Attempting to transform the system through revolution seems pointless, as revolutions only change one state at a time, and because no state or bloc of states has been able to change or exit the system, transformation of the world-system has been thwarted before it could be reached. In attempting to build a "second world," the Soviet bloc found it could not separate itself from military competition or economic influence from the West, and where it did find autarky, it was cut off from scientific and technical innovation that feeds on open and wide exchange. Like Sisyphus, the struggle for social justice may in itself give life meaning and purpose for those revolutionaries who choose to shoulder the burden. But, if fundamental global change is not possible, then the goal of world revolution is absurd. We would do better to seek self-fulfillment, including that which comes from helping others, and leave the trajectory of human history to the invisible hands of uncontrollable circumstances.

Is revolution absurd? That is, are the parameters of the world-system so structurally determined as to be impervious to social action from below? Our answer is no. This answer requires seeing how socialist and other progressive movements have changed the system in the past and what the possibilities are for the future. World revolutions have repeatedly challenged and eventually changed the political rules that govern capitalist relations over the five hundred years of their existence. Abolishing slavery, liberating colonies, and winning democracy have been the three most progressive changes in the world order.

Socialists have long envisioned that each national revolution would give inspiration and support to the next until every state was socialist—a progressive domino theory. A truly new world order would then be created a piece at a time. The problem with the state-socialist countries, from our perspective, is that *they went down the path backwards*. Rather than socialist states cumulating until they produce world socialism, the institutions and relations at the global level must be changed in order to foster equality and end exploitation in every state.

Marx always conceived of socialism in global terms. In one of his last writings he condemned the program of the German Social Democratic Party for inadequate internationalism that failed to place the state within the framework of the "world market" and the "system of states" (1867, pp. 544–545). The same idea can be found in his first scientific work. He was prophetic of 1989 in the following:

> Without this [world socialism] (1) Communism could only exist as a local event; (2) The forces of intercourse themselves could not have developed as universal, hence intolerable powers: they would have remained home-bred superstitious conditions; and (3) Each extension of intercourse would abolish local communism. Empirically, communism is only possible as the act of the dominant peoples "all at once" or simultaneously, which presupposes the universal development of productive forces and the world-intercourse bound up with them. . . . The proletariat can thus only exist *world-historically,* just as communism, its movement, can only have a "world-historical existence." (Marx 1846, pp. 178–179)

The unanswered question is: How is communism created "all at once"? The answer comes in part from understanding the uneven progress of past world revolutions, which more often than not were *societal* failures. Recognizing the global progress, rather than only the societal failures, requires a conceptual leap. Contemporary progressive thinkers present convincing portrayals of the injustice of poverty and discrimination, and the evils of social, economic, and ecological crises. They also present inspiring accounts of local resistance and individual heroism. Rarely, however, is there any discussion of actually changing the world-system. None offer anything more than local resistance, marginal reforms, or anachronistic revolutionary slogans. For many progressive movements, the focus on grass-roots organizing proceeds in a theoretical context in which "globalization" is a novel event understood solely as a source of evil, something to be protected from rather than to be transformed or superseded. What is needed is a long-term historical worldview.

Our fundamental starting point is one of *global democracy.* Global democracy has a dual meaning—democracy at the global level, with democratic institutions governing the ever more integrated world economy, and local democracy, with economic management and social administration as well as politics and the state open to democratic participation. Democracy includes civil and individual human rights, without which democratic institutions are meaningless. Charles Tilly (1995) points to the importance of broad and equal definitions of citizenship for democracy, and we agree that these aspects are central. We add that rights in the economy, and links between the economy and the polity, are also fundamental to any conception of democracy that can actually produce social justice and equality. For us, democracy encompasses political, social, and economic realms, rather than posing an artificial separation among them. However, we realize that democracy, and socialism, are contested concepts.

To some, democracy only means the effective functioning of popularly elected government and political rights. This institutional definition explicitly excludes economic democracy. In highly unequal, class-divided societies the result is an elected polyarchy. This is the kind of democracy that exists in the United States and is promulgated worldwide by the U.S. Endowment for Democracy as the political basis for the neoliberal globalization project (Robinson 1996). Wealthy elites compete with one another at enormous cost to engineer popular support to elect political leaders. Engineering popular support involves massive advertising, but we recognize that it also requires economic growth and social insurance for the electorate. Popular influence on the state and real benefits to the populace are undeniable, even if those who own most of the economy and fund most of the electoral campaigns have far greater influence and receive far greater benefits than the rest. Found in varying forms throughout the core, this kind of democracy is thus greatly superior to the more authoritarian regimes that have predominated in the periphery and semiperiphery. It is nonetheless greatly inferior to substantive popular democracy in which the people actually have powerful influence over the decisions that affect their lives.

As a political and theoretical concept, the term "global democracy" is a global analog for the societal term "social democracy" as it was understood prior to the rise of the communist states. Before World War I and the Bolshevik Revolution, "socialism" and "social democracy" were interchangeable terms. Our definition of socialism is a theory and a practice of progress toward the goals of steadily raising the living standards and ensuring the basic needs of the working class, expanding the public sphere and community life, and eliminating all forms of oppression and exploitation. Global democracy assumes a democratic and collective rationality that promotes greater equality between as well as within countries, greater international cooperation and an end to war, and a more sustainable relationship with the biosphere. Such a system must be democratic because social justice can only be conceived as an expression of the will of the people. Undemocratic socialism is simply not socialism regardless of the good intentions of its creators. Our conception of socialism contrasts with the common one that defines it as collective ownership of the means of production, with the state usually understood as representing the collective will. This is a societal conception of socialism, which we will argue did not work in part because it *was* a societal conception of socialism. We will contend that it is neither desirable nor applicable at the global level.

Even with societal conceptions of socialism, state ownership was in theory never a goal in itself, only a (supposedly temporary) means for achieving socialist goals in the face of hostile opposition. With the advent of the communist states and parties, progressive movements took several different paths, with the main distinction being between reform and revolution. We will discuss the historical twists and turns of socialist politics at a later point. What is important here is to note that, from a world-systems point of view, the split between the Second and the Third Internationals that accompanied the Russian Revolution should have been merely a tactical difference, not a strategic one. Building socialism in the core can proceed legally because core politics are usually democratic. Building socialism in the semiperiphery usually requires the revolutionary taking of state power because semiperipheral states have rarely been democratic (although this is changing). This difference of means evolved into a difference of ends in which the revolutions in the semiperiphery that gave us communist states never achieved democracy, either political or social. They instituted a centralized command economy, based on a military model that was justified, if at all, by geopolitical necessity and the desire to catch up with the capitalist core states, but bore only a rhetorical resemblance to socialism.

In the core, socialists exercised power through the combination of electoral politics and union bargaining in a "democratic class struggle" (Korpi 1983). The best examples are found in Sweden and Norway, to a lesser extent in Germany and Austria, and in some odd ways, France. Although far from constructing complete socialism, of all the countries in the world, they have come closest to attaining socialist goals listed above. In this sense, social democrats have come closer to achieving socialist goals than did any of the countries in which communist parties took power. Even in classic Marxist terms of "surplus value," rates of class exploitation were higher in the former communist states than among the social democracies. To be sure, social democracy fails to change the logic of global capitalism and is limited to marginal reforms within it (and we will contend that those limits have grown tighter of late). But what may be marginal differences among states would be a major transformation of the world-system as a whole. It is in this sense that global democracy is the most desirable and possible at the level of the whole system.

An enduring distinction within social democracy is whether it is possible to achieve socialism through progressive reform of a society or whether reformed capitalism is the best that can be achieved. The latter position has been in the ascendance since World War II (with an added boost since 1989). This has led to the use of the term "democratic socialists" by those who hold to the possibility of a truly socialist system. From a global perspective, we agree that reformed capitalism is the best one can hope for within a single society as long as it exists in the context of the continuing predominance of the world capitalist system. But, democratic socialism is a real possibility for the world-system as a whole. National states are inherently limited in any attempt to fully exercise democratic control over their slice of the world economy. Only world socialism is possible because only a global democracy can govern transnational relations. As a global phenomenon, we will argue that world socialism is inherently limited to very broad parameters of directing capital investment and economic development within a *market* framework. While a command economy has proven to be a societal failure, globally it would be absurd. Both the means and the goals of socialism are important. Basic needs, sustainable development, social justice, and peace are the goals. Global democracy is both a means and goal.

What Is Possible?

Much of this book is about the future of the system, not so much as a prediction of what will happen, although we speculate accordingly, but primarily on what futures are possible. This involves understanding the prospects and possibilities for global change. The collapse of the former state-socialist countries in Europe, along with the rejection of Marxist-Leninist parties throughout most of the rest of the developed world, has left the impression that defeating capitalism and eliminating exploitation is utopian. For socialism of any type to be a reasonable topic, one must not only demonstrate that capitalism is exploitative and that socialism would be a better alternative, but also that achieving world socialism is *possible*.

Goran Therborn's (1980) classic study of ideology explains that any worldview is defined by the answers to the following three questions: "What exists?" "What is good?" and "What is possible?" Determining "what is possible" is the ultimate defense of the status quo. One can empirically demonstrate that exploitation exists and that it is unfair even by capitalist standards of justice, but the goal of eliminating exploitation is irrelevant if that is not possible. The "end of ideology" does not occur, as Fukuyama (1992) suggests, because the evils of capitalism have been muted (quite the contrary) or because the class struggle is no longer a central facet of capitalism (even more the contrary). Rather, socialism has become a suspect ideology, no matter how carefully one constructs a societal model of "real socialism," because past theories no longer seem to have a viable path toward its future realization. The lack of a "utopian" goal against which to organize criticism and more importantly, to direct progress, has led erstwhile progressives and leftist intellectuals into the nihilism and endless relativism of postmodernism (Jameson 1991). Getting past this impasse requires a theory of a realistic alternative at the global level, which we find in the idea of global democracy.

Academics are often reluctant to speculate or predict; our primary job is to explain and educate. Simple extrapolations from what happened before often produce a mechanical notion of history that belies the importance of new departures or cumulative developments. Earlier efforts to scientifically understand the prospects for socialism have been flawed by assumptions of teleology or inevitability. We are properly cautious regarding statements about the future, and we eschew inevitability and teleology. We also are careful with the notion of "progress," though we do not throw it away as have so many others. We cannot predict outcomes exactly or entirely, but structural theories can predict when social conflicts or contingent actions are more likely to influence the course of history. Explanation of the limits on future actions and predictions about probable outcomes given differing conditions has immense value not just for policymakers, but for each of us seeking greater self-determination and a more progressive direction to world history. We hope that our sensitivity regarding the limitations of using theories to discuss the future will permit a degree of tolerance on the part of the reader. Hubris is a danger, but so is reticence.

A good example is the revolution(s) of 1989, which world-systems theory could have predicted, and some did hint at, but all failed to proclaim.[3] Frank (1980) and Chase-Dunn (1982) explained that the communist states had never escaped the powerful military and economic forces of the larger capitalist world-system despite their strong effort to create an alternative and separate socialist world-system. Instead, state communism had become a political program for catching up with the core of the capitalist world-system. Both also separately predicted that the communist states were being increasingly reintegrated into the world market and would become more like other capitalist countries over time, but they did not offer a time frame or predict the revolutions of 1989. Arrighi, Hopkins, and Wallerstein (1989a), in a collection of papers written during the 1980s, explicitly predicted that the decline of U.S. hegemony would have a mirror effect on the East, with the implication being that the Soviet bloc would break up. They too failed to offer a time frame or to predict revolutions. Boswell and Peters (1990, see their footnote 1), writing in the summer of 1989 about the revolts in Poland and China, predicted that they would spread to other state-socialist countries, a prediction that became an outcome by the time of publication. They also hinted that ethnic nationalism would break up Yugoslavia and the Soviet Union. While they predicted revolts, their proximity to the events makes this less surprising, and they did not predict that the other states would fall so quickly.

The failure to predict the fall of Soviet Communism by world-system theory is one of the motivations for this book. This failure was partly a reticence to recognize the importance of making predictions—as much a lack of willpower as an absence of insight. World-systems theories imply greater systemic volatility during periods of economic transition and when no core state is hegemonic over the world economy. Having entered such a period, the value of making predictions about structural opportunities increases dramatically for social movements. Even though we remain scientifically skeptical of predictions, especially at the level of events, the world-systems perspective gives us a powerful tool for visualizing future structural alternatives. This is a politically important task that we urge others to take up as well.

The association of the idea of progress with legitimating capitalism and imperialism has led many contemporary thinkers to discard it altogether. We recognize that progress is a normative concept, not a scientific one. We also recognize that the ideology of progress has been used to justify exploitation and domination. Yet it is nonsense to think that no progress has occurred under capitalism or that no progress is possible. Stephen Sanderson provides a sensible discussion of the notion of progress in connection with long-term social evolution (1994, pp. 337–356). He reasons that considerable consensus is possible among humans regarding the basic elements of a desirable life (health, longevity, autonomy) and thus movement toward attaining the conditions that make these elements possible can be called progress. Sanderson also contends that the evolution from hunter-gatherer societies to agrarian civilizations produced little in the way of progress in this sense for the masses of mankind. However, we agree with Sanderson, and with Marx, that capitalism and the resistance to exploitation that it has engendered have produced changes that ought to be called progressive.

Capitalist accumulation requires economic expansion, yet produces recurring cycles of recession and stagnation. The combination of upward trend and cycle produces a spiraling growth in productive forces that, however unevenly, always offers periods with the possibility of improving people's lives. How much they improve depends on how much of the increase in productivity working people can claim, which is the twin result of market competition and class conflict. While workers in general, and core workers in particular, have improved their lives, it does not follow that capitalism is the best possible system for doing so. Our purpose in writing this book is to show how an even more progressive civilization can be built.

Our theoretical perspective tells us that the solution to current woes lies in *transnational politics*. This focus on world politics means more than just a shift in emphasis. We are also suggesting that politics at the world-system level are more important than was true previously. Global institutions, more than at any time since the origins of capitalism, are directly governing the modern world-system. This has ironically become almost a truism, and yet the muddle of current events and discussions of globalization has produced little clarity of vision regarding possible structural outcomes and sensible strategies.

Our overall stance can be summarized by the following ten points:

1. Capitalism is a global system with a single world economy but multiple competing states. The system is marked by long-term cycles and trends, and is most subject to change by war and revolution during world divides, when the cycles are in transition. This has produced a series of world orders in which the rules and standards of international relations are enforced by hegemonic power and/or core consensus.

2. World revolutions have altered the world order. From the elimination of slavery to the end of colonialism, a rough and tumbling spiral between socialist progress and capitalist reaction has resulted in higher living standards and greater freedom for working people. Fundamental change in the system happens only at the global level. For socialism to replace capitalism, it too must be a global system that embraces a democratic world polity.

3. Building socialism one state at a time is doomed by the costs of transition. State socialism was primarily a strategy for economic development within the system, not an alternative to it. Communist parties came to power in semiperipheral regions and employed strategies that were similar to those of other semiperipheral states that were attempting upward mobility (e.g., trade protectionism, import substitution).

4. State socialism successfully produced economic development until the long stagnation that began around 1968. Stagnation forced industries to restructure in order to restore growth. In communist countries, where the state owned the means of production, this also required restructuring the state itself.

5. The communist states of Eastern Europe housed three internal contradictions that imploded under the pressures of a stagnant world economy and changing social structure of production. Those contradic-

tions were a polity that failed to represent popular interests, yet bore sole responsibility for all social grievances; a development strategy whose initial gains were based on investing in a mass-production model, but continued application of the same model produced economic stagnation and social dissent; and a distribution system that guaranteed jobs and welfare but generated consumer shortages and technological backwardness.

6. In the core industrial countries of Western Europe, North America, and Japan, the long stagnation of the 1970s to early 1990s drove manufacturing to dramatically increase the pace of transnational integration. The growing integration of the world economy has a contradictory effect on states, encouraging them to both shrink and expand at the same time. One result is a growing number of small nations that have their own state. The other is the development of multistate organizations, such as the European Union, that have the potential to become the next hegemon. Growing integration and international organization is also producing an increasingly powerful world polity. A strengthening world polity increases the possibility of transnational organizing.

7. Increased transnational capital mobility produces new waves of short-term immiserization and long-term environmental degradation. Global democracy is not the only strategy open to contest transnational capital. The first response has typically been nationalist. Economic nationalism rather than global democracy has been the most frequently employed counterstrategy for contesting the rule of transnational capital in the past and it will undoubtedly be revived for the next round as well. Denying national identities, even in favor of human universalism, will only inflame ethnic resistance and stall the growth of a true world polity. While we do not rail against nationalism, it is important to stress that going it alone does not do the job and that nationalistic strategies can easily devolve into racism and xenophobia. The strategy of globalization from below values internationalism without attacking the validity of national identities.

8. Global democracy is the equivalent of social democracy at the world level. It is both the first step and the primary goal of world socialism. All other benefits for working people, from environmental protection to banning child labor, flow from their ability to contest the standards and rule of the world order. Most important is the development of a true people's World Bank that would direct investment and adjust interest rates in order to support environmentally safe production for human needs and work to balance development worldwide. The World Bank and other socialist institutions would operate through the world market and through the collective action of national states. No world state could "command" the world economy, nor succeed at denying

national identities. Global democracy also means the democratization of all national states, which along with the development of a united peace-keeping force, could stop the cycle of world wars.

9. Peripheral and semiperipheral workers in industrializing countries are the most motivated agents of global democratic relations; core labor has been the strongest political force opposing capital mobility that degrades labor standards. A strong core-periphery alliance of popular forces is a necessary requisite for building more egalitarian institutions worldwide. Labor, environmental, and women's movements are increasingly transnational in response. At the global level, these progressive movements share key interests and goals that make them inherently intertwined, with democratization at the center of the cord. This is quite different from the labor internationalism of old in which leaders occasionally have meetings. Rank-and-file understanding and interaction across national, cultural, racial, and religious borders can facilitate cooperative action. This kind of direct linking is increasingly feasible with the dramatic decline in communication costs, but it will not happen automatically. One start would be to focus on issues of wide concern, such as child labor and environmental destruction, forming alliances with transnational women's and environmental organizations.

10. The contemporary transnational drive toward heightened exploitation can only be checked by transnational politics. Global labor standards, environmental regulations, and women's rights form a single starting point. Through institutions of global democracy, labor and allied movements can direct market competition away from cheaper wages and toward increasing human productivity. In world historical terms, this is the essence of the term "progressive."

What Follows

We apply our global perspective in three parts. The first explains the structural dynamics of the system, outlining the possibilities as well as the constraints on political agency. The second explains the great failures as well as the limited successes that were the outcome of the effort to build a state-socialist "second world." The third explores the possible futures of the world-system, and how to move toward global democracy.

In order to do these things, we need first to make explicit our definition and model of the normal operation of the capitalist world-system (Chapter 1). We describe the structures, cycles, and trends of the capitalist world-system. Those who are familiar with world-system literature will find that we offer a condensed interpretation of the basic principles, with a few new slants. We differ here from other world-system theorists (including some of our own previous work) by taking a much more political view of the construction and reproduction of the system, including a theory of world revolution. The world-systems perspective has often been criticized for overemphasizing structure and for ignoring agency. We formulate the microfoundations that underlie the edifice of world-system theory, that is, the actions and interactions that constitute and change world structures. We do this by drawing on concepts of rational material action and unintended social interaction from "analytical Marxism" and from the institutional theories of "world order." We also draw on the insights produced by comparing the modern world-system with earlier, smaller intersocietal systems (Chase-Dunn and Hall 1997).

War, and to a lesser extent, colonial conquest, have been the main political foci of past work. We expand on these and add a new stress on agency in the form of social movements and revolutions for explaining world historical outcomes (Chapter 2). World revolutions, in which new global institutional arrangements are initiated and past institutional changes are consolidated, result when the effects of social revolts are widespread or widely emulated throughout the core of the world-system. World revolutions tend to be progressive, in the sense that they shift labor market competition away from lowest wages and toward highest productivity—such as the world revolution of 1848 that ushered in the end of slavery and the beginnings of labor unions. Since 1848, world revolutions have revolved around the issues of socialism.

The most recent world revolution occurred in 1989. Applying a world-systems perspective to the revolutions of 1989 compares these events to prior social transformations in the governance structure of the world economy (Chapter 3). For the first twenty years, forty in the Soviet Union, state socialism was a successful strategy for promoting rapid industrial development. To Third World countries that had been shackled by Western colonialism, the "socialist path" once appeared to promise development, equality, and independence. Yet the socialist states faltered badly in the late 1960s, finally resulting in an economic crisis so deep as to make them vulnerable in 1989 to the spread of popular revolution. What happened in those last twenty years to undermine and eventually topple state socialism? Why was the industrial rise of these states temporary? What can we learn from this failed experiment, both in why it failed and where it managed some success?

One might say that we perform a biopsy on state socialism, rather than the autopsy that most specialists are performing, because a world-systems view shows that the communist states never left the system. Communist states never constituted an alternative "second world," but rather were always states pursuing a specific political strategy for development within the system. The next questions we confront are: How did the state-socialist strategy compare to other strategies and what were the consequences of 1989 for other socialist movements? We offer a world-historical explanation of the relationship between capitalism and socialism in interaction with one another (Chapter 4). By lifting the unit of analysis from societies to the world-system, we seek to place the life history of state socialism in a systemic context. We review the sources of socialist and other progressive movements' past successes, and their current demise. Eastern European specialists will discuss, debate, and describe in great detail the unique sources of revolt in each country for decades to come. Our mission is to focus on a different level of reality and a greater scale of time.

We argue that economic development and social progress are neither linear, as some modernization theorists might have it, nor cyclical, as some Marxists might imply, but rather both. The combination of linear and cyclic processes produces a *spiral*. Hegemonic and economic cycles repeat the opportunity for social change as existing organizational structures break down. But the conditions of cyclic breakdown and the opportunities they produce are always different, depending on the current state of the ongoing development of the system. The future is never predetermined, and it often gets worse instead of better, but the opportunities for transformation are greater at each critical turn in the spiral.

Turning to a consideration of the leftist impasse imposed by postmodern worldviews, we explore how world socialism might be realized (Chapter 5). While some may contest that capitalism was global in its origins, few dispute the transnational nature of contemporary capitalism. The degree of capital mobility has increased dramatically in the last twenty years, producing a qualitative change in class relations and production systems comparable to the development of assembly-line mass production a century ago. State socialism, which originated as a response to the mass society of assembly-line industrialization, has followed its progenitor into the grave. The Left has been left in a postindustrial, postmodern fog without a vision of what is ahead, only a strong conviction that it will be different from what has passed. We examine two such visions: Warren Wagar's utopian vision of a world commonwealth and John Roemer's analytic vision of market socialism. Then we combine elements of both to offer our own portrait of market socialism on a world scale.

Finally, we turn back to the future (Chapter 6). Changes in world capitalist production, combined with the decline in U.S. hegemony and end of the Cold War, reveal the impotence of any state, including any communist state, to fully control its domestic portion of the world economy. In the past, mobility offered international capital an escape from political control. This was a defining contrast of world capitalism with world empires. The upsurge in capital mobility and interdependence, while lessening the importance of national states, is increasing the importance of, and benefits from, interstate authority, choking off capital's own escape route from political authority. The result has been a concomitant intensification of global institutions with intrastate authority. We have seen a meteoric rise of international governmental and nongovernmental organizations since World War II (Boli and Thomas 1997).

The world capitalist system emerges from this presentation as a single world economy with an emerging global polity. With the increasing development of global intrastate institutions comes a rapid rise in the transnational politics of world governance. We pay particular attention to transnational labor movements, as labor has always been the prime mover in major social transformations. The combination of structural constants, cycles, and trends produces a model of world-system structure that is reproducing its basic features while growing and intensifying. For socialism to transform capitalism, it too must be a global system, one that embraces worldwide democracy.

Notes

1. These jokes were repeated by a first-time panel of Eastern European scholars convened at the 1990 Convention of the International Studies Association in Washington, D.C.
2. Stated in 1990, as quoted in Kumar 1992, p. 309.
3. Randall Collins, utilizing a geopolitical model, did predict the demise of the Soviet Union within fifty years, but offered little insight into its social origins (Collins and Waller 1992).

I

The Political Economy of the Capitalist World-System

Global structures are huge, beyond the existing organizational capacity of firms, societies, or states to control them (see Tilly 1995), and global cycles and trends occur over the *longue duré*, beyond the perception of a single generation (see Braudel 1984). As such, global processes are rarely the result of conscious human determination, but rather the immanent result of interaction conceived at more proximate levels of perception.

Extant research has, therefore, focused on identifying and explaining structural dynamics through large and long-term comparisons. About individual psychology, perception, or consciousness, little is said. To connect world-systemic structure and dynamic to individual agency, there remains an implicit assumption in such research that individuals respond to global parameters in a materially rational manner. That is, global structures provide resources and incentives for, and place limits and disincentives against, material needs and goals of the most basic type, starting with the simple biological ones such as food and shelter, or pain and death. For the most part, people are rational actors who use the resources and opportunities available to them in order to fulfill their material needs and goals, and to avoid pain and other disincentives. If one explains the structure of resources and opportunities available to people, then material rationality of the simplest form will explain some consistent patterns of resultant behavior amidst the varying multitudes of individuals. The pattern may only be a tiny fraction of all behavior, but it should exist across different national cultures and group identities wherever the structure weighs heavy. To be sure, there is substantial variation within these broad parameters, but the greater the integration of the world-system, the more important its structure of resources and opportunities.

This sort of material rationality is an assumption so basic to most structural explanation that it is rarely noticed or acknowledged. It is adequate for most research on global processes, as the effects are mediated through a host of intervening institutions, and thus only broad long-term consequences can be observed. The problem arises when one wants to explain how people's actions forge global structures, and more importantly, how they can *change* the world-system. In order to move the system in some direction, social movements cannot be determined entirely by those same processes that they are trying to change. Active human agency, conscious of its purpose, is required for a theory of global change, even if the actor's purpose differs from the eventual result. Social movements constantly try to change some part of the system, and occasionally they succeed, although often in unintended ways. In order to explain the social and institutional interactions that produce emergent structures, it is necessary to complete the full causal logic of determination in its most basic form as follows: STRUCTURE→AGENCY →INTERACTION→INSTITUTIONS→STRUCTURE→.

Completion of the logical sequence entails better theoretical understanding of the microfoundations of the system, especially what structures and processes enable action, as well as those that constrain choice. In order to do so, we expand upon the edifice of world-systems theory by adding a focus on the microfoundations of rational action and unintended social interaction. For this purpose we draw on concepts from the following three schools of thought that approach the relationship of structure and agency at different levels of interaction: "analytical Marxism" (Mayer 1994; Roemer 1982; Wright 1985; Przeworski 1985, 1991; Bowles and Gintis 1990; Boswell and Dixon 1993), and institutional theories of "world order" and "world polity" (Krasner 1985; Holsti 1991; Meyer 1999; Boli and Thomas 1997; Boswell 1995; Ruggie 1998).

Our notion of material rationality begins with the premise that over the long term, people who fail to conform rationally to the dictums of wealth and power lose both. The prime sources of wealth and power are capitalist firms and markets, and state judiciaries and armies, and the relationships to capital and to the state (i.e., class and citizenship) are prime determinants of one's material interests. Our notions of rationality differ from classic rational-choice theory, however, by recognizing that cultural values and norms are often socially constructed in noninstrumental ways. The flows of information that people use to make decisions are highly skewed by one's material relationships (class and citizenship) and by one's group networks and localities (i.e., nationality, race, gender, etc.). As such, ideologies, that is, conceptions of what exists, is good, and is possible (Therborn 1980), differ by relationships and groups, even though most all the people in those relationships and groups are reacting rationally based on the (skewed) information available to them. Most importantly, people encode their interests and ideologies into institutions with varying amounts of the resources and authority to enforce both. Once formed, institutional patterns persist as long as the institutions can muster resources and maintain authority. In so doing they continue to skew information flows and shape ideologies well beyond their origins or original purposes.

At the global level, the world-system has seen a succession of "world orders" with weak institutional patterns based on the current joint interests of the great powers. For the first time ever in world history, the intensified integration of the system is producing a much stronger set of global institutions, a "world polity" of shared cultural conceptions and norms (Meyer 1999; Ruggie 1998). This world polity is potentially capable of directing the processes of the modern world-system. How and why that world polity is forming, and what potential it has for transforming the world-system, is our constant theme, even though our initial focus is on immanent structures, trends, and cycles of unconscious design.

We outline those structures, trends, and cycles in the next section. Those familiar with world-systems literature will find that we offer a condensed interpretation of the basic principles (for elaboration, see Chase-Dunn 1998). However, given our purposes, we differ here from previous work (including our own) by placing greater emphasis on the *political* side of the political economy of the system. This emphasis will be even more evident as we continue in the subsequent chapter with a discussion of world revolutions.

Three Structural Continuities

A world-system is a network of individuals organized in myriad ways—households, status groups, associations, communities, cities, firms, unions, bureaucracies, parties, nations, and states—that are interlinked by an interstate system and a world market. In the modern world-system, these networks cluster into the following three global "zones": core (industrialized, former empires), periphery (agrarian, recently former colonies), and semiperiphery (industrializing, long-independent states, and former small empires). Not all world-systems—or intersocietal systems—are global. In fact, the Europe-centered system only expanded and incorporated all parts of the Earth into itself in the nineteenth century. Before that there were many regional intersocietal systems that were substantially autonomous from one another. These shared some structural similarities with the European, now global, system. Many of them had core-periphery hierarchies in which core regions, usually those areas with the biggest cities and the strongest states, dominated and exploited adjacent peripheral regions.[1]

The Europe-centered system was different in one essential way, however. It was in Europe that capitalism became the dominant mode of accumulation, and this fundamentally altered the nature of the interstate system. The earlier tendency was for interstate systems to be turned into world-empires through conquest by semiperipheral marcher states, such as the Macedonian, Roman, or Mongol Empires. Capitalism was transformed into an interstate system in which hegemonic core states rise and fall but do not create core-wide empires (Chase-Dunn and Hall 1997).

We can describe the continuities of the modern world-system by pointing to several structural features that exist at the level of the system as a whole. Three structural constants define the current world-system: a capitalist world economy, an interstate system, and a core-periphery hierarchy. These are the essential elements of the system and no fundamental transformation can occur without replacing these elements. Although actors change position within them, these structural features of the modern world-system are continuous and continually reproduced. Further, while the scale of the system increases as it expands, the structures have gotten larger without fundamentally changing.

The Capitalist World Economy

Capitalism is the accumulation of resources by means of exploitation in the production and sale of commodities for profit. Capitalist exploitation is an unequal exchange wherein capitalists extract income from economic exchanges solely because they hold legal title to productive assets. There are two types of exploitation—primary and secondary. Primary exploitation, which takes the form of profit, is an unequal exchange with labor wherein capitalists appropriate all the "value added" in production, net of wages, because they own the business in which the production took place. "Value added" is the difference between the price of a product and the price of everything that went into producing it. The idea of unequal exchange does not need to be based on the assumption that all the net value added in production is due to labor, as in the discredited "labor theory of value." Suppose that we presume that after wages, all value added is due to technological and organizational inputs—that is, to capital, and none is due to uncompensated labor. This would require us to presume no costs whatsoever to job changing, no involuntary unemployment, and no labor market discrimination (a situation not yet witnessed in the five-hundred-year history of capitalism). Even if we make these incredulous assumptions, so that all

net value added is due to capital, this would not mean that
capitalist. Why the owner of capital receives a return ratl
people who work with the capital is the main question pose
critique of property rights in a capitalist society (Schweikar
answer in practice, regardless of theory, is decided by a conf
capital and labor, organized and individual, over how much each
receives. The rules and conditions for this conflict are set by the state,
which also extracts its own share.

Secondary exploitation, which takes the form of rent and interest, is
an unequal exchange between the capital-rich and the capital-poor,
including between wealthy and poor countries. The capital-rich appropriate an income because they own large amounts of capital without
directly putting the capital to productive use. Value is added by others,
who must borrow or rent from the capital-rich. In addition, the collater-
al of wealth lowers costs to the capital-rich, so that they can buy or produce more with the same amount of money than the capital-poor.
Lower risk and easier availability result in a higher net return to the capital-rich. Rent of the means of production is the most obvious form of
secondary exploitation. A particularly contentious form is sharecropping. Sharecropping is where farmers pay rent to (often absent) property titleholders in the form of a portion of their crop. The relative visibility of exploitation in this case is a prime reason why sharecropping is a
frequent source of agrarian revolts (Paige 1975).

The two types of exploitation have the following three common
roots: (1) the source of unequal exchange is the unequal distribution of
productive assets, which, globally, traces back to the coercive "primitive
accumulation" of the mercantilists, conquistadors, slave traders, and
colonialists; (2) capitalists as capitalists accrue income exclusively
because they have a legal title to large amounts of capital that is in limited supply, a title that is enforced by the state; and (3) even in "free,"
competitive markets, the average costs of market mobility (transaction
costs) are greater for workers than employers, borrowers than lenders, or
renters than landlords.

As a result, at all points of exchange in production, capitalists have
institutionalized *coercive power* as employers, bosses, lenders, and landlords. Both Adam Smith and Karl Marx considered exploitation to be
the application of coercive power in markets to obtain an unequal
exchange. The difference is in whether one considers it an aberration of
state intervention or an inherent feature of capitalism.

To be sure, individual capitalists may also earn income as managers,
entrepreneurs, or producers, which is not exploitation to the extent that
their income is equal to the value added by their own work. Nor do we
consider risk or deferred consumption (the standard justifications for

profit and interest) as irrelevant costs. Overrated, yes, but these are relevant costs that need be compensated in a market economy. The question is: Who gets to take the risk, afford the deferment, and otherwise control capital in order to reap a return? Because they control capital, managers, entrepreneurs, and producers often receive income through exploitation in addition to, or as part of, their salaries. Controlling investment capital, which is the most important determinant of economic development (and community survival, and environmental degradation, and so on), is an inherently political question. Yet, it is a politics without equal rights or democratic elections. Profit, interest, and rent are forms of exploitation, not because they are superfluous to economic growth (just the opposite), but because they result from legally enforced inequality. Ownership of large amounts of alienable productive assets (money, machinery, land, minerals, etc.) is private, whereas the creation of capital and the effects of investment are social.[2]

Inalienable assets (skill, talent, education, i.e., "human capital") also produce income inequalities, sometimes large ones, but not capitalist exploitation. Elimination of capitalist exploitation would not produce a utopian egalitarian commune, but rather the now-fictional world of inequality produced only by merit and talent found in "functionalist" sociology and mainstream economics. Also, note that we have only been considering capitalist exploitation in free markets, unfettered by states or by status discrimination (i.e., racism and patriarchy). Like clearing labor markets, this is a nonexistent condition. Patriarchy predates capitalism, and like racism and nationalism, it has become intertwined with capitalist accumulation and exploitation since the origins of the capitalist world-system.

We should note a few contrasts between our conception of the world-system and traditional Marxist theory. While Marx always recognized capitalism as a global system, he never completed a proposed book on the "world market." Instead, the emphasis among most Marxists and the definition of most key concepts are in terms of relations within the enterprise and the production process (to which Marx devotes the bulk of *Capital*) or the national economy. This difference in the focal unit of analysis is important, though it does not require that world-systems theory ignore the importance of classes and class struggles as many Marxist critics contend. Another difference is the world-systems contention that capitalism is fundamentally composed of both the interstate system and the world economy of firms and markets and that these together produce the core-periphery hierarchy, which is also a necessary structure for the system of capitalist accumulation (Chase-Dunn 1998).

We differ from past world-systems theorizing by employing a conception of capitalist exploitation that builds upon the "analytical

Marxism" school. In so doing, we explain exploitation without relying on the failed assumption in the "labor theory of value" that prices can be transformed into labor values, which has discredited Marxist theories of analysis. The source of capitalist exploitation, and thus the path to its elimination, is the legally enforced unequal distribution and access to productive assets, and the institutionalized power that flows from and reproduces it. Conceptualizing exploitation as unequal exchange also connects our explanatory theory of capitalist accumulation with a normative theory of justice (Roemer 1988). In most theories of justice in modern societies, justice is conceived as an equal exchange freely made. Injustice is conceived as an unequal exchange, whose source is typically past or present coercion or dependency. Capitalist exploitation is unjust by its own conceptions of fairness, a point we return to in discussing transformations of the system.

Whereas capitalism in localized forms has existed since the origins of trade, it became the dominant mode of accumulation in Europe in the seventeenth century and in the world as a whole since the nineteenth century. As the Europe-centered world-system became capitalist, capitalism became transnational. Capitalist accumulation became an important alternative to the more directly coercive state-based extraction of surplus. The power of merchants, financiers, and capitalist producers transformed the ancient rise and fall of empires into the modern cycle of the rise and fall of hegemonic capitalist core states (Chase-Dunn 1995). Capitalist expansion subsumed or replaced alternative modes of production (kin-based or tributary) into producing for the capitalist market and articulated their class relations into capitalist forms of profit seeking. All states of the world today are strongly incorporated into, and influenced by, global capitalism. To be sure, important national or regional differences continue to exist and, as we will discuss below, uneven development among these states is an important source of the unequal accumulation of capital.

The Interstate System and the World Order

The European interstate system was born in the Thirty Years' War (1618–1648) in which massive bloodletting and destruction forced imperial dynasties to become states sovereign over nations in order to survive. This is an often-told story, but the key principle in the development of the system is that interstate competition prevented full monopolization of markets, while state building (via war, revolution, and conquest) promoted capitalist expansion as a source of state revenue. Class relations expanded beyond the labor process to become institutionalized in state, colonial, and interstate structures. A system of sovereign states (i.e., with an overarching definition of sovereignty) is fundamental to the origins and reproduction of the capitalist world economy. A mixed system of nation-states in the core and colonial empires in the periphery was the main political structure for three hundred years until decolonization brought the periphery into the interstate system as formally sovereign states.

In the interstate system, unequally powerful states compete for resources by supporting profitable commodity production and by engaging in geopolitical and military competition. Capital and labor attempt to use states to limit competition and garner monopoly rents, a use to which state leaders also put the state in order to raise revenues and expand their relative power base. Mercantilism and colonialism are obvious historical examples, along with current policies such as tariffs, quotas, domestic content legislation, military contracting, and so on. Capital accumulation has always involved political power and coercion.

Yet no state, not even hegemonic Britain or the United States who at their respective peaks controlled well over half the world's production, has succeeded in imposing a single political structure or set of policies over the world economy. The United Nations is no exception in this regard. Rather, the UN is an example of the difficulty of realizing global political integration even when a forum exists for facilitating this goal. Nevertheless, common international standards and procedures have emerged to constitute a constellation of "world orders" (Holsti 1991).

World orders are the agreed upon and normative rules of international relations, the major principles of which are represented in treaties or pacts among the major core powers. The world order is the common understanding of "legitimate" or acceptable interstate behavior, legitimate in the sense that most states encourage, and the major powers actively try to punish, gross misbehavior. The world order is encoded in treaties and international organizations (such as the UN, the World Trade Organization [WTO], or the Law of the Sea), but these often only symbolize a more extensive general understanding that is formed and weakly enforced through reciprocal or isomorphic interaction. Common use of the term "world order" usually pairs it with the adjective "new," recognizing that as an emergent practice, the world order is highly porous and fragile in response to individual state actions. Far more world orders are proclaimed than serious scholarship would recognize in terms of legitimate international agreements and norms that states are willing to defend. Further, each world order is built upon the legacy of previous ones, reinforcing some principles over generations so that they become historic institutions within national cultures and states. The most important example is the principle of state sovereignty itself, which was encoded in the 1648 Treaty of Westphalia. Also over time, specific shifts in the order can be identified. The most notable ones in terms of world progress are the worldwide abolition of slavery in the late nineteenth century and the end of formal colonialism in the late twentieth century.

The institutional grounding of shared global principles and ideas in national cultures over generations of their application leads us to a final related concept, termed "world polity" by the institutionalist branch of world-system studies (Meyer 1987, 1999; Thomas et al. 1987; Boli and Thomas 1997) and by the "social constructionists" in political science (Ruggie 1998). Both concepts of world order and polity refer to the international and transnational rules, norms, and organizations that emerge through interaction, and which are structured mainly by the most powerful actors in the system. The processes behind a world order or a world polity differ, however, and the contrast is important. World polity has a greater emphasis on shared cultural definitions of what is legitimate among states and other global actors. It operates more at the *cognitive* level, institutionalizing the parameters of what is a goal worth pursuing or what is a human "right," as opposed to a world order of collective agreements to achieve or enforce goals and rights.[3] A world polity implies shared values that may or may not correspond with economic and geopolitical interests, and which are enforced through international organizations that have at least some coercive power. The major world religions—Christianity, Islam, Judaism, Hinduism, and Buddhism— have been instrumental in spreading common cultural conceptions, with the first three sharing a common epistemology and with the first two being forcibly spread throughout the world. Secular successors that institutionalize common cognitive understandings are more likely to be international nongovernmental organizations (INGOs), such as the Red Cross or Amnesty International, and only secondarily are international governmental organizations (IGOs), which at least in principle respect national sovereignty.

In contrast, the idea of world order has a greater realist emphasis on formal agreements based on geopolitical power interests, in which the world order is a public good. A world order implies common economic interests that may or may not correspond with individual cultural values, and which are followed out of self-interest with little external enforcement. As such, orders are fragile to the actions of free riders or to changes in self-interest, while polities are fragile to the definition of whom is included within the "self" that shares interests. Most important for world-system theory is that a change in a world polity *transforms* the definition of a system's logic and goals, while a change in world orders is a better or worse achievement of preexisting common goals (Ruggie 1998). Thus the question from our vantage point is not a qualitative one of either collective order or shared polity, as it is sometimes debated in the literature. Rather, our question is when and to what extent does the integration of the world order become a shared world polity, and vice versa, when does a shared polity resolve to only the collective goods of state actors with otherwise divergent self-interests. To transform the world-system, rather than just reform it, is to change the world polity. Ruggie (1998) points out that without a theory of the world polity, one simply cannot imagine the system being transformed, a problem endemic to liberal or realist accounts.

This perspective is useful historically in distinguishing the Catholic polity over the European world of the sixteenth century from the world order of realpolitik between sovereign states in the seventeenth century.[4] The Catholic polity was broken by the Protestant Reformation and the Dutch Revolution. With the colonial expansion of the European world-system, realism and racism undermined any strong world polity, at least until recently. In the concluding chapter, we consider whether or not a new world polity of international organizations (such as the World Trade Organization and the European Union [EU]) is replacing the declining world order of U.S. hegemony and whether it can do so without a global war. We also consider if a world polity can be constructed that would transform the logic and goals of the system.

A Hierarchy of Core and Periphery

The final definitional constant of the capitalist world economy is the core-periphery hierarchy, which results from the interaction of the first two structures. The origin of the hierarchy is the story of emergent capitalism and colonialism—the "rise of the West" and the subjugation of the rest, a story we need not repeat here (see Wallerstein 1974, 1980, 1989). The key point is that the hierarchy was more political than economic in origin, although with the dissolution of colonialism, its current reproduction is more economic than political.

The hierarchy reflects three dimensions of inequality: *power, dependency,* and *productivity.* The core zone (Western Europe, North America, and Japan) is made up of former empires. In terms of power, the current core states are generally democratic and legitimate even to lower classes, with a comparatively high level of bureaucratic efficacy and low level of corruption. Their militaries are technologically sophisticated and can project state power at least throughout adjoining peripheral spheres of interest. In terms of dependency, they have multiple trading partners and sources of capital, and produce diverse products and services. In terms of productivity, core zones specialize in high value-added production, typically employing capital-intensive industry with advanced technology and highly educated and skilled labor.

In contrast, contemporary peripheral states are mostly former colonies of the core powers. Although variation is much greater in the periphery, it is there that one finds the weakest states in terms of legitimacy, efficacy, and corruption, and where the military often shades into a dictatorial "protection racket" (see Tilly 1985). The trade of peripheral countries tends to be the most dependent on few partners (mainly the ex-colonial powers) and exports are often mainly composed of a single product. Economically, peripheral zones have limited capital and little choice but to specialize in labor-intensive and low-wage production, especially in agricultural and extractive industries. Despite the end of colonialism, the relative gap in average incomes between core and peripheral zones has continued to increase. This trend has existed since at least the end of the nineteenth century, and probably before. Compare, for example, the similar living standards of agricultural peasants in Europe versus Africa in the sixteenth century (the bulk of both populations) and the large differences now between working classes.

As noted, variation in the periphery on all three characteristics is great and has likely increased since decolonization. The semiperiphery is composed of states that are more stable and that have more-developed economies than do the states in the periphery (e.g., Mexico, South Africa, Korea, etc.). This zone tends to have states that have been independent longer, whose militaries can project power regionally either as core surrogates (such as U.S. allies Israel, South Korea, Taiwan, and Turkey) or as the largest country in the region (such as Brazil, Iran, etc.), and whose trade and product diversity is generally greater than in the periphery, although some are dominated by a single highly profitable product, such as oil. A key definitional characteristic of the semiperiphery is that while these countries are still dependent upon the core, peripheral countries are dependent upon them both politically and economically.

In the last twenty to thirty years, the semiperiphery has seen a huge growth in industrial mass production utilizing semiskilled labor. This development is sometimes known as the "new dependency" in which dependence on agricultural or raw-material exports is replaced by dependence on transnational corporate (TNC) investment in industrial production for export to the core. While less directly coercive than export-agriculture regimes, TNC manufacturing of export goods often relies on political repression and high exploitation, especially of female workers (Bornschier and Chase-Dunn 1985; Ward 1984). The main point is that contrary to the expectations of modernization theory, TNC investment produces less economic growth than domestic capital because TNCs have fewer links to domestic suppliers or customers. Also, a large TNC presence as a percentage of a noncore economy has negative spillover effects on the rest of society ("negative externalities"), producing high levels of income inequality and engendering political policies detrimental to domestic producers (Dixon and Boswell 1996a, 1996b).

The state-socialist countries were mostly semiperipheral in world-system terms, and as we contend in later chapters, they were part of the hierarchy rather than an alternative to it. To provide some background data for this point and to describe the core-periphery hierarchy more generally, Table 1.1 lists socioeconomic data from most of the countries in the world in the later 1970s and early 1980s. The countries are grouped into core, semiperiphery, and periphery categories on the following indicators for the periods of 1980, 1985, 1990: average GDP per capita; average economic growth; the percentage of income concentrated in the top 20 percent of the population; a scale of political and civil repression defined in Western terms of electoral democracy and independent media and organizations; and the rate of exploitation in manufacturing in the late 1970s. These data give a comparative view of the different zones.

Data are listed in a separate category for the past and present state-socialist countries. Revolutionary political changes have mainly occurred in the now former state-socialist countries, along with strong political movements toward democracy that swept through Latin America and parts of Asia. We offer the data for the 1980s to demonstrate the social conditions facing these countries (some of which are now extinct) shortly before the political upheavals that occurred since the last part of that decade. Generally, economic conditions worsened worldwide during another rolling recession in 1991–1993, followed by a long though highly uneven recovery until the Asian crisis of 1997–1998. As we discuss later, this latest economic crisis pummeled the former state-socialist countries (especially Russia) and other emerging semiperipheral states (e.g., Indonesia).

Others might call these groupings first, second, third, and fourth worlds, but by any name these groups are rough approximations of the core/periphery hierarchy. While data are missing for many countries, we can reasonably assume that conditions are somewhat similar within groups. We will not try to explain or defend these data other than to warn that these numbers must be used with caution. They are best for making broad comparisons between core and peripheral groups of countries and worst for making fine comparisons between otherwise similar countries. One broad conclusion is obvious—the core countries completely dominate the world economy. Discussions of radically changing the system or of building socialism without core participation are pointless. Less obvious but also important is that the state-socialist countries resembled other semiperipheral states in the 1980s, including high exploitation rates, poor economic growth, and low levels of

Table 1.1   The Comparative Structure of the World Economy, 1980–1990

Variable	Mean	Std. Dev.	Min.	Max.	N
The Core Countries					
1980 Democracy Index	9.88	.49	8.00	10.00	17
1985 Democracy Index	9.88	.49	8.00	10.00	17
1990 Democracy Index	9.94	.24	9.00	10.00	17
1980 Inequality	39.29	2.13	36.1	43.4	15
1985 Inequality	38.95	2.56	34.74	43.5	13
1990 Inequality	39.52	4.40	33.80	46.4	11
1980 RGDP per capita	11,792	1,553	10,068	15,311	17
1985 RGDP per capita	12,775	1,697	10,808	16,570	17
1990 RGDP per capita	14,266	1,695	11,508	18,073	17
Growth Rate 1980–1985	.08	.05	.02	.17	17
Growth Rate 1985–1990	.12	.05	.01	.22	17
Exploitation Rate	1.07	.30	.75	1.97	14
The State-Socialist Bloc					
1980 Democracy Index	.13	.35	0.00	1.00	8
1985 Democracy Index	.13	.35	0.00	1.00	8
1990 Democracy Index	n/a				
1980 Inequality	34.76	3.11	32.10	40.83	7
1985 Inequality	36.10	2.81	31.53	39.62	7
1990 Inequality	37.27	2.58	34.57	40.98	5
1980 RGDP per capita	3,892	1,848	971	6,118	8
1985 RGDP per capita	4,203	1,856	1,262	7,049	8
1990 RGDP per capita	4,230	1,670	1,324	6,213	6
Growth Rate 1980–1985	.13	.17	−.07	.40	8
Growth Rate 1985–1990	.03	.15	−.12	.30	6
Exploitation Rate	2.47	.96	1.04	3.03	4
The Semiperiphery					
1980 Democracy Index	4.23	4.07	0.00	10.00	13
1985 Democracy Index	5.92	4.05	0.00	10.00	13
1990 Democracy Index	7.15	4.02	0.00	10.00	13
1980 Inequality	43.12	7.64	35.00	61.60	9
1985 Inequality	45.83	9.42	34.42	64.49	9
1990 Inequality	45.03	10.13	35.28	65.18	9
1980 RGDP per capita	4,464	2,072	882	7,391	13
1985 RGDP per capita	4,603	1,972	1,050	7,536	13
1990 RGDP per capita	5,587	2,670	1,262	9,576	13
Growth Rate 1980–1985	.07	.16	−.18	.36	13
Growth Rate 1985–1990	.21	.21	−.12	.58	13
Exploitation Rate	2.01	.96	.61	3.88	24
The Periphery					
1980 Democracy Index	1.92	3.53	0.00	10.00	92
1985 Democracy Index	2.06	3.58	0.00	10.00	93
1990 Democracy Index	2.88	3.82	0.00	10.00	92
1980 Inequality	49.24	7.04	36.82	66.30	15
1985 Inequality	49.55	6.53	38.92	62.10	20
1990 Inequality	50.63	7.46	39.34	63.00	31
1980 RGDP per capita	2,531	2,314	324	11,311	96
1985 RGDP per capita	2,446	2,371	299	12,404	102
1990 RGDP per capita	2,526	2,575	400	14,854	76
Growth Rate 1980–1985	−.03	.16	−.42	.41	96
Growth Rate 1985–1990	.04	.16	−.28	.54	76
Exploitation Rate	2.10	.92	.83	5.07	52

(Table 1.1 continues)

Table 1.1 continued

Definitions and Sources:
Democracy Index: The annual rating on Polity III's ten-point scale of democracy. Higher scores indicate greater democracy. *Source:* "Polity III: Regime Type and Political Authority, 1800–1994," Keith Jaggers and Ted Robert Gurr, Interuniversity Consortium for Political and Social Research (ICPSR) 6695.
Inequality: The share of income to the richest 20 percent of the population. *Source: Measuring Income Inequality:* A New Database @ Klaus Deininger and Lyn Squire, http://www.worldbank.org/html/prdmg/grthweb/dddeisqu.htm
Real Gross Domestic Product Per Capita (RGDP per capita): Laspeyres index, presented in 1985 International Prices. *Source:* Penn World Tables 5.6, Alan Heston and Robert Summers, http://cansim.epas.utoronto.ca:5680/pwt/pwt.html
Exploitation Rate: Value added divided by wages and salaries, in manufacturing, average 1980–1985. *Source:* World Bank, "World Data 1995," CD-ROM, New York, World Bank.
Data are not available on all countries for all variables. For the GDP measures, the core countries were defined as the following: Australia, Austria, Belgium, Canada, Denmark, Finland, France, Germany, Italy, Japan, Netherlands, New Zealand, Norway, Sweden, Switzerland, the United Kingdom of Great Britain, and the United States of America. The semiperipheral countries used were Greece, Ireland, Portugal, Spain, Turkey, Argentina, Brazil, Mexico, India, Indonesia, South Korea, Taiwan, and South Africa. The state-socialist countries used were Bulgaria, Czechoslovakia, Hungary, Poland, Romania, USSR, Yugoslavia. and China. All other countries for which we have data are considered part of the periphery.

democracy, a classic revolutionary combination in Marxist theory (Boswell and Dixon 1993).

Global Trends and Cycles

In addition to the three definitional constants, there are two other structural features that are continuities even though they involve patterned change. These are the world-systemic trends and cycles. The dynamism of world capitalism is often the characteristic most prominent in differentiating it from other modes of accumulation. That the difference in social life between now and five hundred years ago is greater than the difference between five hundred and three thousand years ago is both obvious and remarkable. Industrialization over just the last two hundred years contrasts sharply with eons of agricultural economies. The motor that drives incessant change in the system is competition among firms in the world market and among states in the interstate system. While change is omnipresent, it is also uneven in pace and distribution. Most discernible changes of major significance at the global (and usually the societal) level occur in spurts or clumps. Long-term trends are those spurts that have a general cumulative unidirectionality, while cycles are those spurts of social change that tend to repeat over time.

Long-Term Trends

The trends produced by the world-system make up what is labeled as "development" or mislabeled as "modernization." The five long-term global trends that are normal operating procedures of the modern world-system are the following:

1. *Commodification:* The expansion and deepening of commodity relations requires land, labor, and capital to be increasingly mediated by monetized exchange in both the core and the periphery. Commodification is typically identified with market expansion, but hierarchies are often an alternative form of price setting (oscillating with markets as described below under *Cycles*). Slavery in the Americas, for instance, was used to forcefully commodify labor where the market was otherwise not profitable for large-scale plantations. Commodification can never proceed to the point at which all human transactions take the commodity form because some relations, particularly emotional ones, lose their value if turned into a monetized commodity. However, in terms of raw economic resources, such as land and labor, all the easy conquests have already occurred. There are no more societies even in the periphery in which kin-based or tributary forms of exchange remain predominant. External expansion, the "spatial fix" to economic crises discussed by David Harvey (1995), is no longer possible. The world market now only expands from increased demand, a critical shift in power from producers to consumers.

2. *Proletarianization:* The world work force has become increasingly dependent on wages set by labor markets for meeting its basic needs (the effect of commodifying labor in point one above). This long-term trend may be temporarily slowed or even reversed in some areas during periods of economic stagnation, but the secular shift away from subsistence production has a long history that continues today. The character of proletarianization has differed by zone of the world economy. The initial expansion of capitalism in the sixteenth to eighteenth centuries led to a freeing of labor from feudal obligations in the Western European core, a tightening of serfdom in the Eastern European semiperiphery, and a massive transnational enslavement in the colonial periphery. "Free" labor only became a core-wide standard in the nineteenth century and a worldwide standard with post–World War II decolonization. The occasional ebb but general flow of

increasing women's labor force participation, which has now
become a flood, is also exemplary of the process. The expansion
of the informal sector is part of this trend despite its functional
similarities with earlier rural subsistence redoubts.

3. *State formation:* States with defined territories and citizens have
replaced all other forms of organizing military power, due primarily to the greater military success of states. As a result, states
have become the arbitrators for all societal-level institutions. All
peoples are defined foremost as citizens of a state, rather than
subjects of a king or members of a religion, even if a king or religious order rules the citizens. The power of states over their populations has thereby increased everywhere. State regulation has
grown secularly while political battles have raged over the nature
and objects of regulation, and the definition of the state's population. Nationalism, the desire for an exclusive state by a nation
(an ethnic group with a defined territory), has increased with the
growth in importance of states. The trend for each nation to have
its own separate state rises as global economic and social
exchanges increase in number and importance relative to societal
ones (Boswell 1989b, 1999). Only states are recognized at the
global level, so all nations will want separate states to the extent
that their commerce is global rather than imperial or domestic.
At the same time, and for the same reason, there has been a trend
over the last two centuries toward increasing international political regulation (via IGOs). Both trends have accelerated dramatically since the Second World War.

4. *Increased size of economic enterprises:* While a large competitive
sector of small firms remains and is reproduced, the largest firms
(those occupying what is sometimes called the monopoly sector)
have continuously grown in size. This remains true even in the
most recent period despite its characterization by a new "accumulation regime" of "flexible specialization" in which small firms
compete for shares of the world market (we elaborate below
under *Cycles*). This is the globalization of the competitive sector
rather than the decline of the transnational corporations. The
latest development is cross-national mergers of enormous size
designed to compete across regional trading blocs, such as that of
Chrysler and Daimler-Benz.

5. *Capital intensification:* Increasing the capital intensity of production, not just mechanization but also "human capital" development, has increasingly raised the productivity of labor.
Increasing productivity is what produces "development" as
opposed to simply growth (i.e., development being growth per

capita). Since Toynbee, spurts of intensification have been identified as economic "revolutions," such as the Industrial Revolution, the green revolution, the information revolution, and so on. The trend toward "time-space compression," associated by David Harvey (1989) with the most recent period of technological change, is also an acceleration of a cumulative trend of long standing, rather than a new trend.

Systemic Cycles

Systemic cycles are repetitive processes operating at the level of the world-system. We emphasize two of these, the K-wave and the hegemonic sequence, because we have currently entered transition periods for both of them. We start with economic globalization, which we list here as a cycle, but it is also a trend because the peaks reached by each successive cycle have been higher than earlier peaks. We also describe political cycles of war, imperialism, and revolt, which are cyclical in general because of their relationship to K-wave and hegemonic determinants.

Economic globalization and the transnationalization of capital. Globalization is a multifaceted process that includes foreign investment, information exchange, and world cultural commercialization, as well as the integration of trade and production. The proportion of all production that is due to the operation of transnational firms has increased in every epoch, but the pace of increases has been cyclical. If we calculate the ratio of international investments to investments within countries, the world economy had nearly as high a level of "investment globalization" in 1910 as it did in 1990 (Bairoch 1996). The ratio of world trade to world output is a sensible measure of trade globalization. From 1950 to 1994, world trade grew an average 1.6 times faster than world output. Trade globalization is estimated over the past two centuries in Figure 1.1 by using a measure based on the average trade openness of countries (imports versus GDP). This measure reveals that there has been both a long-term trend and three waves of globalization since 1800—one in the last half of the nineteenth century, a small one from 1900 to 1929, and a large upswing from 1950 to the present (Chase-Dunn, Kawano, and Brewer 2000).

The pace of world capital and market integration increased rapidly in the postwar era, especially in the late 1980s and 1990s with the regional integration of European Union and North American Free Trade Agreement (NAFTA) markets, the opening of China, the demise of the Soviet bloc, and completion of the GATT round that produced the

Figure 1.1 Average Openness of Trade Globalization (5-year moving average), 1830–1995

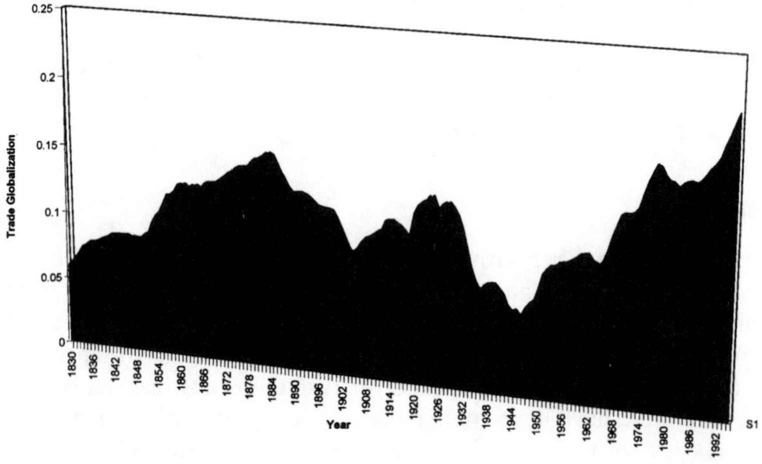

Source: Chase-Dunn, Kawano and Brewer 1999.

World Trade Organization in 1994. Note that these are mainly political changes that accelerate a global trend. The contemporary focus on transnational sourcing and a single interdependent global economy as if they were novel developments is due to the heightened awareness produced by the acceleration of a cyclical trend that has long been in operation.

The Kondratieff long wave (K-wave). K-waves are core-wide economic cycles with a period of forty to sixty years in which the relative rate of economic activity increases during "A-phase" upswings and then relatively decreases during "B-phase" periods of slower growth or stagnation (Kondratieff 1979). K-wave research has empirically demonstrated a cycle in real GNP growth rates about every twenty to thirty years since 1848, accompanied by similar patterns in trade volumes (Misra and Boswell 1997) and in prices since about 1500 (Goldstein 1988 and Barr 1979 offer reviews of the literature).

Periods of economic expansion result when a cluster of combined social and technical "accumulation innovations"[5] accelerate production in what become the leading sectors of the world economy. "Leading sectors" are the most dynamic elements of the economy, which prove over time to have been the driving force of development (Rostow 1978; Modelski and Thompson 1996). Innovation occurs in five basic ways: reducing the cost of capital, increasing the rate of exploitation, increasing the size of markets, increasing turnover rates, and reducing the degree of ruinous competition (Mandel 1975). The effects of these clustered or "bunched" (Mensch 1978) innovations are prolonged by the multiplier effect of bunched investment, and by the addition of modifying innovations. Note that innovations may be social or organizational (including political innovations) and not just technological or scientific. Key innovations increase profit rates.

Stagnation follows the exhaustion and saturation of core markets for the accumulation innovations. Once innovations become commonplace, intensified competition reduces profit rates relative to the previous period (i.e., the new product cycle). Recessions deepen and sluggish demand and cautious investment hinder capital accumulation. A crisis situation develops when the length and intensity of a long stagnation indicate that expansion will not automatically reoccur, and self-conscious innovative restructuring (rather than modifying) is necessary to restore growth. The crisis phase is thus one of experimentation (Gordon, Edwards, and Reich 1982) during which individuals, firms, and polities eventually produce successful accumulation innovations. The successful innovators then become models of development whose widespread imitation leads to renewed expansion.

Table 1.2 lists long-wave periods and some of the more important leading sectors and accumulation innovations.[6] While data are missing and the timing of waves is rougher in the earlier periods, the table nevertheless demonstrates the general historical pattern. Note that the accumulation innovations occur during the stagnant, experimentation phase, which launches a leading sector that the rest of the economy follows into a sustained expansion. The list of sectors and innovations is intended to indicate the key features of a broader complex, and should not be read as a simple determinism. For instance, the dating of innovations is not based on when this or that technique was invented, but rather, when its widespread use became economically important. The pattern of sectors is the historical pattern of capitalist development: from maritime trades in the sixteenth century to colonial trades in the seventeenth, and with the Industrial Revolution, a familiar succession of industrial products from the late eighteenth through the twentieth century.

The widespread adoption of model forms of accumulation innovations by individuals, firms, and polities changes the social structure, so that each wave has an identifiable "social structure of accumulation" (Gordon, Edwards, and Reich 1982), also known as an "accumulation regime" (Lipietz 1987). K-waves are cyclical because the accumulation regime, which is managed by the state, aligns infrastructural investment and organization innovations with a cluster of product cycles. K-waves

Table 1.2   K-Waves, Leading Sectors, and Accumulation Innovations, 1495–1974

K-Wave Phase	Price Change	Leading Economic Sectors	Selected Accumulation Innovations
1496–1508-B[a]	2.73	Direct Spice Trade	Exploration Voyages
1509–1528-A	2.80		
1529–1538-B	−2.18	American Silver	Colonial Conquests
1539–1558-A	3.25		
1559–1574-B	3.28*	Baltic Trade	"Fluyt" Ships
1575–1594-A	2.95*		
1595–1620-B	−0.75	Asian Trade	East India Co.
1621–1649-A	0.68		
1650–1688-B	−0.59	Atlantic Trade	Slave Plantations
1689–1719-A	−0.28		
1720–1746-B	0.53*	Colonial Trades	Colonial Expansion
1747–1761-A	1.09		
1762–1789-B	0.52	Cotton Textiles; Iron	Mechanization/Steam
1790–1813-A	3.52		
1814–1847-B	−0.55	Railroads	Factory/Wages System
1848–1871-A	0.81		
1872–1892-B	−1.95	Steel; Chemicals	Mass Production
1893–1916-A	2.06		
1917–1939-B	−3.46	Autos; Air; Electric	Multinational Corp./ Welfare State
1940–1967-A	4.40		
1968– -B	n/a	Information Industries	Flexible Specialization

Sources: K-Waves: Goldstein (1988); Price Change: percent annual average change during the period for all twenty-six price series from nine core countries found in Goldstein (1988, appendix I, pp. 436–437); Leading Sectors: Modelski and Thompson (1996), Rostow (1978) [we added American silver from our historical research. The timing of waves and sectors differs frequently but usually in small amounts and is variable at the margins in any case]. Accumulation Innovations: Boswell (1987, see his tabular citations); additions from our interpretation of Modelski and Thompson (1996) and other historical research.

Notes: a. K-Wave Phase: A = expansion period; B = stagnation period.
* The direction of the annual average price change does not correspond with the phase. Modelski and Thompson (1996) have a second wave of colonial trades as leading about where we have starred (*) the B phase of the K-wave.

are global because interstate competition produces isomorphic commonality around an ideal regime type, especially during periods of hegemony (see below). Each accumulation regime must facilitate a more productive K-wave expansion than the previous period in order to succeed it. *Each wave of expansion thus builds upon and supersedes the previous period,* rather than replacing the infrastructure produced by the last expansion. World development occurs in logistic-shaped steps rather than a linear progression. However, the distribution of this increased product is an outcome of class and state struggles that cannot be foreordained by technical selection.

The hegemonic sequence. Hegemony is a condition of dominance without resort to coercion, due to the dependence of subordinates on the fortunes of the hegemon. Gramsci (1971), in perhaps the most prominent conception, describes how the dependence of economic growth on profitability gives capitalists a hegemonic position over state and cultural institutions even without instrumental control. In world-economy theory, a hegemon is a state that predominates over the world economy to such an extent that it sets the major trading patterns and the political rules of the world order to match its own interests (see literature reviews in Goldstein 1988; Chase-Dunn 1998).

In world-systems theory, the rise and fall of states results primarily from uneven economic development. There are two interacting, yet contradictory, principles of uneven development—the *advantages of backwardness* and the *multiplier effect* of resource expansion—that guide the mobility of economic innovation and thus the rise and decline of states.[7] First, the "advantage of backwardness" is such that the clustering of economic innovations occurs most often and most profitably in areas that were somewhat left out of the previous application of an innovation in production. This is due to institutional inertia and high fixed investment in the previously leading sectors. As a result, there is a pressure or tendency for the next "revolution" in production to be concentrated somewhere else, giving us a mobile pattern of rise and decline. At the same time, however, an innovation-driven expansion in one sector has a multiplier effect on the rest of the economy, generating resources for further development. One long-term expansion will lay down the infrastructure and provide the resources for the next. As a result, we historically find the geographic clustering of K-wave expansions to occur in pairs. Why only pairs? By the time of the second expansion, institutional inertia and the depreciation costs of aging infrastructure have accumulated to the extent that the advantages of backwardness outweigh the benefits of prior resource expansion. Exceptions to these patterns are possible, of course, such as the repeating British leadership described below.

The unequal and uneven development of the world capitalist economy periodically results in core powers with leading economic positions. These world leaders have only become hegemons as a result of a global war, which destroyed competitors and forced the leaders to manage the world order. Hegemonic phases are followed by multicentric periods in which wealth and power are more evenly distributed among core states. There have been only three hegemonies—the United Netherlands (1648–1667), the United Kingdom (1815–1873), and the United States (1945–1974).

Not all world leaders achieve global hegemony. Modelski and

Thompson (1996) identify five "world leaders," states that have reigned over a geographical concentration of leading economic sectors. These are the three hegemons mentioned above plus the Portuguese in 1517–1562 and a second, earlier, English leadership in 1714–1763 that failed to achieve hegemony. Table 1.3 combines the world-system approach to hegemony with Modelski and Thompson's (1996) long-cycle approach to leading sectors in order to distill the key set of causal factors from the detailed historical narratives in these and related studies (see tabular sources). For comparison the table repeats the list of K-waves by type and a measure of average price increases for select goods during the period, along with associated leading economic sectors and selected accumulation innovations developed during a long stagnation. Also listed are where the subsequent economic expansions were concentrated, and consequently, what states became world leaders and hegemonies.

Through impressive empirical investigation, Modelski and Thompson demonstrate the long waves and leading sectors associated with each world leader (compare Tables 1.2 and 1.3). While they emphatically point out that world leaders are not necessarily hegemons, they neglect to explain when leaders become hegemons and why. However, their recent convergence with world-system theory, along with their pathbreaking empirical work, allows us to fill this gap by combining insights from both theories.

The pattern of paired geographic concentration of K-waves producing a world leader, first described by Modelski and Thompson (1996), can clearly be found in Table 1.3. In the first pair, there is a shift from Portugal to a shared concentration with neighboring Spain. There was also a prior K-wave (ca. 1480s) centered in Portugal, according to Modelski and Thompson, which was fueled by expansion in North Africa and the exploitation of Guinea gold. Afterward, the pattern is largely one in which the first wave in the pair tends to be less concentrated, including two or three countries, while the more exclusive second wave produces a world leader among the competitors. In the second pair in Table 1.3, a general expansion in the Low Countries becomes centered in the Netherlands in the second wave of the pair. The third pair goes from the Americas in general to primarily the English colonies. The fourth pair has both waves centered in the United Kingdom, one mainly due to its colonial success, and the second time from being the center of the Industrial Revolution. Industrialization was nearly as high in France during the first of these paired waves. Both waves of the fifth pair are centered in the United States, but again, during the first wave the United States is not far ahead of Germany in concentration. Finally, what is the

Table 1.3.   Economic Sources of World Leadership and Hegemony: K-Waves, Leading Sectors, and Concentrations, 1495–1974

K-Wave Phase	Price Change	Leading Sectors/ Innovations	Geographic Concentration	World Leaders/ **Hegemonies**
1496-B[a]	2.73	Direct Spice Trade	Portugal	
1509-A	2.80	Exploration Voyages		
1529-B	−2.18	American Silver	Spain/	Portugal 1517–1541
1539-A	3.25	Colonial Conquests	Portugal	**Hapsburgs 1526–1556**[b]
1559-B	3.28*	Baltic Trade	Low	
1575-A	2.95*	"Fluyt" Ships	Countries	(Spain 1594–1597)
1595-B	−0.75	Asian Trade	Netherlands	United Neth. 1609–1635
1621-A	0.68	East India Co.		**United Neth. 1648–1667**
1650-B	−0.59	Atlantic Trade	American	
1689-A	−0.28	Slave Plantations	Colonies	
1720-B	0.53*	Colonial Trades	English	
1747-A	1.09	Colonial Expansion	Colonies	United Kingdom 1715–1739
1762-B	0.52	Cotton Textiles	United Kingdom	
1790-A	3.52	Industrialization	(France)	
1814-B	−0.55	Railroads	United	United Kingdom 1816–1849
1848-A	0.81	Wage/Factory System	Kingdom	**United Kingdom 1850–1873**
1872-B	−1.95	Steel; Chemicals	United States	
1893-A	2.06	Mass Production	(Germany)	
1917-B	−3.46	Autos; Air; Electric	United States	United States 1945–1974
1940-A	4.40	Multi-Corporation		**United States 1945–1974**
1968-B	n/a	Information Industry Flexible Specialization	Japan/ United States	

Sources: See Table 1.2, and the following: World Leaders, periods of peak concentration only: Modelski and Thompson (1996). Hegemony, mature periods only: Hopkins and Wallerstein (1979), with adjustments prior to 1700 from Misra and Boswell (1997). See also Holsti (1991).

Notes: a. K-Wave Phase: A = expansion period; B = stagnation period.

b. The United Hapsburgs was an attempted imperial/Catholic world polity rather than a hegemony. It was based more on imperial coercive dominance and cultural imposition than on hegemonic dependence and cultural isomorphism. After the redivision of the Hapsburg domains, Spain managed a relative sea power superiority above 50 percent, but it was too brief to constitute systemic leadership.

* The direction of the annual average price change does not correspond with the phase.

beginning of the sixth pair sees a concentration led again by the United States, but with a close EU and Japan forming a tripolar world. This last wave may be the least-concentrated development of new sectors. The development of information industries spans nearly the entire core, making the major distinction between core and periphery, rather than between core states each with its own imperially associated colonial periphery.

We continue to hold to the hypothesis of continuing U.S. hegemonic decline despite the fact that the U.S. economy has been growing faster than other core countries since about 1993, and the "Asian miracle" states fell on hard times in the late 1990s. A consideration of the U.S. hegemonic trajectory needs to distinguish between economic, political, and military power, with dominance only clear in the last of the three. Let us first look at economic power. Figure 1.2 shows the U.S. share of world GDP, as well as that of Britain, Germany, France and Japan, from 1950 to 1994.

The fairly steady downward trend of the U.S. share is evident in Figure 1.2. Of the five core countries, only Japan shows an upward trend in this period. Britain fell, while the shares of France and Germany rose, but only slightly. It must be remembered that this was a period in which the global GDP was a steady upward trend, so all these national

Figure 1.2   Core Country Shares of World GDP

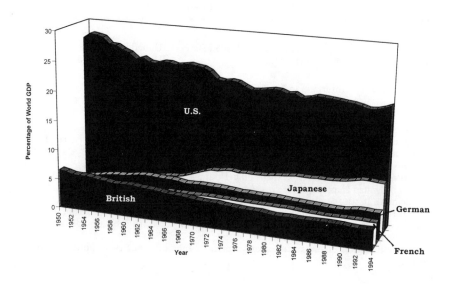

economies are growing while their relative economic power vis-à-vis competing core states is changing in the ways indicated. Bergesen and Fernandez (1999) show that European and Japanese transnational corporations expanded into the industries formerly dominated by U.S. transnationals in this same period.

Figure 1.2 also shows that the U.S. decline in economic power has been gradual rather than precipitous, and that the United States remains several times larger than any other competitor despite its decline. But European unification constitutes a major reorganization of the global power system. If we add the 1994 GDP shares of the countries brought together in the European Union they have a combined share of 19 percent, compared to 20 percent for the United States. To the extent that the European Union functions as a single competing polity, a new economic bipolarity will have emerged. Our best guess is that the U.S. economic hegemony will continue to decline despite the recent period of greater economic growth.

The recent period of relatively greater U.S. growth is a complex phenomenon. Some economists have argued that the U.S. stock market has benefited from the Asian crisis because capital flight out of Asia and the lack of alternative emerging markets has caused investing institutions to further bid up the price of U.S. stocks. U.S. financial centrality is still strong enough that the national economy benefits from demand created by the financial sector itself. The success of the U.S. software business has been largely due to the advantages of scale already enjoyed and the ability of U.S.-made standards to win out over competitors abroad because of the great size of the U.S. domestic market. U.S. capital has also benefited from the historical weakness of welfare and labor institutions relative to other core-state competitors, especially those in Europe. The attack on labor and the welfare state was more successful in the United States, in part because these institutions were already weaker. The effects of these differences are to be seen in the changes in inequality in the different core states in recent decades. The United States already had much greater income inequality than the other core states, and that level of inequality has grown even greater in recent decades (Navarro 1998).

While this "success" has allowed companies to get lean and mean by downsizing their work forces, proletarianizing middle management, and using "job blackmail" (the threat of moving to a "more efficient [cheaper] location"), we doubt that this will continue to be an advantage in future competition among core states. Japan is restructuring and Asian countries are recovering from the crisis, while Europe is restructuring around the Union and the euro.

The United States has greatly increased in military hegemony despite cuts in the military budget, because the main opponent and only alternative superpower (the Soviet Union) collapsed. If we simply add together economic and military power there is little doubt that the United States remains the hegemon. But it is important to recognize that military hegemony is dependent on economic hegemony, because the military is wildly expensive. Declining economic hegemony creates pressure to cut back on military expenditures. This pressure has been temporarily relieved because of the recent economic growth and the new revenues available to the U.S. federal state. But, as we have indicated above, we doubt that this trend of relatively greater economic growth will continue. Indeed, a collapse of the stock bubble could lead to a U.S. economic crisis that would force a major restructuring of its military capabilities and increase the pressure for other core states to take up the slack. Whether this happens quickly or slowly, we predict that the U.S. economic hegemony will continue to decline, and that its military hegemony will follow. This will lead to a new period in which economic power and military power come once again to be recalibrated in a system of more equally powerful and competing core states.

We see the current situation as similar in most structural respects to that at the end of the nineteenth century. Declining Britain was still advocating free trade, while the other core states and upwardly mobile semiperipheries were shifting back to economic nationalism and protectionism. We return to the question of whether or not this happens in the next few years and to what could prevent another cycle of war over world leadership in the last chapter. A new window of vulnerability to warfare among core states will arrive, and the institutional structures of global collective security will again be tested. It is in all humanity's interest that these institutions be strong enough to prevent another war among core states.

Political cycles.   Numerous studies have pointed out the cyclical patterns in the occurrence of major wars, those in which great powers are direct antagonists, and especially global wars, which are major wars in which the rules of the world order and the possibility of hegemony are at stake (Wright 1942; Levy 1983, 1985; Goldstein 1988). In Table 1.4, one finds again the list of K-waves, world leaders, and world hegemonies, with the rise-and-fall phases of the hegemonic cycle added (i.e., ascent, victory, maturity, and decline). We also now find the associated global wars and world orders. Although wars in the core are unlikely when a country is fully hegemonic, major wars are more likely during a K-wave expansion when countries have the resources for a lengthy and expensive war (Boswell and Sweat 1991). As such, those global wars that lead to a hegemony are to some extent paired with the relevant K-waves, but the "twin

Table 1.4   Political Sources of World Leadership and Hegemony: K-Waves, World Leaders, Hegemony, Global Wars, and World Orders, 1495–1974

K-Wave Phase	World Leaders	Hegemonic Cycle	Global Wars/World Order
1496–1508-B[a]	1517	1526 Maturity United Hapsburgs[b]	Italian Wars (1494–1517/25)
1509–1528-A	Portugal		
1529–1538-B	1541		
1539–1548-A			
1559–1574-B		1556 Decline	Dutch Indep./Armada (1584–1609)
1575–1594-A		1575 Ascent United Netherlands	
1595–1620-B	1609 United Netherlands	1609 Victory	Thirty Year's War (1618–1648)
1621–1649-A		1648 Maturity	
1650–1688-B	1635	1667 Decline	Interstate Sovereignty, 1648
1689–1719-A		1672 Competitive	Dutch War of Louis XIV (1672–1678)/ League of Augsburg (1688–1697)/ Spanish Succession (1701–1748)/ Balance of Power, 1714
1720–1746-B	1714 United Kingdom		Jenkins Ear/Austrian Suc. (1739–1748)
1747–1761-A	1739		Seven Years' War (1755–1763)
1762–1789-B			
1790–1813-A		1789 Ascent United Kingdom	Rev. Wars/Napoleonic (1792–1815)
1814–1847-B	1816 United Kingdom	1815 Victory	Concert of Europe, 1815
1848–1871-A	1849	1850 Maturity	
1872–1892-B		1873 Decline	World War I (1914–1918)
1893–1916-A		1897 Ascent United States	
1917–1939-B		1918 Victory	League of Nations, 1918
1940–1967-A	1946 United States	1945 Maturity	World War II (1939–1945) United Nations/NATO, 1945
1968–-B	1974		World Trade Organization, 1995?
1990s?–-A		1974 Decline	

Sources: K-Waves: Goldstein (1988). World Leaders: Modelski and Thompson (1996). Hegemony: Hopkins and Wallerstein (1979)—we changed their UN dates based on Misra and Boswell (1997). Global Wars: Levy (1985); Italian wars from Modelski and Thompson (1996). World Orders: Holsti (1991).

Notes: a. K-Wave phase: A = expansion period; B = stagnation period.
b. The United Hapsburgs was an attempted imperial/Catholic world polity rather than a hegemony.

peaks" pattern hypothesized by Modelski and Thompson (1996) is not found in all cases.

The most obvious relationship is between war and hegemony. All historical accounts include global wars as important, and perhaps essential, for securing hegemony. According to Wallerstein, the hegemon's "economic edge is expanded by the very process of the war itself, and the post-war inter-state settlement is designed to encrust that greater edge and protect against its erosion" (Wallerstein 1984a, p. 106). When the hegemon declines, its inability to enforce the postwar settlement or to coordinate the joint interests of the core vis-à-vis the periphery results in a "scramble . . . among the leading powers to maintain their share" and an "incentive to a reshuffling of alliance systems" (pp. 106–107). The scrambling and reshuffling continue until the next world war secures the hegemony of one of the competing great powers.

Modelski and Thompson (1988) apply the same logic to world leaders, who typically emerge from a global war with a clear preponderance of naval power (i.e., more than half the world total). Lesser states are unlikely to challenge the world leader as long as it retains this concentration of power. This provides a pattern for the concern of "realists" that rational state leaders initiate war only if they expect to both win and profit, and expectations of winning are based on calculations of relative resources (Gilpin 1981). We can put these two perspectives together to point out that if a world leader does not translate innovation and military concentration into a hegemonic position, then its leadership will be challenged, yielding a period of renewed rivalry and potential global war.

On the other hand, when the leader succeeds to hegemony, its dual concentration of economic and military resources enables it to enforce the postwar *world order*. There have been six attempts at establishing a framework for world order—in 1519, 1648, 1713, 1815, 1919, and 1945. Every other one was associated with the emergence of an economic hegemon and the world order lasted as long as the hegemony. Without hegemonic enforcement, the attempted frameworks of 1519, 1713, and 1919 failed to establish a lasting peace and their breakdown kindled subsequent wars (Holsti 1991). We discuss world orders in more detail in the next chapter.

While the hegemony arguments are well known, the finding that war intensity is associated with K-wave expansions may surprise some. Note that intensity applies to the size of wars, not their frequency. The basic argument is that economic expansion provides the resources to wage larger wars and that military expenses drag opponents into peace during stagnant periods. This is a *resource* theory of the size of wars. Internal pressure from stagnations or domestic conflict may encourage core states to wage "cheap" wars of conquest in the periphery (discussed below), but major wars, those that require a massive and sustained supply of military and human resources, are more difficult to prepare for during economic crises. Two psychological biases, egocentrism and ethnocentrism, tend to skew information on resources such that state leaders would typically perceive their own relative advantages to be greater and more important during expansions (Boswell and Sweat 1991). It only takes one core state to start a major war.

Imperialism and colonial conquest follow the opposite pattern of major wars. Hegemons seek to remove political impediments to their market expansion, supporting "free trade" and encouraging (or at least ignoring) colonial liberation of their core competitors (but not necessarily of their own colonies). Conquest rises, on the other hand, during periods of contested hegemony when no single power can enforce a world order. In regard to long waves, exerting imperial control over peripheral resources provides an outlet for internal pressures or crises produced by stagnation. The opposite is true of expansions where the cost-benefit ratio of imperial coercion declines relative to expanding market resources. The overall pattern is manifested in cycles of net colonial expansion and decolonization (Boswell 1989a; Bergesen and Schoenberg 1980).

The cyclical nature of imperialism is bracketed by the shifts in world orders and interacts with the trend in national state formation, such that a convergence of all three in the post–World War II period eventually resulted in the abolition of formal colonialism. The principles of the world order, embodied in the UN and enforced by an overwhelming U.S. hegemony, called for a universal rather than the previous core-wide-only national sovereignty, which was not fully codified nor accepted until as late as 1960 (Boswell 1989a). This came at a time of military defeat or exhaustion of several core imperialists (Germany, Japan, Britain, and France), followed by tremendous economic expansion. This combination made colonialism an increasingly costly anachronism, epitomized by the failed (neo)imperialism in Algeria and Vietnam.

Decolonization is a fundamental change in the operation of the interstate system, following perhaps only abolition in importance. Nevertheless, the end of formal colonialism has not, of course, meant the complete elimination of neocolonial hierarchical relations between core and periphery. There has been an *oscillation between markets and hierarchies,* in which more open market trade periodically gives way to more politically structured interaction (Boswell 1989a). This is currently manifested in the form of emergent regional trading blocs, which include both developed and less developed countries (Junne 1999).

A Dynamic Model: Rise, Fall, and War

Our theories of the world-system explain that uneven development results in shifting geographic concentrations of economic, and thus military, power (Boswell 1995; Chase-Dunn 1998). In Figure 1.3, we present an analytical model that summarizes the trends and cyclical features of the world-system. In this model, cycles result from the interaction of trends. The cycle of hegemony and war results from the interaction of three long-term trends: state formation, economic interdependence, and uneven development. Figure 1.3 displays the causal pathways for each trend going across the rows. At the top, interstate competition drives state formation as polities are forced to develop militarized states to compete with other states. Growing integration of the world economy brings new societies into competition and requires that all global actors have recognizable and even similar institutions to enable interaction. The combination of integration and uneven development results in an unequal interdependence, in which the core states regulate exchange with peripheral ones through imperial means. Imperialism has been the political cement between core and periphery.

Following across the figure, conflicts over imperial spheres lead to wars, which become major wars when a long K-wave expansion provides the resources. Major wars become global wars when the shifting economic balance creates multipolarity among the core states. States that manage to harness the leading economic sectors and to build formidable military establishments become leaders over the system. World leaders may contend for hegemony, and the military outcomes of that contention, along with institutionalization of subsequent peace, are necessary for successful hegemony. A world leader emerges from the global war to forge a new world order for regulating international relations and distributing imperial obligations. If the war has devastated competitors and if the new world order skews relations so that expansion of the leader is in the common good of most core states, then during the next economic expansion, the world leader may translate its position into hegemony over the system. To realize hegemony, it must institutionalize its position in the postwar order. If it fails, the unfortunate result is another round of war. The "ifs" are the historically contingent institutional and political factors.

A hegemon's life-span is limited. The figure displays hegemonic decline as the trends continue. Hegemonic resilience depends in particular on preventing the world order from breaking back down into imperial regulation of competing spheres. It thus benefits from decolonization of competing empires (but not its own). Maintaining the world order also requires the hegemon to extend its military reach over long-

Figure 1.3 Hegemonic Cycles Resulting from the Interaction of Global Trends

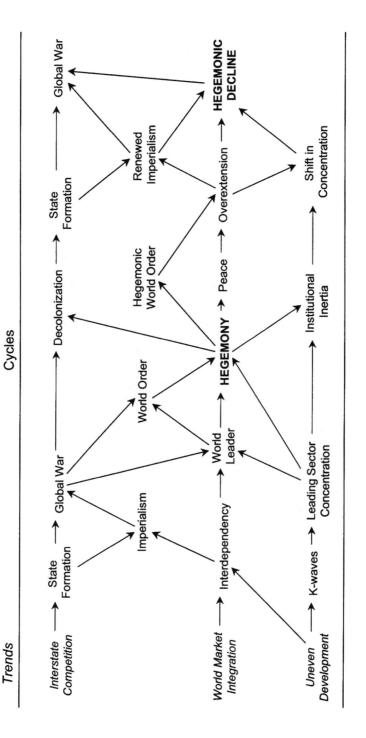

distance transactions. However, other traders benefit from the world order without paying the military costs, leading eventually to an overextension by the hegemon. Institutional inertia slows adoption of innovations by the hegemon as it is located where the past institutionalization was strongest. Decline sets in when the lead shifts to a new economic sector, but the overextended hegemon is entrenched in decaying industries.

The analytical model in Figure 1.3 is intended to display the systemic causal processes involved in hegemony that are common to all three cases. Such analytical models refine historical processes into their necessary and sufficient causes. To do so, they of course must ignore both historical specificity and some important structural changes since the fifteenth century. Giovanni Arrighi's 1994 structural history of the modern world-system specifies the important organizational features that changed the relationships among capitals and states in the successive "systemic regimes of accumulation" that accompanied the rise and fall of hegemonic powers.[8] Historical explanations for the rise or fall of each hegemon also include a great mass of particular history, contingent events, and random occurrence—the highlights of which are summarized above in Table 1.1.

A related question, and central to our overall purpose, is whether a long-term political cycle is evident in social movements, revolutions, and other political upheavals from below. Less empirical work has been completed on this topic than on major wars and imperial conquests, and prior theory is less developed. The lack of world-systemic theories of revolution is surprising given the importance of revolution to world history. But there have been a few pioneering studies (Boswell and Peters 1990; Kowalewski 1991; Silver and Slater 1999). These studies have reached similar conclusions independently, the most important of which is that *transition* phases between cycles appear to be periods of rebellious upheaval. We call these intervals "world divides," periods in which one accumulation regime is giving way to another and the world order is being redefined. Advancing this theory is one goal of the next chapter, with applications to the revolutions of 1989 in the following chapter. But, the importance of revolutions for world-system theory is not just to explain these or any other set of revolutions. Revolutions are key to understanding human agency in the construction and reconstruction of the system, such as the global importance of the French Revolution for expanding individual liberty, of the Russian Revolution for expanding social welfare, or of the Algerian Revolution for ending colonialism. An equally important goal is thus to develop the other side of the theory, explaining how clusters of revolutionary activity restructure the institutions and redefine the cognitive parameters of the world order. These clusters are what Arrighi, Hopkins, and Wallerstein (1989b) call "world revolutions."

Notes

1. Chase-Dunn and Hall (1997) have formulated a comparative world-systems framework for examining the similarities and differences among stateless, state-based, and the modern world-system and for explaining human social evolution over the past twelve thousand years.
2. Roemer (1982) provides logical proofs for the theory of exploitation. See also Bowles and Gintis (1990).
3. Ruggie (1998, pp. 12–13) makes a useful contrast between the Durkheimian concept of "social facts" such as values and norms that exist because people agree upon them, and "brute facts" such as warheads and markets that impose themselves on people regardless of their shared beliefs. A world polity exists to the extent that peoples share social facts of great importance.
4. The terms "world order" and "world polity" differ in emphasis and sometimes in ontology. Meyer (1987) and Boli and Thomas (1997) contend that a Christian world polity prefigured the emergent capitalist/interstate system and that while the new system recast and re-created the world polity, the definition of states and sovereignty has always been determined by the preexisting global political culture. As will be explained in later chapters, we argue that older world polities have been deliberately deconstructed and replaced by a succession of war-born world orders that have, in contested fits, become more integrated over time. That integration has accelerated tremendously since WWII.
5. The theory of sociopolitical "accumulation innovations" developed in Boswell (1987) is a synthesis of long-wave and economic-historical research by Schumpeter (1939), Braverman (1974), Mandel (1975, 1980), Wright (1975), Chandler (1977), Mensch (1978), Edwards (1979), Wallerstein (1980), Gordon (1980), Gordon, Edwards, and Reich (1982), Weber (1983), Bowles, Gordon and Weisskopf (1983), and Piore and Sabel (1984).
6. Extensive evidence for each leading sector can be found in Modelski and Thompson (1996) and Rostow (1978); for the first 250 years in Misra and Boswell (1997); for most of the second half in Gordon, Edwards, and Reich (1982); and in raw form in Goldstein (1988).
7. Alternatively, the combination of two contradictory tendencies could be seen as one dialectical principle.
8. Arrighi (1994) also emphasizes the important shift that occurs in each accumulation regime. The shift is from profit making based on production to profit making based on financial investments and manipulations.

2

World Revolutions and the Political Economy of Socialism

Revolutions in the World-System

Consider the following definition:

> Social revolutions are rapid, basic transformations of a society's state and class structures; and they are accompanied and in part carried through by class-based revolts from below. Social revolutions are set apart from other sorts of conflicts and transformative processes above all by the combination of two coincidences: the coincidence of societal structural change with class upheaval; and the coincidence of the political with social transformation. (Skocpol 1979, p. 4)

Here is another:

> "Revolution" is a thoroughgoing social transformation, a prolonged process altering basic economic, political, and cultural/ideological structures. (Moghadam 1989, p. 148, synthesizing Johnson, Huntington, Petrovic, and Skocpol)

One more:

> [Revolution is] An abrupt change in the form of misgovernment . . . revolutions are usually accompanied by considerable effusion of blood, but are accounted worth it—this appraisement being made by beneficiaries whose blood had not the mischance to be shed. (Bierce 1911, p. 292)

Each of these definitions of revolution, along with a thousand more like them, includes an assumed definition of the economy and the class structure as parts of a society. This assumption is necessary to distinguish revolutions from rebellions that fail to transform society or from

51

coups that only change governmental personnel (with Bierce questioning whether the changes are either real or worth it). The distinction is also necessary in order to understand the conditions that cause people to revolt.

Cross-national research has produced an increasingly consistent list of societal causes of revolution (Boswell and Dixon 1990, 1993; Muller 1986, 1988; Muller and Seligson 1987). The primary causes are the following:

- *Class exploitation* (the ratio of total value added in a society to total wages and salaries, implying at high levels, intense work at low wages)
- *Income inequality* (the concentration of income and, by causal implication, income-producing capital and land, among a small elite)
- *Economic crises* (low and declining rates of economic growth, such as recessions; the effects of crises are greatest where exploitation is highest)
- *State repression* (lack of a representative voice for grievances, giving no alternative to revolt—note that extreme repression can, however, deter open revolt)
- *Ethnic separatism* (nationalist liberation movements within a state, typically by oppressed minorities)

Exploitation, inequality, and economic crisis incite rebellious grievances from those seeking a larger share and a more equitable distribution of income. The aggrieved also may struggle for more control over their working conditions and those features of the system that are thought to cause their deprivation. Grievances are more violent and revolutionary where repression has closed off democratic sources of social change and civil outlets for protest, but extreme repression can prevent people from mobilizing large-scale revolutionary actions.[1]

While more extensive and more violent rebellion is found with increases in this combination of causes, popular support is no guarantee of a rebellion's success. Cross-national research usually stops with the causes of rebellion, but comparative historical research on revolutions offers evidence on the issues of success and consequences (e.g., Skocpol 1979; Walton 1984; Boswell 1989b; Goldstone 1991; Wickham-Crowley 1991). Successful revolutions usually require an additional source of state breakdown, frequently caused by fiscal crisis and/or international military pressure.

Revolutions are directed at capturing, using, or amplifying political institutions and as such, their main long-term effect has been to strengthen the state. Skocpol (1979), for instance, echoes Tocqueville in claiming that the primary result of revolution is a strengthening of the state, typically through increased centralization and bureaucratization. The revolutions of 1989, however, run counter to this prior trend.

From a world-systemic viewpoint, the state-building effects of revolution should come as no surprise. State formation is one of the long-term trends of the system, driven mainly by war and geopolitical competition, which revolution contributes to and defines. Economic changes brought by a revolution also tend to meld with long-term global trends of the system as a whole. Domestic economic institutions are constrained by the basic global parameters required for international interaction. Understanding the long-term consequences of a revolution by contrasting postrevolutionary domestic structures with those in other societies will thus always disappoint. Organizational forms, of course, may differ in ways that are quite significant for the people involved, but they cannot become entirely incommensurate with the existing world order without suffering isolation or invasion. From a world-systems perspective, the ultimate consequences of revolutions can best be understood by the effects that they have on the world order itself.

There are two types of revolutions with long-term world-systemic effects: (1) state-building revolutions and (2) world revolutions. State-building revolutions are those social upheavals that have been the focus of most of the recent social-science literature on revolution and the object of the several definitions quoted at the beginning of this chapter. World revolutions are clusters of revolutionary activity and social movements that can restructure and redefine the normative rules and cognitive assumptions of the world order. State-building revolutions are the most common type and the only kind of revolution that is studied by those who proceed from a societal perspective. From a global perspective, however, world revolutions are more important. In world-system theory, world revolutions and associated social movements are a missing key to understanding human agency in the systemic operation of international relations and world markets. We address each type of revolution in turn.

State-Building Revolutions

War has been the driving force behind modern state formation in the core, with revolutions often following if state breakdown occurs as a consequence of wartime destruction, defeat, or fiscal crisis. These revolutions have typically produced stronger states in their wake. Revolution also often includes its own war, either a civil war or a war of independence. State building has the contradictory results of both strengthening and expanding states, and of breaking up multi-ethnic states into a proliferation of nation-states. This gives us a distinction between social revolutions versus separatist and colonial revolutions, each with distinct features and causes. Social revolutions are those where the rebels build an alternative state within the existing society, either in direct competition with the old regime—a dual power situation—or on top of the ruins of the previous regime—a state breakdown situation. Separatist revolutions are those where a minority ethnic group with a regional concentration builds a separatist state that rejects the authority of the previous regime. Colonial revolutions are those where the rebels (which may or may not be an ethnic minority) seek to build an independent state in a colony or other subordinate political subdivision of the old regime.

A general theoretical difference between world-system versus societal studies of revolution is a greater emphasis upon and inclusion of separatist and colonial revolutions. Social science literature has traditionally focused only on social revolutions, leaving separatist or colonial revolts unanalyzed. While the major causal arguments listed above usually apply to all three types, at the societal level there are good reasons to consider each type separately. Most important is the differential class character of revolts, with social revolutions usually dividing between a coalition of lower classes versus an upper-class/state-elite bloc, while separatist and colonial revolts divide between ethnic and national identities that usually span classes. The difference in organizing principles between class solidarity and ethnicity or nationality is one of the enduring contributions of the social movement literature.

From a global perspective, however, these differences lose some of their distinction and prominence. Class exploitation crosses national borders and often overlaps with ethnic or national conflicts. This is obvious with overt colonialism and to a lesser extent with transnational corporations, both of which are entangled with states and policies. Secondary exploitation between large and small capital owners adds to international and regional/ethnic conflicts as well. Ethnic, national, and religious conflicts within societies are generated to a large extent by global uneven development and transnational migration (Bonacich et al. 1994).

Most important is that national "sovereignty" itself is a principle imbedded in the origin and functioning of the capitalist world-system. War may have been more central to state building, but revolution and war are frequently intertwined. Since the end of the sixteenth century, all the different types of state-building revolutions have had as their result the formation and reformation of sovereign states as recognized actors in the interstate system. While we tend to think of social revolutions as fundamentally different from separatist and colonial revolutions, all share the aspect of a conflict over which political bloc and associated military force will rule over a territory that is or could be recognized internationally as sovereign. A rebel bloc in a social revolution contests the status quo for state power in an already recognized territory; a colonial or separatist rebel bloc contests the status quo in a new territory that must be recognized internationally in order for the rebellion to succeed.

As noted in Chapter 1, revolutionary state building, starting with the Dutch Revolution of the sixteenth century, was responsible in part for the origins and reproduction of the interstate system. From that point forward, creating new states, whether via separatism or colonial independence, changes the structure of the system. The change may be small—unless revolutions cluster or their ideas spread. The cumulative effect of separatist and colonial revolutions that spread national self-determination throughout the system is one of the most significant changes in its five-hundred-year history.

In principle, people can make a revolution at any time the conditions demand it and the political situation allows it. Societal revolutions are scattered throughout time and space in world history, but within that scatter are clusters whose size, breadth, and effects are far greater in importance than others. These revolutionary clusters make a pattern that is not entirely contingent on particular historical conjunctures. These have a rough proximity to world-systemic cycles. We examine the historical pattern of revolutionary activity below and link the clusters to shifts in the world order in the next section.

Historical Patterns of Revolt: 1492–1992

In his *European Revolutions,* Charles Tilly (1993) provides an exhaustive review of revolutionary situations in most of Europe since 1492.[2] Revolutionary situations exist when two or more organized groups hold state power over a territory, or some portion of it. In Figure 2.1, we display the pattern of all these revolutionary situations over time. Various clusters and spikes are evident that we will discuss below. But first, it is important to recognize how the character of revolution has changed over time.

Tilly centers on how changes in the interests and demands of populations shift over time as both their social conditions develop, and as the character of polities and the powers of rulers evolve. The basic trends of

Figure 2.1   Total Revolutionary Situations in Europe, 1492–1992

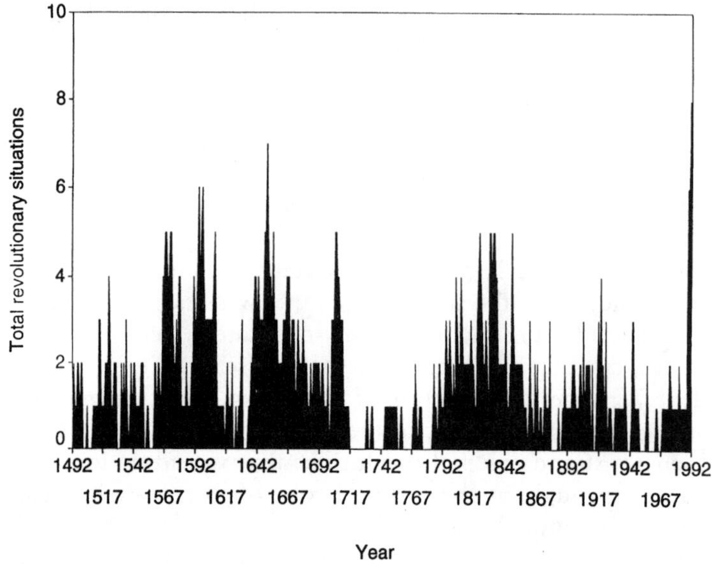

capitalist development—commodification, proletarianization, urbanization, capitalization, and transnationalization—result in greater emphasis over time on prices (instead of supply), labor (instead of craft), hous-
ing (instead of land), and debt (instead of duties). Regarding the state,
the general trend since 1492 has been one of central-state expansion,
subordination of the autonomy of princes and churches, and political
intensification, wherein populations are counted, conscripted, coerced,
consoled, coddled, and otherwise converted into citizens. The very
process of subjecting populations, Tilly points out, also created state
obligations and responsibilities, such that states become increasingly
subject to popular consent.

   We have gone through the history of every revolution in the data set
to characterize it according to three overlapping features: religious
struggles, anticentralization conflicts, and class conflicts.[3] Figure 2.2
plots religious struggles and is distinguished primarily by the falloff of
events in the seventeenth and again in the eighteenth centuries (these
were dominated by the Anglo-Irish conflict thereafter). This pattern represents the impact of the Reformation and the eventual transition of
polities from dynasties to modern states.

Figure 2.2   Religious Struggles in Europe, 1492–1992

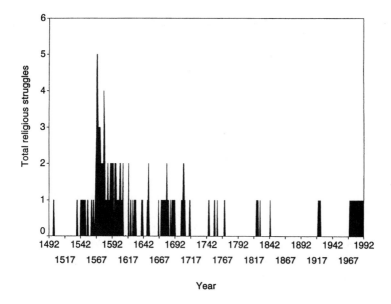

Figure 2.3   Anti-Centralization Struggles in Europe, 1492–1992

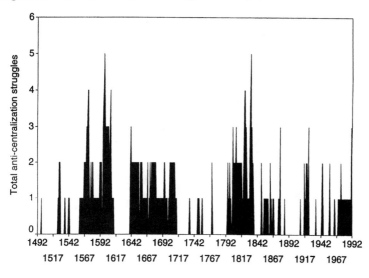

Figure 2.3 reflects the anti-centralization struggles over state building. These include both revolts that are a resistance to attempts to
expand central authority and independence struggles by internal
colonies and nations, or other distinct regions. This latter type of revolt
was often confined to a particular region or provincial state (Ireland,
Serbia, Catalonia, etc.), and did not threaten the imperial state as a
whole. As such, these were often the internal equivalents of colonial
revolts in the periphery, and were thus frequently intertwined with
interstate wars.

Revolts that included significant class conflicts appear in Figure 2.4.
Clear indication of peasant revolts, artisan armies, worker uprisings,
massive strike waves, factory takeovers, and so on fit this category.
Peasant revolts decline over time and shift geographically with early
industrialization as one might expect. Indications of urban artisan or
worker revolt rise correspondingly, although even the earliest revolts
would often involve urban uprisings. Many of these revolts started for
other purposes, but gained a class character as combatants conscripted
the lower classes and elicited their support, or when interelite conflict
created the opportunity for the lower classes to press their interests. The

Figure 2.4   Class-Conflict Struggles in Europe, 1492–1992

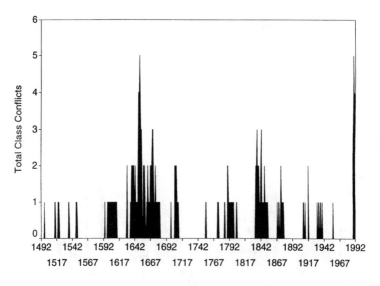

pattern for revolts with a clear class component shows sharper peaks and longer fallow periods than the trends shown in previous figures. The geographic pattern over time is one where class-based revolts end first in northwestern Europe and last in the undemocratic semiperiphery of Eastern Europe. As a general principle, where class conflict forced states to become democratic, large-scale class violence has disappeared. Classes pursue their interests through organizations and nonviolent electoral means of representation in what Korpi (1983) calls the "democratic class struggle."

Revolutions in the core of the world-system, most of which are represented in the Tilly data, should be the most important for the system as a whole. The impact of revolutions outside the core is mainly felt in terms of decolonization of the periphery and of socialist revolutions in the semiperiphery. The most important socialist revolution outside Europe is the Chinese Revolution of 1949 (followed by Cuba in 1959). After World War II and the hardening of the Cold War, most all decolonization revolts added a socialist character (a topic to which we will return). As one can see in Figure 2.5, decolonization occurred in two distinct clusters, in the Americas in 1776–1820, and in the rest of the

Figure 2.5   Waves of Decolonization

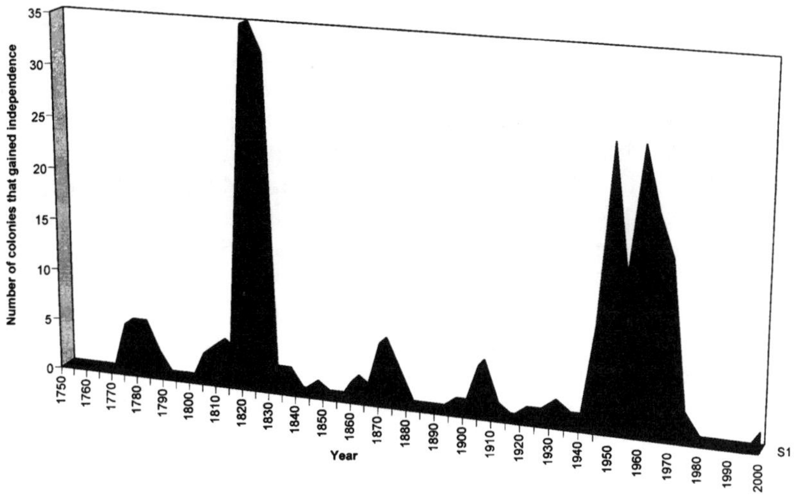

Source: Henige (1970).
Note: Colonial empires of Britain, Italy, Japan, the Netherlands, Portugal, Spain, France, and the United States were coded.

periphery following World War II (Bergesen and Schoenberg 1980). Within the postwar cluster, there are two distinct spikes. The first is in 1945–1949 with the dismantling of Japanese imperialism and the decolonization of the South Asian subcontinent, and the second is around 1960 with the dissolution of the French Empire in Africa and a further dismantling of empires generally following the 1960 UN Declaration on the Granting of Independence to Colonial Countries and Peoples [Resolution 1514 (XV)].

Since World War II, these two huge waves of state-building revolutions have vastly expanded the number and global dispersion of independent states through the decolonization of former colonial empires. Add to this a third wave in 1989–1992 caused by the breakup into national states of the former multi-ethnic USSR and Yugoslavia, as shown in Figure 2.3. The result is a much different and far more complex interstate system than the prewar system. Such state-building processes are likely to continue, for reasons we explain elsewhere, although the pace should decline over time as the number of nations without states decreases.

Starting with the European-centered world-system around 1492 and including all the rest of the globe by the end of the nineteenth century, we can now identify a few periods over the entire five hundred years during which state-building revolutions and revolutionary situations were most heavily clustered.[4] The most important revolutionary clusters are the following:

- 1522–1525: Peasant Revolts, beginnings of Protestant Reformation, various revolts against centralizing authority
- 1556–1581: Wars of Religion throughout central Europe
- 1640–1648: Portuguese independence (1640), Dutch independence (1648), English Revolution (1640), and multiple revolutionary uprisings throughout Europe in 1648[5]
- 1776–1820: North America (1776–1783), Netherlands (1785–1787), French Revolution and revolutionary wars (1789–1792), Latin American independence (1811–1820), Haitian Revolution (1804–1806)
- 1848: French Revolution, revolutionary uprisings throughout continental Europe
- 1916–1919: Breakup of Austro-Hungarian Empire (1918–1919), Arab Revolt (1916), breakup of Ottoman Empire (1918), Russian Revolution (1917)
- 1944–1950: Decolonization in Asia, notably India and Indonesia (and to a lesser extent Africa), Chinese Revolution (1949)
- 1959–1969: Decolonization in Africa (especially French colonies,

notably Algeria in 1962) and in Asia, Cuban Revol
and various armed uprisings in Latin America
* 1989–1992: Eastern European revolutions, breakup
  Union and Yugoslavia

A few smaller clusters are worthy of note, including Belgian and Greek independence, a French political revolution and minor uprisings elsewhere in Europe in 1830, or the Chinese Nationalist and the Mexican Revolutions (both in 1911). The 1974 Portuguese Revolution and independence of its African colonies form a small cluster. Vietnamese independence spans several clusters, but also ends in 1974. Revolutions in Nicaragua, Iran, and Zimbabwe, along with uprisings in Poland and China, make another small cluster in 1979–1980. Several other important events were relatively isolated or otherwise hard to classify, such as Garibaldi's expedition of Italian unification (1860), the American Civil War (1860–1865), or the Paris Commune (1871).

The geographic spread of revolutionary state building follows the imperial spread of the system, first concentrated in Europe and the Americas, then mainly comprised of decolonization of Asia and Africa following World War II. The decline of revolutionary activity in the core also reflects the expansion of representative democracy, and with it, a decline in inequality and exploitation rates. As noted above, with democracy, class and other struggles have the alternative of nonviolent means. One alternative is union organizing and strikes. Examining strike waves and other large-scale protests in the core countries, we find a similar pattern to that of revolutions, with large spikes in 1917–1919, 1948, and 1966–1969.[6] The clusters were related in part, we will theorize, by common reactions to world-systemic dynamics. More importantly, we argue below that each of the major clusters, especially when coincident with a major war, was part of the process that produced a world revolution. Each world revolution shifted the character and political principles of the world-system over time.

World Revolutions: 1492–1992

World revolutions are accompanied by, and are in part carried out by, social and political revolutions within societies. They are also often intertwined with interstate wars and entail changes in interstate relations. However, they differ from societal revolutions in that world revolutions cannot involve the overthrow of the government, as there is no world state. While the term "world revolution" finds common use, as an analytical concept it has been little developed and empirical investigation is largely absent. Hegel (1956) offered some interesting (although not entirely comprehensible) ideas about the French Revolution as the penultimate culmination of the Enlightenment and Napoleon as the "world soul." More generally, Marx and most Marxists argue that revolutions are the deciding events in the class struggle that propel world development beyond the fetters of antiquated but heretofore entrenched social relations. Trotsky's (1931) theory of "permanent revolution" is probably the most relevant, particularly his notion that revolutions have a "two steps forward, one step back" character. Egalitarian ideas and unfettered institutions brought forward by revolution are forced back by counterrevolution, but rarely all the way back to the prior status quo. In the next revolution, progress ends up where it had last advanced before being forced back.

In world-system theory, we find a similar concept in essays by Arrighi, Hopkins, and Wallerstein (1989b, 1992), who argue that world revolutions are only firmly incorporated by a subsequent "consolidating" revolt. They identify only two world revolutions, 1848 and 1968, with the 1871 Paris Commune, 1917 Russian Revolution, and 1989 East European revolutions serving as consolidating revolts. Although their empirical criteria are not entirely clear, the designation comes from the effects of a revolution on the character of antisystemic movements. Specifically, the development of socialist movements makes 1848 a world revolution, while the New Left origins qualify 1968. Arrighi, Hopkins, and Wallerstein (1989b, 1992) lack a concept of the world order, although Wallerstein (1995) discusses similar ideas. Developing a theory of world orders (and polities) is critical, we contend, for explaining the effects of human agency on world structures.

We build upon this prior research, but our approach incorporates institutional theories to explain how revolutions matter at the world level. We connect the institutions of the world order and polity with ideas and institutions of revolutionaries and social movements, completing the duality of structure and agency. In so doing, we provide the empirically grounded frame missing in Arrighi, Hopkins, and Wallerstein (1989a), without falling into the cultural determinism of traditional institutional theory (Meyer et al. 1997). Much more is to be done to fully flesh out a theory of world revolutions, but our beginnings here start to tell us what we need to know.

In the absence of a global state, the national states can codify changes in the world order only by joint pronouncements, treaties, and pacts among themselves (and among firms and other international actors). Major war, which by definition means that the prior world order had failed, is the impetus for most new forms of world order. Designed to restore peace, the order defines what state behaviors and forms are "legitimate," that is, what will not be challenged by other states. Free trade, self-determination, democracy, and human rights have been raised as justifications for war, that is, as state behaviors and forms worth fighting over. To widely varying degrees, all have been incorporated into postwar world orders. In defining legitimate states, the world order thus includes far more than just the terms of a treaty (Meyer 1999). For a state to be legitimate, it must also engender internal peace. Revolutions, even those that fail to capture state power (and most do fail) can render a state illegitimate and force it to adopt new forms and policies. Revolutions often follow a major war, when states have been defeated or fiscally strapped, and when populations are disgusted with their state. If accepted as legitimate, revolutionary states will have changed the world order, although they may have had to go to war to get recognition. Also important is that even when state elites are not directly threatened with revolt, they may adopt a mild version of the new political forms and polities to avoid the same. Thus the effect of revolution may far exceed its direct political success.

World orders proffer only weak forms of international enforcement in themselves. However, on occasion rogue states are boycotted, contained, or invaded, especially when they embody and promote radical new state forms and behaviors. Containment of revolutionary Russia in 1918 and again with China in 1945–1949, and of France in 1815, was fundamental to postwar orders. Containment also included preventing or overthrowing revolutions inspired by the above.

Although its most obvious enactment, active military enforcement of a world order actually represents a weakness of its influence. The main source of enforcement is reciprocity, most powerfully when going "tit for tat" with a hegemon. The substance of a shift in the world order is found not only in collective action or international organization, but also in innovative organizational forms that are emulated throughout the system and that institutionalize a new standardization of relations. New organizational forms are widely adopted because they are successful at *containing social conflict* or *promoting economic development,* with the most successful doing both. Once a standard is set, it is further enforced by the advantage of facilitating interaction among like forms, and sometimes by the active shunning or boycotting of divergent forms. The classic example is the modern state itself, which with few exceptions is now in the form of a republic. Except for a few very rich and a few very poor cases, once-ubiquitous monarchies are nearly extinct. Nor does any state dare use the name "empire," common only a generation ago. An at least partially representative legislature has become a nearly universal political standard (Meyer et al. 1997). In most cases, representative elections were hard-fought victories of social movements or revolutions. Where states are less representative, they generate high levels of rebellious conflict and lower economic growth (Boswell and Dixon 1990).

Revolution is the ultimate form of societal conflict. Institutional change following an attempted revolution tends to be progressive in part because it is designed to satisfy or at least pacify rebellious populations. This includes elite concessions to avoid the spread of more-radically egalitarian movements. The alternative to concessions is sustained coercion, which can be used, but is costly and is a drag on innovative development. The cost of coercion increases with industrialization. The more firms or states are dependent on technical skill and cooperative social interactions, the more vulnerable they are to social unrest. Vice versa, coercion can be quite efficient in extracting physical labor in unskilled production. Plantations used slavery to produce raw materials for capitalist factories for four hundred years. Sweatshops survive today in unskilled textile production. However, despite exceptions and periodic setbacks, the long-term trend has been one of global progress.

Global Progress

Shifts in the world order that are brought on by revolution tend, over the long term, to be *progressive*. By progressive, we mean changes in the rules and norms of typical behavior that increase the freedom and autonomy of the working classes, and in so doing, reduce their exploitation and raise their living standards. Both sides of the definition must apply—increases in freedom that reduce living standards are not progressive, and vice versa. But, the two are strongly linked in most cases. World revolutions set global standards that reduce the ability of capitalists and landlords to employ coercive means to extract labor or to force workers to compete over lower living standards.

Progressive standards proscribe the ability of capitalists and states to hold down wages, limit labor mobility, restrict women and ethnic minorities, break unions, and so on. Abolition is the most obvious example. The increase in freedom and autonomy forced employers to compete for labor, reducing exploitation and raising living standards not just for former slaves, but also for wage workers who once had to compete against slave labor. Although the scale is far different, removing gender and ethnic discrimination or other coercive impediments to labor mobility and organization has a similar effect. The progressive effects of standards that ban coercion are easy to see and are consistent with the idea of free labor markets. The same logic applies to standards that increase labor mobility, that is, make it easier for workers to change

jobs and to move to places that pay higher wages (coercion is also difficult where labor mobility is high). Also obvious are the benefits of standards that facilitate labor organization and legal rights. Related, but
more difficult to enforce, are proactive standards that limit employment
of vulnerable populations, such as bans on child labor, and that set minimum wages and standardize working conditions. Even more difficult
and volatile, but also important, are welfare standards and land reforms
that provide workers with alternatives to wage labor.

Setting standards in a labor market reduces the profits from seeking
lower wages and raises the return to investments in technology or in
training that raise productivity, further raising living standards.
Technological development itself is not inherently progressive, but
increases in productivity make it easier to set progressive standards. In
general, the value of pacifying (rather than coercing) labor increases
with technological development that requires educated or skilled workers. At the same time, technology that raises productivity increases the
ability to pay higher wages. Most important for social progress are standards that encourage investment in human capital (training, skills, experience, education, etc.). Again, while highly uneven, a long-term view
shows general trends toward more-educated labor with fewer restrictions on their mobility and organization.

All combined, these progressive shifts have a distinct effect on the
labor market. Employers increase profits by either utilizing cheaper
labor than their competitors or by increasing the productivity of labor
through capital investment, both human and physical. In either case, the
profit increase tends to be temporary, as competitors emulate anything
that works, making for strong trends in one direction or the other. It is
difficult to go in both directions at once. Highly productive labor is
harder to come by where wages and investment are low, and workers are
unlikely to increase their productivity unless it raises their wages.
Competing simply over cheaper labor costs results in a never-ending
drive to move to lower-cost areas, break unions, and otherwise reduce
workers' freedom and their living standards. Global limits on such
behavior put none at a disadvantage (although they do raise the benefits
of cheating) and instead shift competition to the advantage of firms and
states that raise productivity by investing in technology and education.

Since the world revolution of 1848, the general long-run trend has
been a rise in productivity and in wages for industrial labor in core
countries (Mitchell 1992, 1993, 1995). The trend is highly uneven and
sometimes reverses for years during K-wave stagnations, but from a five-
hundred-year perspective, there is a vast increase in the ability of labor
to organize, move, vote, and protest. Social movements and world revolutions have correspondingly become less violent. They also no longer

accomplish vast changes, such as abolition or decolonization, in part because they change a less rapacious and despotic system to the extent of the success and consolidation of prior world revolutions. Progress is not guaranteed, however, because conservative reaction and countermobilization most often reverses initial radical changes. What gains that do survive from any one revolution are typically not institutionalized into the world order until after a subsequent world revolution. As such, world revolutions always seem to fail in their stated goals. Where they succeed is in winning past revolutionary goals, some now twenty to fifty years past, or longer if it takes more than one subsequent revolution to institutionalize a change in the world order. In general, major changes in the world order would occur with the second in linked pairs of world revolution.

Revolutionary changes in the social structure are usually incorporated back into the existing class and state structure, with only those social innovations that increase labor productivity or eliminate waste being retained. A new social structure of accumulation is adopted that is superior in profits and productivity to those of the past. In so doing, the revolutionary period stimulates experimentation in organizational forms, even by states and firms far removed from the locus of revolt who seek to avoid similar conflicts. Every world revolution thus both consolidates acceptance of past demands and initiates a new set of concerns. The result is neither linear progress nor cyclical politics, but instead a combination of both that produces a historical spiral that is only recognizable as progressive over the *longue duré*.

The legacies of past world revolutions are institutionalized by the conservative reaction to existing ones as an attempt to reinforce the status quo and to prevent further social uprisings. Often, the only immediately obvious change that lasts past the conservative reaction is a shift in the terms of ideological concepts and debate. Challenges from below are formulated in egalitarian ideologies that frequently threaten the institutional bases of capitalist accumulation or hegemonic order. The discourse of world order is inherently universalistic. It must apply to multiple states and classes. Universalism becomes egalitarian when expressed by the subordinate classes (Gramsci 1971). This usually comes in the form of indirectly changing existing definitions of grand ideas by changing the assumptions that are taken for granted in making the definition. Liberty is the classic example (Sewell 1985). It is always defined in universal terms, but the assumed meaning of those terms has shifted over time to include the bourgeoisie, core workers, nationalities, minorities, and women left out in previous conceptions.

In Table 2.1 below, we list world revolutions along with a date of prime symbolic importance in the cluster of events. To the left, the revolutions are preceded by listings of the K-waves, leadership and hegemonic cycles, and global wars and world orders (see Table 1.1, Chapter 1, as well). We include only the modern world-system, and focus necessarily on the system's core. The first two cases are bracketed because, as we discuss the individual world revolutions below, revolutionary activity prior to 1648 differs from later instances. These early cases should be considered precursors or transitional instances, and while historically important, they do not fit the pattern seen in more recent examples of a concentrated set of events that topple states and realign the system in a relatively short time period. Religious and dynastic issues predominated prior to the Thirty Years' War, when the interstate system was consolidated. States fought a near continuous series of wars and imperial conflicts for the next 150 years before the next world revolution. Since 1648, world revolutions have come with increasing frequency and declining violence, while world wars have become less frequent and more violent.

Note that each world revolution initiates social experimentation of new ideas and organizational forms, listed below each event, and it institutionalizes ideas and organizational standards that were initiated in the prior world revolution. The list should be read looking up to the previous event to see what a world revolution institutionalizes and down to see what it introduces. If we compare the columns for world orders and world revolutions, we see a rough pattern of a linked pair of world revolutions for each major change in the world order, the latter typically associated with a major war.

World revolutions are rare events. We suggest that only nine cases merit inclusion, two less than the number of world wars listed, and of these, the first two we bracket as precursors to the modern state system. Each case occurred within a cluster of revolutionary activity and produced a significant change in the world order. Arrighi, Hopkins, and Wallerstein (1992) only recognize two cases, 1848 and 1968, as world revolutions. They mention the events of 1871, 1917, and 1989 as being global in scale and consequence, but exclude them from consideration because they see these actions as only consolidating movements initiated by the prior revolutions. Wallerstein (1998) elsewhere gives great importance to 1789, but leaves it out of world revolutionary status for reasons that are unclear.

In contrast, we determine the presence of world revolutions by observing a clear cluster of powerful events. We separate this from determining their effects, which is the extent that they affect the world order. While expecting that all world revolutions both consolidate and initiate social movements in linked pairs that restructure the world order, the extent to which this happens is a historical question that may be affected by a multitude of intervening factors. Most cases are well known to his-

Table 2.1   World Revolutions: Relationship to K-Waves, World Leaders and Hegemonies, and Global Wars and World Orders, 1492–1992

K-Wave Phase	Leader/ Hegemonies	Global Wars/ World-Order	World Revolutions (Initiatives)
1496-B			
1509-A	1517 Portugal	Italian Wars (1494–1525) [Catholic, 1519]	
1529-B	1526 [United Hapsburgs]ᵃ		[1526+ Reformation] (religious sovereignty, antiserfdom)]
1539-A	1556		
1559-B			[1556+ Religious Wars] (anti-imperial/Catholic polity; state sovereignty)
1575-A	1609 United Netherlands	Neth. Ind./Armada (1585–1609)	
1595-B		Thirty Years' War (1618–1648)	
1621-A	1648 United Netherlands	Interstate Sovereignty, 1648	1648 Sovereignty (republicanism, Enlightenment)
1650-B	1667	War of Louis XIV (1672–1678)	
1689-A		League of Augsburg (1688–1697) Spanish Succession (1701–1713)	
1720-B	1714 United Kingdom	Balance of Power, 1714	
1747-A	1739	Jenkins Ear (1739–1748)	
1762-B		Seven Years' War (1755–1763)	

		Rev./Napoleonic (1792–1815)	**1789 Liberal** (liberal rights, abolition, "universal" suffrage, utopian socialism)
1790-A	1816 United Kingdom		
1814-B	1850	Concert of Europe, 1815	
1848-A	**United Kingdom**		**1848 Democratic** (women's suffrage, labor movement, social democracy)
1872-B	1873		
1893-A			
1917-B		World War I (1914–1918)	**1917 Socialist** (self-determination; socialism)
1940-A	1945	League of Nations, 1918	**1949 National Liberation** (civil rights, developmental state)
	United States	World War II (1939–1945)	
1969-B	1974	United Nations, 1945	**1968 New Left** (women's liberation, cultural autonomy, environmental protection)
1991-A?			**1989 Global Democracy?** (world polity, universal rights, globalization)
		World Trade Organization, 1995?	

Sources: Long Waves (A = expansion; B = stagnation): Goldstein (1988). World Leaders: Modelski and Thompson (1996). Hegemony: Hopkins and Wallerstein (1979) after 1700; before 1700, Misra and Boswell (1997). Global Wars: Levy (1985), Italian wars from Modelski and Thompson (1988). World Orders: adapted from Holsti (1991), except for 1519 and 1995 speculation. World Revolutions: constructed with dates and insights from Boswell (1987); Boswell and Peters (1990); Boswell and Stevens (1997); Bergesen and Schoenberg (1980); Tilly (1993); Arrighi, Hopkins, and Wallerstein (1989a, 1992).

Notes: Years listed are symbolic turning points.

a. As the interstate system was not set until 1648, the United Hapsburgs dynasty was not hegemonic in the same sense as later states. Instead, it attempted imperial sovereignty over western Christendom. Likewise, the Reformation was not a world revolution in the same sense as later events.

torians of political philosophy and social movements, and it is clear that some results were much more significant than were others. Also, some cases produced more distinct results than others, such as the origins of modern socialism in 1848 and of communism in 1917. Our list is thus longer, but we do not ascribe equal importance to every event. As mentioned above, it appears that the radical sweep and importance of any world revolution may be declining over time, even as their frequency has grown.

Some of the cases may not deserve the name "event" at all, as a world revolution is not made from a singular episode of capturing power in this or that particular state. Instead, it is composed of multiple uprisings, mobilizations, and social movements—that mostly "fail" in their stated objectives. Nevertheless, we can usually point to a momentous event within the larger cluster, often lasting less than a single year, which so rapidly upsets social relations as to initiate experimentation in new institutional forms and consolidate acceptance of prior social demands. The list in Table 2.1 designates key revolutionary events of this sort. In most cases, the final outcome emerges over decades and new principles are not institutionalized globally until they are consolidated in a subsequent world revolution. Many initiatives are lost or reversed, and those that survive may be fought over in more than one subsequent revolution before they become institutionalized. Once-revolutionary propositions, like abolition, suffrage, or self-determination, are now taken for granted throughout the core and even most of the rest of the world. Only when revolutionary initiatives are institutionalized to the extent that they are taken for granted could we say that the battle has been won. In this sense, all revolutions are failures in their own time.

World Revolutions and Systemic Processes

There appear to be links between the pattern of world revolutions and world-systemic processes, some obvious and some more speculative. Statistical analyses will be required sometime down the line to further substantiate the apparent historical and theoretical relationships,[7] which include the following four connections. First, revolutions are intertwined with wars. Losing wars can destroy a state, and even winning can be so expensive as to bankrupt it. Revolutionaries not only have a better chance to topple a weak state, and receive assistance from the other side, but the taxes, conscription, and deaths from war can also incite rebellion. These factors have long been known to have played a large part in the English, French, Russian, and Chinese Revolutions. What world-systems theory adds is that the occurrence of war is in turn related to systemic dynamics. In short, major wars tend to be bigger during K-wave expansions, fewer wars occur during hegemonic periods, colonial conquests were more frequent during K-wave stagnations, and colonial independence more frequent during expansions (see Chapter 1). The coupling of revolution with war greatly expands the possibility for movements from below to impact the legitimacy of states and with it, the parameters of the world order as it is reconstituted in the postwar peace.

Second, the size and breadth of societal revolutions appear to be greatest during the two transition points in the K-wave, that is, both when the long expansion has first begun to stagnate and when, after a long stagnation, the economy shows signs of a sustained rebound. We will discuss the causality by which the K-wave transitions produced revolutionary clusters below. Consider for now our third point, which is that comparing the two transitions, the effects of revolutions are greater in the latter, during the transition from stagnation to expansion. The reason is that the latter period is when states and firms are applying experiments that showed promise in getting them out of the long stagnation. World revolutions can break the inertia of existing structures in order to implement innovations that have been found to be successful elsewhere. This is especially true where elites and intellectuals sense that their states and firms are losing out in economic or political/military competition with other states or firms. Losses in economic competitions are most evident in countries that lag behind in adopting the innovations that are producing renewed growth elsewhere. People rebel in order to eliminate not just the governmental and class elites who reigned over losses, but also the political and social structures that gave elites the power to enact failed policies. The Russian and Chinese Revolutions were both obvious cases where a war loss, coupled with a long-term lag behind economic competitors, generated massive revolutionary aspirations for rapid economic development.

Fourth and finally, the effects of world revolution are modified by the cycle of hegemony. Hegemons rise to world leadership through a geographic concentration of leading sectors that produce a K-wave expansion, and then consolidate that leadership into hegemony through a second such concentration during the next K-wave expansion. World revolutions that occur at the height of hegemony are least capable of affecting the world order because its key precepts are infused by hegemonic interests. Hegemons can undermine or contain challenges to the world order. In contrast, world revolutions are most efficacious in shifting the world order during the correspondence of a K-wave transition from stagnation to expansion with periods of hegemonic transition. We call such periods of corresponding and linked transition "world divides." These are periods in which human agency has the greatest possibility to affect systemic structures (Wallerstein 1998).

We will briefly outline our rationale for all the cases up to 1848 below, then examine the events from 1848 to 1989 in greater detail in the last section of this chapter. Our focus is on the revolutions and movements that lead up to and become socialist ones, and we select material for discussion accordingly. A less selective history of world revolutions, particularly those prior to 1848, awaits their being the primary subject of discussion. In the next chapter, we focus on the events of 1989 alone.

Historical Outline: 1500–1848

Our first case, the Protestant Reformation, coincided with major peasant revolts starting around 1525. This is the least clear case of world revolution. This was not an abrupt change. If viewed from a Europe-wide perspective, the Reformation was a long series of revolts and religious wars directed against the Catholic world polity, and later, against the imperial reach of the United Hapsburgs, which was Catholicism's prime political patron. It might better be seen as a precursor to revolutionary changes in the system, and a source of the consolidation of the European inter-state system. The revolutionaries fought for religious "freedom"—escape from Catholic and imperial controls, not for religious tolerance in general. Expropriation of church properties sweetened the deal and hastened the accumulation of capital (Hill 1958). Liberal tolerance emerged only as an alternative to the wars of religion, especially where intolerance interfered with commerce.

Most often, the Protestant revolts were organized by noble patrons with their clients as part of a general opposition to central control, along with a demand for traditional local liberties. As such, these revolutions were also typically interstate wars as well. As Tilly (1993) points out, Protestantism survived where ruling noble classes joined the Protestant coalition of bourgeois and working classes. Hence, the Reformation has a "democratic impulse" (p. 61). None other than Phillip II, the Spanish Hapsburg ruler and staunch defender of the Catholic polity, recognized in 1559 that "a change in religion doesn't occur except in the company of movement toward a republic, and often the poor, idlers, and vagabonds take on new colors to attack rich people's property" (quoted in Tilly 1993, p. 61).

Revolutionary upheavals surge again starting in 1556 partly in response to Hapsburg imperialism and the Counter-Reformation. Conflict continues for another quarter century. Political and religious resistance merge in the Low Countries and in the Germanic principalities against the "Spanish Papist-beast." The case here is one of tearing down an oppressive world order (or polity), rather than consolidating a new one. These struggles lead eventually to Dutch independence and to the Thirty Years' War, which the other powers (France, England, and Sweden) joined in a constant interplay of war and revolution. One could even argue for a single process of revolt stretching from 1556 to 1648. The eventual results were crucial for world history in that they initiated the European interstate system, and in so doing, prohibited a Hapsburg-Catholic empire that could have snuffed the burgeoning development of the capitalist world economy.

The Dutch Revolution, which garnered de facto independence for the Netherlands from the Hapsburg Empire in 1609 and de jure sovereignty in 1648, was a critical juncture on the road to world capitalism. The Dutch revolt and other revolutions prompted by the carnage of the Thirty Years' War denied the Hapsburgs imperial sovereignty over the prime source of commercial wealth in Europe, guaranteeing commercial rivalry between states. "The crisis of the Seventeenth Century" in 1640–1648 saw the most contemporaneous rebellion across Europe prior to 1848, with a peak in 1648 of eight revolts in England, France, Catalonia, Portugal, Naples, Netherlands, Sicily, and Ukraine (Hill 1958, p. 121). Revolution did wonders for political philosophy. "Killing the King" required acknowledgment of the legitimacy of revolution against tyranny and some recognition that authority requires consent of the governed.

National sovereignty for core imperial states became the defining principle of the world order in 1648 with the Treaty of Westphalia, which ended the war. For the rising Dutch commercial state, independence both made possible and required investment in expanding trade. The Netherlands went on to become the prime mover in the geometric expansion of trade during the first half of the seventeenth century and the first hegemon over capitalist trade. Dutch hegemony was felled after a revolution in England brought the state-builder Cromwell to power, whose mercantile policies were deliberately modeled after the Dutch success. Freed from landed obligations and desperate for income from commercial expansion to pay the costs of state, Cromwell launched a series of market-share wars against the Dutch. Following the Fronde, and in need of commercial expansion to recoup its costs, France eventually joined with England to bring down the Dutch hegemony and to issue in a new round of colonial expansion. The solution to the seventeenth-century crisis, colonial and commercial expansion, would maintain the status quo for the next hundred years.

With power balanced in the newly formed interstate system, there was a long gap until the next world revolution. If British leadership had translated into hegemony during the eighteenth century, the world order might have been revolutionized. The 1701–1714 War of Spanish Succession enabled the other core power (France) to maintain the balance of power, which was set in the Treaty of Utrecht in 1713. Relative peace after 1713 and a long prosperity starting around 1747 produced a flowering of scientific and social thought that we now call the Enlightenment. While Enlightenment ideas of liberty and rights had contemporary sources, they were also a legacy of the prior epoch of wars and revolution. They reflected recognition that where war and revolt threatened absolute power, the rule of reason and tolerance was increasingly necessary for peace and profits.

No major institutional changes swept the European-centered system until a series of liberal revolutions starting in North America (1776–1783), followed by the Netherlands (1785–1787), and especially France (1789–1792). The Latin American revolutions followed (1811–1820) once revolutionary France had conquered Spain and Portugal, expanding the effects of this world revolution, but not constituting a second one. Although far short of adopting "liberty, equality, and fraternity," these revolutions were critical in initiating shifts in the world order that made space in which social movements could fight for these ideals. As Tilly (1993) points out, the modern structure of "social movements" themselves were formed with this world revolution, and with the development of huge conscripted armies for the revolutionary and Napoleonic wars. The national state became the locus for protest because it haltingly moved toward becoming based on popular consent and the assumption of greatly expanded responsibilities.

The last world revolution at the end of the eighteenth century was the cumulation of Enlightenment ideals. Perhaps more than any other event, this world revolution stretched the conception of "what is possible" for human society. It ushered in romanticism as the popular idiom of the Western civilization. This included the belief in the heroic individual, personified in Napoleon, whom Hegel called the "world soul" (1956). The furthest conceptual stretch occurred when Babeuf articulated the "universal" goals of the French Revolution in utopian-socialist terms of the lower classes. This was perhaps the earliest formulation of the socialist movement that was to grow stronger and less utopian by the middle of the nineteenth century.

The Concert of Europe was a reaction against popular revolution and sovereignty, but in the very act of reaction the Concert formulated the first core-wide recognition of popular consent and state responsibilities. The argument against liberalism ensconced it as the alternative to the conservative order of king and church, making liberals of all those for whom the current order was illegitimate (Wallerstein 1998, pp.

14–20). The Concert was also a consolidation of the interstate system against the possibility of a core-wide empire of the sort that Napoleon had tried to construct. Napoleon's effort was not the last of this sort. Germany tried the same trick in the twentieth century. In both cases the move toward world empire was thwarted by rising capitalist core states that became hegemonic within a still multicentric interstate system— the British in the nineteenth century, and the United States in the twentieth. Neither of these, despite their great powers, tried to construct an empire within the core. This is a critical difference between a capitalist world-system and earlier world-systems in which the tributary modes of accumulation were predominant.

The world revolution of the late eighteenth and early nineteenth centuries occurred in both the European core and among Europeans in the periphery. Obviously, the fledgling United States was yet in the periphery despite the strong conviction that it was showing humankind its future. A capital city fit for a great power was laid out in a wetland on the Potomac. The Monroe Doctrine of 1823 told the European powers not to interfere or try to restore colonies in the Americas and the United States (along with Great Britain) aided Latin American revolutions against Spain. But there were even more threatening rumbles in the periphery.

In the new United States, the revolution produced the "first emancipation" among those northern states with slaves (Zilversmit 1967). Revolutionary France freed its Caribbean slaves, and then Napoleon sought to re-enslave them. This spurred a massive slave revolt led by the Black Jacobins of Haiti (James 1963). Although small and poor, revolutionary Haiti was a powerful world symbol of antislavery and of black power in the domestic politics of the great powers (Stinchcombe 1994). The Haitian Revolution served as an example of a dreaded possible outcome for slave-owning societies, encouraging both the French and English imperial states to contemplate more controlled transitions to wage labor in their colonies. This illustrates the spiraling effect of the world revolutions, where a revolutionary gain of freedom is withdrawn and isolated, but the eventual result is an end to slavery nonetheless. The effect on the southern U.S. landlords, on the other hand, was to tighten internal surveillance and to pressure the U.S. government to isolate Haiti internationally. As a result, Haiti remained an isolated anomaly in the Americas.

The Haitian Revolution and other slave revolts were an important stimulus to the abolitionist movement. The movement crystallized in 1848, led by religious and middle-class reformers, and supported by workers and capitalists where they were not dependent on slave production. The resistance and revolts of slaves would not of themselves have been powerful enough to produce abolition without the sympathies and political action of large numbers of people who were not themselves slaves but who objected morally to slavery. This was partly a question of economic interest, but it was also a strong indication that the people were taking seriously the values that their leaders were espousing to justify the social order. Abolition was the first global movement and its success a fundamental change in the operation of the world-system.

The 1848 revolutions occurred in all of Europe. The biggest revolt was again in France, with substantial actions in Germany, Austria, the Balkans, and the Italian states. Only England was immune. The key importance of these revolutions was the initiation of socialist movements, which is discussed in the next section. In addition, this world revolution was important because of the institutionalization of the world abolitionist movement. Social movements for women's suffrage and rights also emerged, most famously when women were banned from international abolitionist meetings. Also important was the development of modern labor unions and social movements for labor rights, especially the ten-hour day. Sewell (1980) explains that the concept and organization of "liberty" shifted during the 1789 revolution. Liberty came to mean individual rights rather than communal or local privileges. It shifted again in 1848 to include group rights as an association of people with individual rights. Most important from the 1848 revolutions was the consolidation of democracy as universal suffrage, although women's suffrage was not (yet) included in the patriarchal conception of "universal" (Markoff 1996). The revolutions of 1848 fell to their own subsequent counterrevolutions. Despite the massive upheaval, Europe added only one republic and it would take the next world revolution to finally discard the dynastic mandate of the 1815 Concert of Europe.

"Realism" replaced romanticism after the bloody counterrevolution made heroic individuals seem foolish. Gone too were utopian or communal dreams of transforming society, replaced by attempts to ground social movements and social change in scientific understanding of social forces. Since 1848, the progressive shifts in the world order produced by revolutionary initiatives have been defined in terms of socialism, including colonial, separatist, and social revolutions. This was a great ideological success of socialist movements, but was also far more than just a conceptual success. Capitalism generates the desire—and the resources—for anticapitalist movements.

The Political Economy of Socialism

[Socialism is the] abolition of private property.
—*Karl Marx and Friedrich Engels, 1848*

Socialism is the economic side of the democratic ideal.

[There is] not a hint of socialism in the Soviet Union.
—*Leo*

[Socialism is a] society without exploitation.
—*Max Horkheimer, 1937*

Compared to the tragicomic definitions of socialism as a system in our introductory chapter, the above characterize an ideal, a set of goals toward which humankind should strive. Socialism is in this sense a social movement, deliberately analogous to the abolitionist and political democracy movements, but applied to wage labor and employer absolutism it becomes the abolition of exploitation and the establishment of economic democracy.

In the history of the world-system, socialism as we know it today was institutionalized with the revolutions of 1848. The only place Marx and Engels defined socialism at length is in their 1848 pamphlet, *The Communist Manifesto*. They summarized the definition with the following single phrase: "Abolition of private property" (1848, p. 219). By property, they meant the means of production, that is, capital, not personal property, or even "self-earned" (saved) productive property of artisans, peasants, and the like. Their direct analogy was to the elimination of feudal property rights during the French Revolution. As income garnered from holding a title of nobility was exploitative in capitalist terms, income derived from holding title to property is exploitative in socialist terms. Only income from work is *just,* they believed. Enacting socialism was the political movement of the working class against capital, in the same way that spreading capitalism was the political agenda of bourgeoisie against the feudal landlords.

The point of eliminating exploitation for Marx and Engels was not only juridical and substantive fairness, although this was one goal, but primarily to ensure prosperity and autonomy for the working class by planned rational development, freeing it from the misery, alienation, waste, and monied despotism of capitalism. In order to accomplish this goal, they proclaimed: "[t]he first step in the revolution by the working class is to raise the proletariat to the position of ruling class to win the battle of democracy" (1848, p. 226). To this central point was appended a list of complementary demands, which included income taxes, no inheritance, free education, and a vague discussion of women's rights. The list ends with the elimination of national differences and antagonisms (pp. 227–228).

Marx returns repeatedly to the *Manifesto* in the course of his later

,vork for a theory of class rebellion and for a political statement of the socialist program (e.g., Marx 1867). While multiple volumes have been written interpreting these goals and their implementation, some common themes emerge. These themes include the following: fairness, equality, prosperity, worker autonomy, basic needs, rationalization, planning, democracy, rapid development, international equality, and world peace. In all disputes, definitions of the purpose of socialism and what it should accomplish override definitions of what means or what form socialism should take. Much of the dispute over defining socialism is, nevertheless, over means rather than goals. What is appropriate, that is, what is both productive and egalitarian at one time or in one part of the world, may breed inefficiency and inequality in another time or place. No matter how elevated one's list of goals, including the ones listed above, they are worthless if unachievable.

Prior to the revolutions of 1848, political democracy and cooperative ownership were considered adequate means to achieve socialism. Political democracy would put the state under the electoral rule of the masses, and its economic analog, cooperative ownership, would put the workplace under the democratic control of workers in nonalienating (craft/artisan) labor. Artisan or craft work required the active participation and intellectual development of workers for high productivity, making socialism both a more productive and less alienating alternative to capitalism. Early socialism was thus a reaction against the onslaught of deskilling mechanization and wage labor proletarianization as well as being a proactive movement for democracy. The slogan "abolition of the wages system" (or of "wage-slavery," an even more direct analogy to the abolitionist movement) summed up this socialism. Socialism would be a society of artisans paid prices rather than wages and who own equal amounts of capital. In principle, the labor theory of value would apply under such circumstances of equal ownership of capital because with variation of capital held constant, prices would be proportional to labor values. As capital inputs would be the same for every artisan, solely their labor efforts and individual abilities would determine product values (assuming also, free exchange of science and technology). Capitalist exploitation would be thus eliminated and productivity would be the only basis for unequal incomes. Democracy would likewise enthrone political equality.

Marx and Engels (1848) call this type of socialism "petty-bourgeois" (and not "scientific") because it looks back to guilds rather than ahead to modern industry. Their scientific socialism was to retain the premise that equality would enhance growth, but also recognize that the mechanized factory, which utilized unskilled proletarians, made a return to a workshop of artisan equality a reactionary utopia. The proletariat emerges from the Industrial Revolution as the agent of social revolution. With the deepening division of labor, cooperative ownership by the unskilled would leave large disparities in capital accumulation, and thus unequal returns to capital owners (i.e., exploitation), even if these capitalists were also workers. Socialism was to eliminate the brutal alienation of the nineteenth-century factory, not simply redistribute its profits.

Their solution was to fuse economic and political democracy into state ownership of the means of production. Economic expansion brought on by industrialization and the increasing division of labor could proceed without producing class inequities because state ownership would use profits for public goods, including increased growth. Exploitation would decline without threatening growth of any particular enterprise as the state could set minimum standards for all production, the most important being a reduction in the length of the working day. A democratic state would also provide living standards based on needs (welfare) in contradistinction to the capitalist logic of individual self-sufficiency and market anarchy. Alienation would be overcome by shortening the workday and by continued deskilling that would enable switching jobs according to individual interest.

Marx and Engels, as many have noted, never explained in detail how the socialist state should be organized. This was due in part to the materialist belief that new social conditions would call forth new political and social forms of administration. At the same time, they also took for granted the widely shared notion of state ownership that traces back to Babeuf, the early French "communist" who was executed in 1797 for leading a "conspiracy of the equals" that sought to defend and extend the French Revolution. Babeuf's rhetoric repeatedly shows up in later Marxist and other socialist writings. It also foreshadows the militaristic application of state socialism under Stalin, making a brief quote a useful guide in explaining the historical development of socialism. In defining his beliefs at his trial for attempting to overthrow the state, Babeuf declared the following:

> The sole means of arriving at this [equality] is to establish a *common administration:* to suppress private property; to place every man of talent in the line of work he knows best; to oblige him to deposit the fruit of his work in the common store, to establish a simple *administration of needs,* which, keeping a record of all individuals and all things that are available to them, will distribute these available goods with most scrupulous equality, and will see to it that they make their way into the home of every citizen.
>
> This form of government, proven by experience to be practicable, since it is the form applied to the 1,200,000 men of our twelve Armies (what is possible on a small scale is possible on a large scale as well), is the only one that could result in unqualified and unalterable universal

welfare: *the common welfare, the aim of society.* (Babeuf 1797, pp. 67–68)

From 1848 State Socialism to 1968 Post-Marxism

The revolutions of 1848 institutionalized socialism as state socialism and socialist parties as revolutionary. The defeat of the 1848 revolutions by state repression proved that success would require state power. The 1848 uprisings were primarily revolutions for popular sovereignty (Arrighi, Hopkins, and Wallerstein 1989b). The rebels sought to fulfill the promise of the 1789 French Revolution, using the same slogans of democracy and citizenship, but now articulating them in class and national terms rather than as individual and/or natural rights (Sewell 1980, 1985). Democracy was the clarion in the north and west of Europe, while national unity and self-determination were also salient in the fractured principalities and imperial holding tanks of nationalism to the south and east.

That the 1848 revolutions failed as social revolutions, that is, as popular uprisings that were intended to initiate a rapid transformation of political and economic structures, is obvious. But they succeeded as a world revolution by initiating a progression toward goals that ultimately succeeded. The growth of industry and the expansion of states were strong trends. Marx's dialectical method was to analyze what the system was becoming, rather than what it was at the moment. This left Marx in a constant battle with anarchists and syndicalists until the infamy of the Paris Commune in 1871 frightened away reformers and cemented the necessity of state power for socialism. It also meant that revolutions, being as they were reactions to current conditions, would, no matter how "successful," always fall short of socialism. Revolutions were over control of the state; only state power, it was thought, would bring about socialism.

The 1860–1865 American Civil War and the 1870–1871 Paris Commune certainly helped solidify abolitionist and socialist movements, but fell short of being world revolutions. The commune may have helped spur Bismarck's welfare reforms, which were designed in part to pacify support for socialist revolutionaries. In most of the European core of the world economy, popular democracy in the form of universal male suffrage was won between 1871 and 1917, with suffrage for women soon following, although the variance is wide among states and among minority groups. A K-wave expansion during the latter half of the period (1893–1917), the so-called second industrial revolution, brought assembly-line mass production, scientific management, monopolistic firms, and a new wave of imperialism. States expanded not only geographically, but also as protowelfare states along Bismarckian lines. These innovations accelerated world production after the first "great depression" of the 1890s, which was the finale of the long K-wave stagnation that began in the 1870s. The finale of the K-wave expansion that followed was, of course, the "Great War," and with it, the Russian Revolution.

The welfare provisions of social-democratic movements, which offered a capitalist alternative to a socialist revolution, got a boost during World War I, when core states expanded to rationalize production and sought to contain labor conflict for the war effort. Reactionary governments, including the fascist counterrevolutions, eliminated much of the war-born welfare provisions, preventing the welfare state from being fully institutionalized in the 1920s. Isolationists in the United States also prevented the League of Nations from establishing a secure world order. Both the social-democratic welfare state model and the League were failed attempts at constituting a new world order. However, many of the welfare state provisions were revived or expanded during the Great Depression and especially during World War II. Also important is that war and revolution broke apart the Austro-Hungarian Empire in 1918 in favor of national self-determination.

The Russian Revolution consolidated a socialist state that, for better or worse, was finally able to last past the initial counterrevolution (Arrighi , Hopkins, and Wallerstein 1992). In so doing, however, it also initiated a split in socialist movements that has lasted past the demise of state socialism. Although suffrage was still far from universal, democratization in the developed west of Europe and the United States split socialist movements into electoral and revolutionary camps, known since 1917 as Social Democratic versus Communist Parties. A second fissure (or expansion from a revolutionary perspective) was the post–World War II development of national-liberation movements. Successful socialist liberation revolutions in Yugoslavia, China, and Vietnam took state power following World War II. Large armed resistance armies enjoined numerous revolts for liberation elsewhere, notably in Algeria, Greece, and the Philippines. The choice for imperial powers shifted from colonization versus independence to capitalist independence versus socialist liberation. Gandhi's nonviolent movement also inspired an alternative to armed revolt. Britain, and later France, eventually supported a controlled transition strategy to independence that became fully institutionalized in the world order with the 1960 UN Declaration. The national liberation, civil rights, peace, and nonviolence movements that flourished during 1968–1969 were all inspired by, and took tactics from, the postwar decolonization movements.

Each movement—social democratic, communist, and national liberation—represented an alternative strategy to achieve state power, corresponding roughly to the conditions found in the three zones of the world economy. Following the format laid out by Arrighi, Hopkins, and Wallerstein (1989b), we can categorize the three alternatives in Table 2.2 and in the subsequent discussion.

To be sure, the three movements could be found in each zone, such as black liberation movements in the United States, communists in Italy, or social democrats in Jamaica. However, in these and similar cases the parties either modulated their strategies to fit the prevailing circumstances or were relegated to marginal status. In the core, for instance, communists became Euro-communists and some revolutionary groups devolved into terrorism. Euro-communism was a strategic mix of social democracy and communism. Nor was every liberation movement directed at formal colonialism. Cuba was a mixed case where the movement was against neoimperialism rather than direct colonialism. Variation within the movements was also important, especially communist movements that produced market versus state socialism. Nevertheless, it is analytically useful to consider each of the three socialist movements separately.

Social democracy. In the developed West, waiting for the revolution was like waiting for Godot—it never came. Social-democratic parties retained at least some affiliation with Marxism through the interwar period and like Marx, many considered elections a democratic path to state socialism. Elections were available for a movement that claimed to represent the majority, and failure to pursue democracy would isolate socialists. Evolutionary socialists (Bernstein 1965), for instance, sought to avoid the pitfalls of the dictatorship of the proletariat so amply demonstrated by Stalin, as well as the economic disruption of a civil war, also well illustrated by the Soviet example. An electoral path was

Table 2.2   Socialist Movements and Zones of the World Economy

Movement	Strategy	Actors	Prototype	Zone
Social Democratic	electoral/ reform	workers & middle	Sweden	Core
Communist	revolution/ state control	workers & peasants	Russia	Semiperiphery
National Liberation	revolution/ decolonization	peasants & workers	China	Periphery

considered appropriate for the developed core democracies, not only because it was available, but also because the entrenched bureaucracies and extensive civil society required a "war of position" to replace capitalist institutions with egalitarian and democratic ones (Gramsci 1971). Otherwise, capitalist authority lost in the state alone would continually resurface in other institutions to again challenge the socialists for state power.

Przeworski (1985) points out that socialist movements achieved a measure of state power and many others verged on victory during the 1920s and 1930s. However, electoral socialism repeatedly reached two internal limits to success. First, in order to win elections, socialist parties had to garner voters from outside their traditional base of support in the industrial working class. This included service-sector workers and state employees, as well as "middle strata" intelligentsia and professionals, newly enfranchised women, and so on. Diluting the platform to accommodate diverse groups threatened loss of base support among industrial proletarians. Viable parties thus had to produce tangible gains, such as wage increases and health insurance, to maintain support. They could not remain in total opposition to reform nor remain purely parties of the industrial proletariat.

With electoral victory, social democrats faced their second limitation. Once the party's fate rested on providing tangible benefits to workers of all types, then any policy that disrupted economic growth could lead to an electoral defeat and programmatic reversal. Growth is necessary to pay for programs and to prevent unemployment. Nationalization and other transformative socialist goals would produce capital flight and investment strikes as long as the changes fell short of a revolution. Przeworski (1985) calls this problem the "valley of transition," where in order to reach the benefits of socialism the state must undergo a period of substantial economic decline in transition. Rather than benefits, the transition offers tangible losses to workers and their allies, with the promise of socialist benefits still uncertain. No elected socialist party could remain in power through a transition, so all parties turned to piecemeal reform instead.

The solution, worked out initially and most extensively in Sweden in the 1930s, was a corporatist compromise between capital and labor. The compromise was, in short, a social contract where wage growth was traded for profits. The socialist and allied unions would allow capitalist profit with the proviso that capitalists reinvest sufficiently to produce economic growth that would benefit worker wages. Unions would refrain from demanding a greater relative share of the product in return for investment in growth that would garner a larger absolute product size. Capital benefited from labor peace, equalization of some labor costs (i.e., minimum wages and working conditions), and socialization of certain risks (health and other insurance). The class compromise had the long-term benefit of focusing competition on increasing productivity, so that wages and profits could increase simultaneously. The key to the social contract was, like all contracts, that the state could guarantee compliance on both sides. The bargaining structure was corporatist, with state-mediated nationwide contracts between whole industries and industry-wide unions. Most importantly, the state employed Keynesian policies to stimulate growth by increasing demand.

When the Second International was reborn in 1951, social democrats abandoned Marx to become the parties of Keynes and compromise. To their credit, the social-democratic parties produced a highly successful class compromise in the postwar period that achieved a high standard of living and a low level of alienation for the working class. No matter how egregious the failure of social democrats in other areas and despite their essential abandonment of the socialist project, the social-democratic corporatist countries have had the lowest rates of exploitation, least inequality, and best provision of human needs. But of course, they operated in the developed core of the system.

In the 1970s, and especially the 1980s, economic growth in the social-democratic countries stagnated, as it did everywhere during the long down K-wave period. Conservatives who were elected in this period slashed welfare spending, which has not been fully replaced by social democrats even where they have returned to power. Suggestions such as Korpi's (1983) that the core social democrats pursue economic democracy as a solution to the crisis have not been followed. All these countries face a structural problem—greatly heightened international exchange makes it increasingly difficult for individual states to finance welfare or to protect wages through high tariffs (especially in small but active traders such as Sweden or Belgium). The European Union is recognized as a possible long-term solution to this predicament by equalizing inter-European competition and setting common standards. The question that remains is whether European-wide is wide enough in the increasingly integrated global economy.

Communist states. The strategy of 1848 finally succeeded in 1917 (Arrighi, Hopkins, and Wallerstein 1989b). In the interim, the idea of a popular uprising to seize state power was modified by the experience of 1871 to include the forming of a revolutionary dictatorship. Arrighi, Hopkins, and Wallerstein (1989b) call the socialist movements that emerged in 1848 a "rehearsal" for the Russian Revolution. Such was the Paris Commune. After 1917, revolutionary socialists would attempt revivals of Lenin's script on national stages all over the world.

We will explore the contradictions and consequences of the state-socialist model in detail in Chapter 5. What is important here is that above all, state socialism was a *development strategy* for rapid industrialization by a semiperipheral state. The semiperiphery is where state-run development was found most attractive. As a development strategy, the Soviets and to a lesser degree their imitators (a forced imitation in most cases) were largely successful industrializers until the 1970s. Some say that they could have had equal success as capitalist countries. This cannot be known, but what is known is that most countries until that time had failed to industrialize, and the few newly industrialized countries (NICs) are a more recent phenomenon and they used some similar approaches (described in Chapter 4). The last country to successfully industrialize prior to the USSR was Japan. Soviet success was therefore striking to most semiperipheral and peripheral countries.

When the Russian Revolution occurred, the world's most productive factories consisted of mass-production assembly lines run by industrial armies. This became the model for the first socialist state. The goal was for the whole society to become "a single office and a single factory" subject to "'factory' discipline" as a first step toward communism (Lenin 1970, p. 121). The adoption of Taylorism in industry during the 1920s (Lenin 1967, p. 513; Fisher 1964, pp. 258, 605) and Stalin's consolidation of power over the party bureaucracy in the 1930s fused the military-style bureaucratic organization of party, state, and industry. The Stalinist party/state was self-defined as the only leader of the working class, one whose "line" was the only true representative of working-class interests. Alternative parties, internal factions, or other forms of dissent represented, by definition, the interests of other classes. The party line included a teleological theory of history, used to justify undemocratic statist means to reach the ends of stateless communism. The party line was also the political analog to the bureaucratic concept of a "standard operating procedure." Deviation from the line or procedure without approval from superiors was *defined* as irrational and detrimental to the organization. Stalinism divorced political democracy from the socialist project, redefining it as a total institution dedicated to expanding mass production and providing social welfare.

Political democracy was inherent to socialism in all Marxist and other socialist literature until World War I, and remains so in most Western Marxism. The fact that socialists in predominantly democratic countries supported the war (especially Germany, which had the most powerful socialist party) led Lenin and his followers to dismiss capitalist democracy with scorn as corrupted by the power of capital and the dependence of labor (Lenin 1970). However much this may have been apt, the converse was false. An undemocratic state cannot be socialist. If the state is undemocratic, workers cannot be in control of capital and, as was often the case, they may be exploited for the benefit of party/state bureaucrats.

Recall from Table 1.1 in Chapter 1 that several state-socialist countries had strikingly high rates of exploitation just prior to their overthrow. To be sure, the data are sketchy but, as we will see in the next chapter, they coincide with reports on work life in Eastern Europe. Exploitation is a deliberately inflammatory term. What we measure is the ratio of value added in manufacturing to wages and salaries (Boswell and Dixon 1993). Under "real" socialism, value added (surplus value) would not be exploitation because it would be retained by the workers who have produced it in the form of higher growth or better public goods. The low inequality and the provision of health, education, and other public goods indicated some such use of surplus value under state socialism, although one can argue that the lack of democracy meant that it was still exploitation even if for supposedly egalitarian purposes (Elster 1978).

By the 1980s, an increasing portion of this value added in Eastern Europe and China was going to pay foreign debt or for military spending (and some to elite privileges and corruption everywhere). In these cases, the so-called socialist state had become a manager of labor for global capital. Communist Poland, a major meat producer, rationed domestic meat consumption in order to increase exports. Romania even rationed electricity to pay its debt. Ironically, Marx's prediction that high exploitation, low growth, and limited democracy would produce proletarian revolutions was proven most accurate for state-socialist countries (Boswell and Dixon 1993).

This state of affairs has been labeled "state capitalism," "bureaucratic collectivism," a "degenerated worker's state," and other derogatory terms in order to separate "real socialism" from the Stalinist model. Trotsky pointed out over fifty years ago, regarding "state capitalism," that "this term has the advantage that nobody knows exactly what it means" (Trotsky 1937, p. 245). The same could be said of a variety of other monikers for the "really existing socialist societies." So, we will stick with the term "state socialist."

Our point is that neither social democracy nor state socialism were, or could have been, "real socialism." There was a great confusion between means and ends. Socialism is a set of principles for a just world. While societies may enact institutions that embody socialist principles, an individual society can no more be socialist than can an individual person be an institution. To restate our operative premise, capitalism is a world-system and thus to succeed it, socialism must be organized at the global level as well. In that sense, all societies are "state capitalist," if

what is meant by this elusive term is using the state to promote economic development within the capitalist world-system. State socialism is
only more "statist" in its methods of development. If the comparison is
with other semiperipheral states, then the differences diminish. A semiperipheral position offers unique pressures and opportunities for state-
led development (see Chapter 4). Yet it is the social-democratic countries, which have by and large abandoned the goal of socialism, that have
nevertheless embodied more socialist principles than the avowedly
socialist states. One conclusion is thus clear from a comparison between
social democracy and state socialism: progress toward socialist ends cannot be made by employing nonsocialist, undemocratic means. Let us
consider socialist movements in the periphery and then return to the
discussion of world socialism.

National liberation. National movements are those of groups, usually eth-
nically defined as a "nation," seeking state sovereignty over a particular
territory; liberation movements are those of an oppressed status group
(usually ethnic, religious, or gendered) seeking equal citizenship and
removal of impediments to political power in the state. The combination of *national* and *liberation* applies to independence movements in
both external colonies (subject populations outside the territorial
boundaries of the imperial power) and internal colonies (populations
within the imperial power's boundary that have some separate national
identity). What constitutes the boundary of the imperial state versus a
subject colony is, of course, a matter a dispute. French imperialists considered Algeria internal; Gandhi's prewar movement in South Africa
demanded treatment as if the colony were internal rather than external.
The United States is perhaps the most successful state at turning external
boundaries into internal ones, even a former overseas colony in the case
of Hawaii. The United States is, however, an exception to the otherwise
general trend of resiliency of national identities. The resilience is obvious in places like the ex-Yugoslavia or ex–Soviet Union, but also in
multinational states unified hundreds of years ago, such as the Basques
in Spain and the Scots in the United Kingdom.

   Prior to World War I, most colonial independence movements were
national without being much in the way of liberation movements. That
is, they were the products of elite (usually aristocratic) local rulers seeking sovereign state power for their territory, without removing the subject status of the working population within the territory. As such, these
were a part of the widespread anticentralization revolt of the nobility
and other elites against attempted absolutism, with the key difference
that they produced independent nations. The Dutch Revolution of
1581–1609/1648, which was the first major independence revolution in

the capitalist world-system, was of this type, as were the American revolutions of Washington and Bolívar. While these national revolutions accelerated moves toward equal citizenship, only the Haitian Revolution of 1806 (James 1963), made by the slave population, ought to be considered a national liberation.

The imperial system remained remarkably stable until World War I, when the defeated empires—the German, Austro-Hungarian, Turkish, and Russian Empires—collapsed. Internal colonies became independent nations in the former three cases and were reorganized on a somewhat more equal, state-socialist basis in the case of the Russian Revolution (although ultimately much less equal than claimed). Lenin's twelve theses, countered by Woodrow Wilson's fourteen points, defined self-determination as inherent to the accepted practice of international relations. It did not become a practice in reality until after World War II and was not fully institutionalized in the world order until after 1960 (Boswell 1989b). Thus while the imperial system faltered with World War I, the interwar period saw its greatest expansion and the peak number of 168 overseas colonies was reached during the K-wave stagnation of 1917–1939 (Bergesen and Schoenberg 1980). Imperialism reached its highest stage, then shattered into hundreds of states.

After World War II, the confluence of rising national-liberation movements and the wartime devastation of all the core empires undermined the imperial system. The decline became terminal with the support for "free" market relations by a rising U.S. hegemony and the support for liberation by its primary contender, the USSR. The postwar period was also a K-wave expansion of unprecedented size. Colonial ties weakened and decolonization increased during the economic expansion because core imperialists could expand markets without resort to costly coercion. Resources also expanded for the lower classes, increasing their ability to mobilize (Boswell 1989a). Thus, the underlying structural conditions were opportune for widespread success by colonial liberators.

The Russian and especially the Chinese Revolutions were models for national-liberation movements and, like the Haitian Revolution but to a much greater extent, they served as alternatives to, and incentives for, controlled reform by the imperialist states. To a much greater extent than the abolitionist movement, decolonization was a liberation movement fought from below. The effect of World War II was critical in that it weakened imperial authority not only morally, but also literally in the sense of less money for colonial affairs. This opened opportunities for organizing resistance, and where the resistance fought invaders, for arming the resistance.

Given their nationalist character, one may wonder why the post–World War II national-liberation movements were articulated as socialist. National-liberation movements were like the socialist movements in the 1848 revolutions in that they were movements for popular sovereignty. This applies to rebels in nominally independent states opposing neoimperialism and great-power manipulation as well as colonial liberators. The periphery is larger and more diverse than the core or the semiperiphery, and thus it is much more difficult to characterize. Despite some exceptions, in most colonies anti-imperialism was also anticapitalist because large-scale capital was imperial. This includes not only former colonies where communist parties now rule and that were once connected to the Soviet bloc (China until 1961, Cuba, North Korea, Vietnam), but also the avowedly socialist liberation movements throughout Africa, Asia, and parts of Latin America. By implanting imperial landlords, employers, and managers, colonialism forged capitalist exploitation in ethnic/national as well as class terms. Max Weber's (1946) axiom that status group affiliation undermines class cohesion, which applies in the core, is reversed for the periphery where status and class were often indistinguishable. In the periphery, nationalism was class consciousness wrought international. As a result, even indigenous middle classes of farmers, business owners, and professionals often articulated their opposition to imperialism and to big business in socialist terms.

Preventing the periphery from going the "communist road" became, after 1949, the central tenet of U.S. foreign policy in the area. While it opposed immediate decolonization if it would directly lead to communist rule, the main U.S. policy (eventually supported by European imperialists) was to cultivate, or where necessary, to implant an indigenous national elite that could carry on containment from within. Most often, this was a "moderately repressive" military dictatorship, to quote Jeanne Kirkpatrick (U.S. ambassador to the UN in the 1980s). U.S. anticommunism was ubiquitous (see accounts by ex-CIA agent Phillip Agee, 1975, for example). The most spectacular attempts at implanting anticommunist state power were the "hot" wars of containment in Korea and Southeast Asia, the invasions of the Dominican Republic and Grenada, and the covert or proxy attempts in Greece, Iran, Cuba, the Philippines, Guatemala, Chile, Nicaragua, Angola, El Salvador, and Afghanistan. Only in Cuba and Vietnam did the United States ultimately fail to install an anticommunist regime, failures that served to inspire numerous other communist-led revolts. In each of these cases, the U.S. effort to create anticommunist governments by setting up indigenous regimes also undermined the global legitimacy of formal colonialism or other nonindigenous regimes.

The dismantling of the imperialist system was thus the combined result of a double war—a war of national liberation against imperialism, mostly led by indigenous nationalists who were nominal socialists, and an imperialist war against state socialism, led by the U.S. hegemon, which was nominally for "free markets." In most cases, both the nationalists and the United States won, accepting the compromise position of a decolonization controlled by an indigenous elite. This has only become obvious in the last decade as socialist rhetoric in liberation movements is being shed in exchange for access to U.S. and other markets. Like state socialism in the semiperiphery, national-liberation movements were a revolt against the global hierarchical division of labor that assigned peripheral colonies and countries a dependent position (Arrighi, Hopkins, and Wallerstein 1989b). In global terms, national liberation could only be fully successful if it also entailed economic development. This created a constant tension between pursuing sovereignty versus development, in which the former typically sacrificed foreign investment and preferred trade relations. The primary trading relationship for most former colonies is their former colonial ruler (or a substitute, such as the USSR for the United States in the Cuban case [Scott and Cochran 1989]). Most of the NICs, as well as the resurgent Japan and Germany, owe no small part of their economic success to their close political, and especially military, ties to the U.S. hegemon.

Judged in narrowly economic terms, national liberation failed as a development project, just as state socialism failed, and for the same reason—national states control an ever-decreasing share of the world economy. The difference in economic wealth between core and periphery is, if anything, worse than fifty years ago although the NICs are an important exception. Nevertheless, colonial liberation was a significant change in world-systemic relations, replacing the system of colonial empires in the periphery with an extension of the interstate system and at least formal national sovereignty. This transition is still going on, in often unbelievably bloody forms, in places such as Rwanda and Bosnia, and will continue for the foreseeable future.

From a long-term global perspective, the end of colonialism may have been more important than the Russian Revolution and the spread of state socialism for progressive change. But, the latter was necessary for the former, and was itself anti-imperialist. In this sense and *because of* other world consequences, the Russian Revolution remains a progressive event despite its failure as a socialist event (Wallerstein 1998, p. 26). In its origins, capitalism survived and expanded as a world-system through colonialism. Imperium in Europe was defeated, and then supplanted by the exterior colonial expansion of competing states. This colonial conquest shifted the flow of resources to the European capitalist core for the next four hundred years. While previous waves of decolonization occurred, followed by renewed imperialism, the postwar liberation was so thorough and disruptive as to "shift" the world order against any other renewed formal colonialism (Boswell 1989a). Only the abolition of slavery was as momentous as a conscious movement to change world-systemic relations.

It is possible to wonder whether decolonization is only an intensification of capitalist relations in the periphery. One result of decolonization is that market relations increased in importance relative to administrative state controls. Certainly, decolonization did not change fundamental economic processes of the world-system. Nor did it reduce the amount of inequality in the system. Rather, discarding the imperialist rubbish eliminated a political obstacle to capital mobility, trade, migration, and, unfortunately, intraperipheral wars. Thus, decolonization accelerated the long-run cyclical trend of economic globalization. The extension of the interstate system to the periphery, like the abolition of slavery, made the periphery somewhat more like the core, but it probably has not yet reduced the overall power differential between core and periphery. It is nevertheless still the case that formal national sovereignty is better than colonialism, just as limited representative democracy is better than an authoritarian regime. These gains, though limited, would not have occurred without the struggles and sacrifices made by the people who resisted exploitation and domination.

Assuming that increased marketization means less potential for socialism, however, would be to equate socialism with the state and to ignore that states have been used mainly to pursue capitalist accumulation and monopolistic advantage. This is inherent to capitalism rather than contrary to its expansion. Decolonization has altered that logic, limiting colonial relations and requiring that world trade increasingly follow competitive market precepts. To be sure, neocolonial relations still exist and continue to oscillate, but neocolonialism increasingly resembles and merges with the hegemonic relations of an increasingly global capitalist class.

Moreover, the growth of the NICs and the acceleration of capital mobility in the last twenty to thirty years have been predicated on the demise of colonialism. Decolonization has reduced the political sources of global inequality and laid bare the economic ones. Most importantly, the proliferation of sovereign states has created a constituency for a secular world polity (the subject of Chapter 6).

Social Liberation Movements: "The New Left"

The same forces that set national liberation into motion—an expanding economy, a declining return to coercion, a rising U.S. hegemony, and a weakening of the traditional order—contributed to the rise of new social movements in the core during the postwar period. These include racial, ethnic, student, environmental, cultural, antiwar, women's, consumer, and human-rights movements. Other contributing factors at the time included the "baby boom" generational division, the expansion of education, and the increasing incorporation in the paid labor market employment of women and ethnic/racial minorities. While the first wave of national-liberation movements spurted with the breakdown of imperial authority during the war, the new social movements came to force during the second wave of decolonization in the 1960s when the world economy was peaking. The experiences of the baby boom generation maturing during a K-wave expansion and U.S. hegemonic phase contrasted sharply with the Great Depression and wartime experiences of their parents, producing a generation gap in how they saw the world. Most of the new movements originated in the core, especially in the hegemonic United States, although they spread throughout the rest of the world in varying degrees and in differing forms.

The success of the national-liberation movements in the periphery also redounded back on the core. Notably, the civil-rights movement by blacks in the United States was initially inspired by national liberation, especially by Gandhi in India in 1948. Inspiration is not simply a moral uplift, but also a concrete indication of potential risks and payoffs that actors use in deciding which actions to take and what strategies are viable. As such, successful actions in analogous settings are a key element in mobilizing resources for collective action (Tilly 1978). These resources and opportunities for using them were concurrently expanding, for the reasons listed above, making for a reinforcing circle of social action. The success of the civil-rights movement inspired several other similar movements, including other minority ethnic groups and women, but also "New Right" groups, such as antiabortion groups that have copied civil-rights protest strategies. Outside the United States, and to some degree within, the civil-rights movement has become a global human-rights movement.

There are four legacies that constitute the major New Left movements: peace and freedom, women's liberation, environmental activism, and national liberation. Several of these movements have had previous incarnations in prior world revolutions. A striking example is women's liberation. Women's suffrage movements were initiated in the 1848 world revolution and consolidated in the post–World War I upheaval. But as is often the case in consolidating a progressive agenda, states and other powerful actors only acquiesce to what is necessary to pacify or demobilize the movement. Further progress requires reorganization and reorientation of the movement, in this case to a broader agenda of social equality. Whether the reorganization is a new or a resurgent movement depends on the extent of institutional continuity. In this case, the institutional linkages between the suffrage and the liberation movements were rarely significant. Substantively, while the women's liberation movement of the 1960s consolidated or regained legal and civil rights fought for previously by the suffrage movement, it also initiated fundamental social changes in the family and the workplace. On both organizational and substantive dimensions, it is thus analytically appropriate to treat the women's liberation movement as "new."

The New Left was also new in that a great deal of its energy was directed against the Old Left of communists and social democrats. Arrighi, Hopkins, and Wallerstein (1989b) point out that a central theme common to all New Left movements was an attack on bureaucracy for its oppressive authority, inflexibility, and agency for exploitation by a managerial elite. Militarism and military-style bureaucratic authoritarianism, including Stalinism and other forms of "democratic centralism," were criticized as increasingly ineffective as well as irrational and oppressive. Common to all the new movements, including New Right movements, was the attack on central bureaucracy that fettered information flows, work rules, communication systems, and social relations in general. Successful attacks on bureaucratic rigidity as a general principle of society allowed for growth in information technologies and flexible production that, in turn, fueled anticentralization in a reciprocal fashion. This may have been the most important unforeseen and unpredictable effect of New Left movements and the change in sensibility associated with the 1968 world revolution.

Labor relations also changed during the postwar period and especially in the 1960s through the expansion of higher education, an increased mobility of labor, a further decline of agricultural labor, transfer of low-skill jobs to the (semi)periphery, and a further increase in the size of the service sector. Two results were the huge expansion of scientific/technical professionals who were disconnected from, and do not identify with, the industrial working class, and the growth of female, minority, and nonunion employment outside the industrial sector. Immigration was loosened worldwide and heightened mobility spread south, fueling migration to core labor markets and ethnic mobilization therein. These changes became a resource for women's and minority movements and a second source of the conflict between the New and Old Left in the labor movement.

Consolidation and Disillusionment

As with prior world revolutions, the main success of the one that centers on 1968 is the institutionalization of progressive movements brought to the fore in the previous one, national liberation and its core counter-point, civil or human rights. National liberation was, in retrospect, unstoppable after 1960, although it was 1974 before the United States finally withdrew from Vietnam and Portugal lost the last major colonial empire in Africa. Civil rights, in the legal terms of equal treatment of ethnic minorities, were largely won by 1968. Segregation's proponents became official pariahs in the world order (i.e., Rhodesia until 1979 and South Africa until 1991). Women's rights would, again, lag and come in a diffuse manner that is still not complete. Institutionalizing national liberation and civil rights was to take their final success for granted and to initiate new conceptions of what is desirable and possible given the new granted baseline. This included a more fundamental level of gender and ethnic equality, a higher quality of life and environment, and the acceptance of human rights and democracy as global principles, rather than national creeds.

Around 1968, the new social movements took a radical turn. The success of liberal and social-democratic movements opened political space for radical movements whose constituency expanded as frustration grew with the limitations of 1789 liberalism or 1917 communism. The Soviet invasion of Czechoslovakia in 1968 was a capstone rather than the initiation of New Left disillusionment with Old Left communism and the Soviet model, especially among 1968 radicals in Eastern Europe.

A second wave of revolutionary upheaval spread throughout Latin America during the 1970s and 1980s, which began with radical student and other groups originating around 1968–1969 (Wickam-Crowley 1991). These formed new movements or reinvigorated old ones. Similar processes occurred in Asia and Africa. For many radicals, inspiration shifted to the Cultural Revolution in China and the war in Vietnam. These symbols became deterrents to radicalism, especially in the better-off core, once the appalling social and economic consequences of the Cultural Revolution overshadowed the glorious and perhaps sincere egalitarian rhetoric, and once Vietnam had become just another communist dictatorship and Cambodia had become the "killing fields."

While these shifts in symbols and inspiration were of grave importance to the New Left, deradicalization was mainly driven by the simple fact that the current social programs and future possibilities of these movements were predicated on economic growth. From Medicare to child care, the social programs of the New Left were rolled back in every core country once the K-wave stagnation switched funding from a slice of a growing pie to a redistribution of a shrinking one. The New Right adopted "freedom," "empowerment," and other antibureaucratic rhetoric in an ostensibly populist counterattack on the welfare state. A core-wide conservative counterattack was launched against the taxes required to sustain it in a stagnant world economy. The attack was supported not only by capitalists, managers, and other likely suspects, but also by the better-paid strata of the industrial working class. Thatcher, Reagan, and Kohl, the conservative triumvirate of the 1980s, were elected in response to these changing global conditions as much as to unique national circumstances. The state itself, as a bureaucratic institution and as a source of social change, lost efficacy and lost legitimacy among the New Left as well as the New Right.

We have offered few details, but this period and the New Left movements it spawned have been written about copiously by their now academic participants (a good example is Gitlin 1987). The question for us is what is left from the New Left? And, what of the Old Left social-democratic, communist, and national-liberation movements still constitutes an opposition and a possible alternative to world capitalism? How can we reorganize and reorient social movements in order to achieve further progress? We return to these questions in the last two chapters. But first, let us continue with our narrative by turning to the world revolution of 1989.

Notes

1. Muller and Seligson (1987) describe the relationship between repression and revolt as an inverted U curve. Rebellious activity increases as repression eliminates democratic alternatives, but extreme repression can prevent rebels from assembling or communicating, arrest their leaders, and so on. States are often most vulnerable when they reduce repression from what were very high levels, allowing long-grieved populations to finally express their discontent. Also, as inequality is associated with, and a source of, high repression, its causal effects on rebellion are often masked by the demobilizing effects of high repression. This hidden effect of inequality led some early researchers to mistakenly assume that inequality was not an important source of rebellion (Weede 1981).

2. Germany and Italy are the two missing regions from Tilly's data set of European revolutionary situations (why is unclear). Inclusion of these areas (a current project) would add several well-known events, such as 1848 and 1918, that correspond to the patterns found for Europe as a whole. Unknown is the pattern of lesser-known events. Inclusion of the United States and Japan, once they became core states, adds virtually no variation.

3. Using the sources Tilly (1993) cites and a variety of supplementary sources, we coded each event according to obvious characteristics mentioned in the texts. Religious struggles were coded when combatants held different religions or were fighting over different religious interpretations, and religion was a prime source of organization and inspiration. Anticentralization conflicts were those where a major source of conflict concerned control over a region or principality. These were often the internal equivalents of colonial revolts. Class conflicts were identified where the lower classes of peasants, workers, or artisans

were central actors in their own right. In a similar vein, we also identified revolts where succession was a major issue. See Boswell and Marsh (1998) for more detail.

4. Tilly (1993) provides a European compilation of revolutionary situations, which we have summed over time to identify clusters. Bergesen and Schoenberg (1980) do the same for decolonization periods. Others were identified from cited sources on revolutions.

5. In 1648, Catalonia, England, France, Naples, Portugal, Netherlands, Sicily, and Ukraine saw revolutionary uprisings, peasants revolted in Austria and Poland, and Turkey had a Janissary revolt (Hill 1958, p. 121).

6. See Silver (1995); Mandel (1975).

7. Boswell has begun some preliminary analyses that show promising results along the lines indicated here.

3

The Revolutions of 1989[1]

First Poland, then China, then all of Eastern Europe underwent mass uprisings of workers and intellectuals against state socialism. Under state socialism, states were ruled solely by a Communist Party (CP), which claimed to be the vanguard of the working class. Yet, workers and intellectuals rebelled against CP rule. Although these rebellions focused mainly on transforming the state, state ownership of the means of production meant that a fundamental political change inherently involved a transformation of class relations as well.

Research on the revolutions of 1989 has proliferated (Rady 1995 provides a useful review). Our intention in this chapter is not to question historical accounts of particular national revolutions, but to explain the events from a world-systemic point of view. Despite a reaction against the static and polemical theories of totalitarianism (Curtis 1986) that dominated the field until the late 1960s, most recent studies have still used a highly state-centered approach (see the literature review in Nee and Stark 1989). One reason for this is obvious: the distinction between state and civil society, an important ideological and social distinction under capitalism, was deliberately bridged under state socialism. The "party/state" of intertwined party and state apparatuses wielded tremendous institutional power, but its overwhelming strength was also its greatest vulnerability (Bunce 1989). While taking credit for any success, the party/state also had to assume all blame for every socioeconomic, political, or international defeat. If an economic crisis thrusts the population into political action, then the state and only the state was the focus of the struggle. What state-centered studies failed to explain, then, was how and why socialist party/states that had survived absorption of all social conflict up until 1989 proved so fragile in that year.

State-centered research explains a crucial structural vulnerability of the party/state. Yet, as Jones (1983) points out, the focus on the unique political features of state socialism ignores that their polities are shaped by dynamic industrial and social structures that are basically similar to those in capitalist societies. The party/state reacted to unanticipated changes in the social structure as much as it "commanded" the development of that structure. Certainly, no party/state planned an economic crisis. Nevertheless, the "industrial society" approach (Jones 1983), like modernization or convergence theories, is also flawed because it treated industrial society as an ideal type from which state-socialist or other societies diverged depending on their degree of development toward the ideal. Marcuse (1964) mistakenly saw this as the inexorable march of all industrial societies to a unidimensional society of mass production, mass consumption, and mass conformity. This approach is overly focused on values at the expense of organizational structure (Nee and Stark 1989, p. 7) and excludes the uneven development and unequal dependency inherent to the world economy as a whole (Chase-Dunn 1982; Brucan 1989).

We agree entirely that examining the relationships between state and socioeconomic structures is necessary for understanding class conflict. But, the ability of class conflict to hold the entire economy hostage to peaceful resolution varies dramatically. Because of its political focus, state-centered research searches for conjunctures of debilitating political events, such as wartime fiscal crises, to explain when structurally weak states will topple (Skocpol 1979). Revolutionary conjunctures are thus only idiosyncratic events resulting from the interface of various external and particular internal political configurations. Unexplained are the systemic connections between the external world conditions and the internal social structures. Also unexplained are why some revolutions are instances of widely sweeping transnational transformations, such as the changes that have taken place in nearly all former and the few remaining state-socialist societies. What a world-systems perspective offers is a theory of long-term industrial change in the world economy to explain why popular revolts are so powerful at certain points in time. The socialist states promoted rapid industrial development for twenty years, forty in the Soviet Union; why did they find themselves in economic crises in the 1980s? They had always concentrated political protest; why were they suddenly so vulnerable?

What we suggest (as outlined in the previous chapter) is that the rebellions in the socialist states were in large part reactions to the national consequences of an ongoing "world divide" between expansion and stagnation, innovation and obsolescence, and core and periphery, in the global economy. World divides are the critical turning points during the transition from stagnation to expansion in a long K-wave. During the divide, firms, industries, and states must develop extensive sociopolitical accumulation innovations in order to foster renewed economic growth and development. Those that fail to adopt the accumulation innovations are left stagnating, and eventually are reduced to dependence on the innovators.

After a long postwar boom, the world economy was relatively stagnant from about 1969 to 1992. Growth following recessions was robust, especially in 1983–1984, but extremely uneven. A world-economic divide was taking place between high-skilled flexible production (such as biotechnical, electronic, and information processing) and low-skilled mass production (such as textiles, toys, appliances, and other assembly-line work). The latter was shifting to the semiperiphery (Piore and Sabel 1984; Hearn 1988). State-socialist societies experienced extremely difficult economic reactions to the world divide because they had concentrated so heavily on low-skill mass production in the postwar period. These reactions fomented rapid social change. Negative economic consequences and failed political adaptations to the divide, in turn, generated the popular rebellions. These were self-conscious attempts by workers and intellectuals to gain some political control over how the social changes would take place.

We use the term "intellectuals" as a convenient reference that includes not only traditional intellectuals such as students, professors, and teachers, but also those "organic" intellectuals in the working class and petite bourgeoisie whose position in the labor process requires *creative* intellectual activity and wide access to constantly changing information (Gramsci 1971). The latter includes highly skilled technical and scientific workers and many mid-level white-collar employees and professionals, what Reich (1992) calls "symbolic workers." It would also include most creative artists, performers, writers, and journalists. What unites and motivates intellectuals to political action is that productivity and success typically require a high level of individual autonomy and a wide and deep access to information. This is true in terms of personal, spiritual, career, economic, and even employer and national goals. To a significant extent, restrictions on the freedom of information or on creative decisionmaking result in economic inefficiencies and waste, along with personal alienation and frustration. High productivity requires high levels of autonomy and flexibility. Wanting increased freedom is thus an integral part of their labor process and lived experience, as well as an attractive philosophical or political ideal. An increase in intellectuals and the intellectual content of all labor was a key component of the world divide.

Our world-systems perspective does not constitute an exclusive monocausal lens through which we can analyze every popular revolt. Nor in this chapter can we fully explain the multiple sources or outcomes of rebellion. This would require a thick description of the full history of the specific Chinese, Polish, and other cases.[2] We leave this to the area experts. Our goals are more analytic and more exploratory. We want to situate the rebellious events in the world historical context rather than to explain their particular unfolding. We argue that the world-economy perspective provides an understanding of the structural precipitates for fundamental social change. Once these precipitates are set in motion, the style, course, and outcome of social changes are conditioned by a country's contextual configuration along economic, political, and cultural lines.

In the sections that follow, we first examine the long-term development of mass production, its current crisis, and its transformation. Next, we explain how this general world economic development generated particular problems in socialist states. Rather than a defining or endemic feature of "socialism," from this historical context, the development of unified party/states is a particular result of the application of Stalinist bureaucratic politics to mass-production industry. We then outline the responses to the world economic divide in Poland and China that led to popular rebellions. After comparing these cases, we briefly contrast them with the revolts in the other socialist states that soon followed.

World Divides and National Revolutions

Why did most Stalinist party/states falter in promoting industrial development since the late 1960s? The first answer is that almost all states faltered because the entire world economy stagnated for twenty years. In Table 3.1, we have listed the growth rates for the capitalist core (broadly conceived) and the state-socialist semiperiphery. Average annual growth rates clustered around 4–5 percent in the 1960s, around 3–4 percent in the 1970s, and 1–3 percent in the 1980s. The exceptions were Japan, which grew at nearly 12 percent in the 1960s, and China, which was alone in increasing its rate of growth over time. While Japan maintained high growth for longer than the rest of the core, it also stagnated longer in the 1990s. The increase in China, however, is even more dramatic than it appears in Table 3.1 since Chinese growth was negative in the early 1960s.

As one can see from the percent change in growth rates (far right columns), growth in the capitalist core declined on the average 35 percent between the 1960s and 1970s, and declined another 18 percent from the 1970s to the 1980s. The comparable figures for the state-socialist societies are declines of 26 percent and 34 percent respectively. A 50 percent decline in growth rates occurred in both regions over the

Table 3.1 Economic Growth in the Capitalist Core and State-Socialist Societies, 1961–1988

	Average Annual Real GNP Growth Rates			Recession and Recovery Rates		Percent Change in Growth Rates		
	1961–1970	1971–1980	1981–1988	1980–1982	1983–1988	1960s–1970s	1970s–1980s	1960s–1980s
Capitalist Core[a]	4.95	3.20	2.62	0.90	3.25	–35	–18	–47
Western Europe[b]	4.75	3.00	1.79	0.43	2.35	–37	–40	–62
United States	3.80	2.95	3.02	0.03	3.97	–22	2	–21
Canada	4.95	4.25	3.15	0.26	4.23	–14	–26	–36
Japan	11.70	4.70	4.06	4.03	4.23	–60	–14	–65
State-Socialist[c]	4.70	3.45	2.27	1.60	2.08	–26	–34	–52
Soviet Union	4.90	2.85	2.08	2.03	2.02	–42	–27	–58
Eastern Europe	3.85	3.40	1.26	–.07	1.98	–12	–63	–67
China	4.05	5.70	8.68	5.20	9.85	41	52	114
Comparative Ratios State-Socialist to Capitalist Core								
East to West	.95	1.08	.87	1.78	.64			
Europe	.81	1.13	.70	–.16	.84			
China to Japan	.35	1.21	2.14	1.29	2.32			

Source: Economic Report of the President 1985, 1989 (Table b-109).
Notes: a. OECD (Organization for Economic Cooperation and Development) countries (1971–1980 also includes Israel, South Africa, and non-OECD Europe)
b. European Community.
c. China, Eastern Europe, North Korea, Soviet Union, Yugoslavia.

entire twenty-year period (1960s–1980s). The percentages show that the stagnation of the 1960s–1980s was a *world* phenomenon. The effects in the periphery were more varied, with even worse declines in some areas (i.e., central Africa). The exceptions were the newly industrializing countries of Southeast Asia (which we compare and discuss in the next chapter). Nevertheless, the decade averages disguise the fact that, outside of China, the stagnation was much worse in the communist countries during the 1980s. The ratios of socialist to capitalist growth rates, and especially of East to West European rates in the bottom rows of Table 3.1, show that growth rates were similar until the 1980s. In the 1980s, East European growth dropped to 1.26 percent, only 70 percent of Western Europe's own meager rate of 1.79 percent. The recession of 1980–1982 hurt Eastern Europe more than any other developed area. While the capitalist countries recovered to a (highly uneven) average growth rate above 3 percent since that recession, Eastern Europe was stuck at a meager 2 percent (or less). The recession of 1989–1991, although not as severe, came on top of this lackluster recovery.

The importance of these comparisons is augmented by the fact that the state-socialist countries were considerably less developed to begin with, so that higher rates of growth would have been necessary to achieve the same absolute increases in living standards. Even more importantly, investments and loans were planned according to expectations of future growth. Since the socialist states developed detailed national plans, the unexpected declines of 50–60 percent in growth rates produced disastrous investments and calamitously high debts. This was the immediate source of the desperate restructuring and revolutions by exasperated populations in the Eastern bloc.

World Divides

During the long period of economic stagnation, firms, industries, and nations are divided in the following two ways: between those who first develop basic innovations and those who later imitate, and between those who restructure and those who only attempt to modify. Firms, industries, and nations on the latter side of both forms of the divide may continue to stagnate until the innovative sectors increase the pace of growth in the world economy—making the laggards dependent on the innovators. This process is what drives the rise of world leaders in the core and the phenomenon of newly industrializing countries in the periphery. It also results in the "deindustrialization" and decline of past leaders and former innovators.

The central accumulation innovations and model industries for each expansive wave since the Industrial Revolution are outlined in

Table 3.2. Mass production was introduced during the pre–World War I expansion of 1893–1916. Ford's assembly-line production along with scientific management of time and motion (or Taylorism) were the key sociotechnical innovations that broke the control of skilled craft labor and increased the rate of exploitation. But as Chandler (1977) points out, mass production also required organizational innovations of mass marketing and of monopolistic integrated firms in order to be profitable.

The success of deskilling mass production eventually resulted in even greater overproduction and widespread conflict during the erratic and often stagnant period following World War I. States and firms experimented with various innovations to control markets, and to pacify or repress labor. Bureaucratic coordination of management and labor, external state regulation of monopolistic markets, and Keynesian welfare policies (i.e., state-monopoly capitalism) proved to be a solution to both problems. Most importantly, the bureaucratic organization and state welfare innovations were built on top of the mass-production edifice without reducing its high levels of productive output. Other models, such as business welfare capitalism in the United States or worker's councils in the USSR and Italy in the 1920s, although possibly more productive, did not survive the market and class conflicts. During World War II, military organization and discipline eliminated residual alternatives and accelerated adoption of the bureaucratic welfare model.

This is not to say that a military-style bureaucratic organization is the only functional form for mass production by unskilled labor. Managers and workers determined the organization of production, not technology. However, it was the form that was adopted, and it did prove to be highly profitable. Of course some forms of organization produced more efficiently, but were also more prone to class conflict than others. Mass production based on a military bureaucratic organization was primarily invented in the United States to deskill rebellious craft workers and to utilize the influx of low-wage unskilled immigrants (Braverman 1974; Edwards 1979; Gordon, Edwards, and Reich 1982). The military was the model because armies can run on unquestioning bureaucratic discipline.

Thirty years of unparalleled expansion after World War II saturated the core markets for *new* mass-produced uniform products and the productivity gains from *new* applications of mass-production techniques or bureaucratic organizations became rare. Declines in productivity growth upset the entire macroeconomy (Bowles, Gordon, and Weisskopf 1983).[3] Wages and social welfare continued to rise in the 1970s as they had done in the 1960s, but they could not now be fully compensated from increased productivity. As a result, price inflation and national

Table 3.2 K-Waves and Accumulation Innovations

Expansion: Stagnation:	1790 1825	1848 1871	K-Wave Phases 1893 1916	1940 1968	1991
Model:	British textiles	British railroads	U.S. steel and automobiles	U.S. oil and chemicals	Global information technology
Mechanization:	Power	Machinery	Extraction	Agriculture	Information
Control:	Patriarchal control	Direct control	Scientific management	Bureaucratic segmentation	Flexible specialization
Production:	Manufacturing	Proletarianization	Assembly lines	Continuous process	Computerization
Markets:	Merchant marketing, American expansion	Liberalization, abolition	Mass marketing, imperial expansion	Mass media, Keynesian welfare state	Globalization: global media, marketing
Coordination:	Merchant financing	Limited liability	Integrated management	Multinational & divisional	Transnational firms
Turnover:	Canals	Railroads	Automobiles	Airlines	Internet
Competition:	Colonial monopolies	British hegemony	Monopolistic firms	American hegemony	EU, NAFTA, WTO

Sources: Schumpeter 1939; Braverman 1974; Mandel 1975, 1980; Wright 1975; Chandler 1977; Edwards 1979; Gordon, Edwards, and Reich 1982; Piore and Sabel 1984; Bowles, Gordon, and Weisskopf 1983; Boswell 1987; Goldstein, 1988. Modified from Boswell's (1987) synthesis.

debts skyrocketed worldwide despite high unemployment. Class conflict over income distribution became decidedly more zero-sum. Conservative politics designed to cut welfare and undercut unions surged in popularity among the middle and upper classes throughout the capitalist core, such as the election of Thatcher, Reagan, and Kohl we discussed earlier.

Saturation of mass production in the core countries did not mean its elimination, but rather that it was no longer a growing and innovative sector. The technology became commonplace, so firms using low-skilled mass production were rapidly moving investment in new plants to the (semi)periphery where labor costs were comparatively low. As noted, the result was the rise of newly industrialized countries such as South Korea, Taiwan, Singapore, and Brazil. In regions of the core, this appears as a "deindustrialization" (Bluestone and Harrison 1982). But this is a misnomer, as is "postindustrial." The new forms of organization and technology are equally "industrial," but they are no longer the mass assembly lines that have been associated with the term since the 1890s.

Core production cannot compete with the (semi)periphery on the basis of labor costs. Where the technology is largely standardized, as in auto or steel production, differences in productivity and quality depend more on the skills and motivation of labor. This means upgrading rather than deskilling labor, and increasing worker input and control rather than enforcing military-style bureaucratic discipline. It also means scientific-technical research to develop innovative (high) technology to produce nonstandard (specialized) goods, all of which are less available in the (semi)periphery. Experimentation and innovation advance the pace of product obsolescence, making the long production runs of a uniform product found in mass production an increasingly risky investment. This is especially true in a more integrated world market where few products are protected from competition.

While various accumulation innovations were adopted, a common factor in the more successful adaptations has been "flexibility" (Piore and Sabel 1984; Friedman 1988). Flexible organizations include decentralized management with much more cooperative participation from below, higher-skilled and relatively more-autonomous workers, increased scientific and technical labor, variable-batch production runs, and rapid adoption of new technology. A key element in international trade is subcontracting production and limiting ownership to design and marketing (Gereffi and Korzeniewicz 1994). While the transformation is far from complete, the more popular models of flexible organization in firms range from corporations like Nike and Hewlett-Packard, to the small-scale Italian artisan firms, to worker-owned cooperatives in Spain and the United States (Piore and Sabel 1984; Weitzman 1984;

Hearn 1988). Among U.S. business managers, the favored model in the 1980s was "Japanese management," with an increasing emphasis on self-managing teams (Boswell 1987; Hoerr 1989). Among the state-socialist managers and bureaucrats, the preeminent model was the Hungarian market reforms (Kolko 1988, p. 26; Kornai 1989; Nee and Stark 1989).

The Rise and Fall of State Socialism

When the world divide occurred in the 1980s, the state-socialist countries were ill-prepared to make the transition. Industrialization in the state-socialist societies occurred from the 1930s to the 1960s without the benefit of individual liberties or much in the way of popular democracy. Why did popular democracy and political liberalization, in the original sense of the terms, become so important in the late 1980s?

When the Russian Revolution occurred, the world's most productive factories consisted of mass-production assembly lines run by industrial armies. This became the model for the first socialist state. The adoption of Taylorism in industry during the 1920s (Lenin 1967, p. 513; Fisher 1964, pp. 258, 605) and Stalin's consolidation of power over the Party bureaucracy in the 1930s, fused the military-style bureaucratic organization of party, state, and industry. The Soviet economic model was to mobilize the entirety of society for development the way an army mobilizes forces against an enemy in war. Born during the Great War, baptized in a civil (class) war, and raised on intervention, invasion, and "containment," the Soviet party/state was, at some level, always at war.

Wartime states are rarely fully democratic and they invariably suspend even their own laws and principles in pursuit of either presumed necessity or hoped-for victory. In addition to the international conflict, the Stalinist party/state was self-defined as the only true leader of the proletariat in a class war.

Ironically, the Bolsheviks initially capitalized on the efforts of workers to reorganize both mass-production factories and the state into democratic worker councils or "soviets." In the absence of a world revolution, foreign intervention and civil war quickly subverted all functions of the new state to its military one, and the Party organized accordingly. While other options were available, the adoption of Taylorism and military-style bureaucratic control is not surprising because it appeared to be the most advanced form of capitalism at the time. Defeat of the Kronstat rebellion in 1921 ended hope for renewed direct worker control. While the New Economic Policy (NEP) period was relatively more liberal socially, it continued the trend of adopting capitalist management practices. With the collapse of the world grain market in the 1930s, the alternative of export financing of industry was also eliminated and the party/state turned to more coercive accumulation, primarily at the expense of the peasantry. We disagree with those who claim that given the Leninist beginnings and these subsequent conditions, the inevitable development was Stalinism (which we consider to have been a betrayal of socialist principles, and a major impediment to the development of democratic socialism). Trotsky's (1937) and Deutscher's (1949) critiques of Stalinism are still relevant, but so are more recent ones (e.g., Gorbachev 1987). The purges of the 1930s, which eliminated scores of educated and talented leaders, were surely detrimental to economic development. Nevertheless, the options for development were greatly constrained as the Depression set in during the 1930s. That the forced mobilization of capital accumulation and industrial development succeeded under these dire conditions was still a remarkable feat.

Far less industrialized than the core countries, the Soviet economy expanded during the depressed 1930s as the party/state rapidly employed the mass-production model without the market saturation and financial crises that had crippled capitalist expansion. The ability to develop mass-production industry and expand social welfare brought popular support despite the lack of democracy. Industrial development could have been achieved by other, more democratic, means. Although undemocratic and coercive, armies generate mass loyalty because they are paternalistic, total institutions. They provide for all the social welfare of dependent soldiers and indoctrinate them into the goal of serving a higher moral purpose. Loyalty, even devotion, to the military "uniform" is expected and common (although far from complete). Such was true for the Party, at least through Stalin's reign.

We agree with Eric Hobsbawm's (1994) scathing criticism of Stalinism, but also with his overall assessment of the historical role of the Bolsheviks and the Soviet Union. The Bolsheviks had wanted to create a new socialist world. In this, they failed and many were killed for trying. They could not have succeeded in building a new world in a single country. Instead, the result was undemocratic, statist, and nationalist. Nevertheless, the failed Soviet experiment offers many lessons and cautions for socialists. Its impact at the global level is far different from its sad internal history (Wallerstein 1998, p. 26). The Bolsheviks held the USSR together while the other large empires disintegrated, and the Soviet Union was the key to defeating Nazi Germany in World War II. Thus ironically, at the global level, the USSR was a key element in saving liberal democracy in the core against the real onslaught of fascism and racist imperialism. Despite its own imperial policies, the existence of the

Soviet Union provided space for national-liberation movements in the periphery and an incentive for core capitalism to reform itself, as emphasized in the previous chapter.

Great-Power Imperialism Versus Hegemonic Stability

Following World War II, the United States and the USSR both promoted, often violently, their versions of "classless" bureaucratic welfare states as models for development. The promise of development was the key ideological element underpinning support for both sides in the Cold War in Europe and hot wars in the periphery. The huge postwar expansion gave credence to the claims of both models, at least until the late 1960s.

Stalinist organization was exported by force to Eastern Europe, with only Czechoslovakia exhibiting sizable support. Even there the 1948 coup overthrew a government that had sought friendly relations with the Soviets. In Asia, on the other hand, indigenous communist revolutionary movements launched revolutions following the war in the Philippines, Malaya, Vietnam, and of course, China, winning in the latter two countries (Goodwin 1989). North Korea falls somewhere between the exported and indigenous models. The difference is due in no small part to the differing relationships to hegemony and to colonialism.

Throughout East Asia, and soon after spreading to Africa and Latin America, socialist and anti-imperialist movements were fused ideologically and organizationally after the war. With a colonial or neocolonial state, a colonial settler-landlord class, and an imperial capitalist class, national and class conflict became inseparable. Both maintained a statist orientation, due to the overtly political sources of class power in colonial societies, enhancing the appeal of state socialism despite its undemocratic structure (Frank 1989).

Revolution erupted first in East Asia because the atomic bomb had produced a Japanese defeat before European imperial authority could be restored or U.S. occupation was complete. The negative examples of a bloody stalemate in Korea and the French defeat in Vietnam, along with the positive examples of defeating the communist insurgency in the Philippines and Malaya, led the United States to temper its traditional support for self-determination with guarantees of a transition to conservative, anticommunist governments. As hegemon, the United States had the most to gain from decolonization of its competitors, and did not want those gains to be lost to nationalizations and Soviet influence. Although adamantly opposed to decolonization immediately after the war, Britain and France eventually acceded to U.S. neocolonial strategy.

By 1960, the international regime in the periphery had shifted from imperial competition to hegemonic stability; decolonization was inevitable (Boswell 1989a). Ironically, this controlled transition reinforced the fusion between state socialism and anti-imperialism as it maintained the connection between neocolonial states and class structure. As noted, the result was a renewed wave of revolutions as the 1960s progressed, this time in Africa and Latin America.

In Europe, Stalin forcibly claimed a sphere of influence as the fruits of victory. The Soviet action was, despite the ironic socialist rhetoric, in accordance with prewar "Great Power" traditions wherein imperial expansion at the expense of a vanquished enemy is accepted by other imperialists up to the point of their own sphere of influence. Spheres are set by implicit and sometimes explicit agreement in order to reestablish a stable balance of power. While the Yalta, Potsdam, and other Allied conferences contained multiple intrigues, establishing an agreed-upon balance of power and influence was certainly one of them. What went on in the conferences is a matter of much dispute in diplomatic history, but ultimately was irrelevant because the prewar balance-of-power international regime was replaced by the postwar hegemony of the United States.

As the ascendant hegemon, the United States eschewed balance-of-power politics because it far surpassed the economic and military capacity of all combined competitors. As Britain had done in the 1820s after the defeat of rival hegemon France, the United States in the 1940s supported self-determination for all nations within the spheres of influence of its competitors (even its allies). Neither the United States nor Britain applied the same principle to its own sphere. Britain supported Latin American independence from Spain but firmly maintained its own colonies; the United States opposed Soviet intervention in Eastern Europe but intervened frequently in Latin America.

The United States abandoned any idea of direct support for East European liberation after failing to support the 1956 uprisings. While nuclear politics overshadowed any decision, in simple economic terms the prospect for expansion in Eastern Europe, and even in the Soviet Union, was trivial in comparison to the opportunities in Western Europe and Japan, and the ones opening in the former colonial world. What this meant for potential revolution/liberation was that the United States accepted the limits of its hegemony within Eastern Europe but contested any Soviet challenge to it elsewhere. The Soviets, in turn, saw strict control over Eastern Europe as necessary as long as there was no counterbalance to U.S. hegemony. This would hold for thirty years, until Western Europe and Japan were again full competitors.

Deconstruction of the Soviet Model

In organizing totally around mass production, the Stalinist party/states built in both economic and political contradictions that came to the fore as mass production became antiquated. Economically, these contradictions led to three endemic problems—constant shortages, poor quality, and inefficient sectors.

Starting with shortages, the party/states' interests were in long-term development and modernization. State investment in long-term development, however, is a zero-sum proposition vis-à-vis state investment in short-term consumption. In theory, the former should pay for itself and eventually provide funds for the latter. In practice, resources were concentrated in heavy industry and military production at the expense of light industry and consumer production. The practice was reified politically by the party line and the political influence of military and heavy-industry leaders. What benefits consumer production received indirectly from expansion of heavy industry declined as the latter's products became widely available. The result was constant shortages of consumer goods relative to the purchasing power of workers who were guaranteed employment and social welfare, producing ubiquitous long lines and immense pent-up inflation.

Concerning quality, bureaucratic rigidity along with international isolation retarded innovation in production in the Soviet system relative to that produced by competitive markets in the West. Throughout the late 1940s and 1950s, when the world economy was booming, capitalist firms focused on only modifying existing production techniques. Emulation of U.S. firms, which were the most productive in the world, created a global isomorphism in the direction of modifications, even if the national starting points were quite different. Technological differences between East and West were thus mainly due to the much lower starting points in the East, and as a result, the socialist states would grow at a faster rate simply by applying existing technology. Huge investments in science, although heavily militarily oriented, also produced occasionally spectacular exceptions to the trend of technological lag (e.g., Sputnik). Because of the military orientation, however, the postwar regimes failed to grasp the increasing relevance of science and technology for consumer production (Brucan 1989). This would come back to haunt them.

In addition, there were multiple sources of inefficiency, which is true of any economy. Most unique, however, was ideological commitment to the mass-production model that resulted in its application where batch production would have been more efficient, or where information flows are nonstandard. Examples of the former included delicate agricultural products and of the latter, most intellectual work. The result was inefficient state farms and dissident intellectuals, to name the most prominent.

Turning to the political contradictions, these were between state and civil society in general, and between party/state bureaucrats and workers in particular (Bunce 1985, 1989). Because party/states were employers and managers for virtually all of labor, every conflict over wages and working conditions became a *political* conflict. While this created conflict on the shop floor (Burawoy 1985), repression and co-optation usually prevented workers from producing a sustained organized opposition as long as the economy was growing and the state provided extensive social welfare. This also hindered collaboration with dissident intellectuals, who as intellectuals were oppressed by application of the mass model that was producing the workers' benefits. The Party periodically campaigned to alienate intellectuals from workers and peasants, and from the Party itself. Kundera writes,

> In the political jargon of the day "intellectual" was an expletive. It designated a person who failed to understand life and was cut off from the people. All Communists hanged at the time by other Communists had that curse bestowed upon them. Unlike people with their feet planted firmly on the ground, they supposedly floated in air. In a sense, then, it was only fair they have the ground pulled out from under them once and for all and be left there hanging slightly above it. (1978, p. 5)

Occasional bursts of protest, as in East Germany in 1953, or in Poland and Hungary in 1956, demonstrated the continuing internal weakness and external dependency of these party/states. Reforms from above in 1953–1956 set critically important precedents for change and began a slow shift of power from the party/state to civil society (especially in Poland). Attempts at fundamental change, however, were violently repressed in Hungary in 1956 and in Czechoslovakia in 1968. As in the rest of the world, however, 1968 marked a turning point.

After the world revolution of 1968, the pace of change quickened. The restoration of Japan and Germany in the core, along with decolonization in the periphery, vastly increased world market diversity and competition. Declining U.S. hegemony led to a proliferation of models to emulate (most notably the Japanese) and of sources of innovation. The slowing growth rates, especially growth in productivity, along with the economic shocks of recession and oil crisis of the "B phase" (the stagnation phase of the K-wave) in the 1970s and 1980s, led to basic innovations in production technique and social organization. The result was acceleration in the pace of obsolescence internationally for several critical products, most notably in electronics, including computers.

Some long-term investments would never pay a return before being replaced by cheaper and better alternatives. The party/state commitment to long-term investment compounded the problem. Starting in the late 1960s, Western-made products were increasingly higher in quality at lower prices (relative to quality), escalating demand for foreign technology and consumer goods (Abonyi 1982). The effects were slow at first, but cumulative. By the late 1970s, *Sputnik* was long forgotten and the overriding goal for party/state leaders was to obtain hard currency in order to purchase Western technology.

Planned adoption of the mass model spread it rapidly, so that by the late 1960s extensive applications had become saturated (Szelenyi 1989). What had been innovative and productive during the past fifty-year-long wave was by then being increasingly applied where it was least efficient. Andrei Sakarov[4] summed up what would be a growing divergence between East and West when he wrote the following:

> [A]ny comparison must take into account of the fact that we are now catching up with the United States only in some of the old, traditional industries, which are no longer as important as they used to be for the United States (for example, coal and steel). In some of the newer fields, for example, automation, computers, petrochemicals and especially industrial research and development, we are not only lagging behind but are also growing more slowly. (Sakarov 1968, p. 31)

During the 1970s and 1980s economic growth dropped dramatically (as described in Table 3.1). Even where production was robust, product quality lagged behind the West and shortages were common. The worst effects of the structural crisis were not initially felt, however. As an oil exporter, the 1974–1979 increase in oil prices gave some respite to the USSR and its allies. Buoyed by cheap Soviet oil, and by access to petrodollars, several socialist states (although not the Soviet Union) followed the pattern set by semiperipheral countries in the West: they borrowed heavily from the West to finance continued development. This eventually made the problem worse.

Debt financing was a bargain in the 1970s as long as inflation rose faster than interest rates. The bargain went bust in the 1979–1980 "Volcker recession," which combined high interest rates with high inflation and high unemployment (so named after the head of the U.S. Federal Reserve who continued to push up interest rates to fight inflation even as unemployment rose). Debt payments rose drastically in real terms as inflation receded, while at the same time, the recession cut Western demand for exports (the only source of the hard currency that was badly needed to make the payments). Overreliance on cheap Soviet oil intensified the decline when prices fell in 1980–1982. Growing discontent pressured the party/states to expand paternalistic benefits and retain militaristic repression. The former increased inflationary pressure, while the latter decreased worker and intellectual productivity, further exacerbating the problem. By 1980, state socialism was in crisis.

Reconstruction

Why did mass production in the less developed socialist states suffer more from the industrial devolution than mass production in the West? To be sure, the capitalist core was suffering through a painful industrial transformation. But capitalist market economies also have a greater variety of organizational forms, and thus more adaptive flexibility, than the military-style conformity of state socialism. Nor are capitalist states as ideologically committed to equality and social welfare. Quite the contrary, the legitimizing economic myth in Anglo-American countries is free enterprise among petty-commodity producers.

The social-democratic countries of Central Europe (Scandinavia, Germany, Austria, and perhaps northern Italy) also have greater adaptive flexibility, in part because craft traditions and unions remained powerful. Even mass-production workers in Germany and Austria are often still trained through apprenticeships. As a result, participatory involvement by workers has remained strong and was more easily increased. Craft traditions, once considered backward, are proving to be an advantage in positioning these countries in the forefront of flexible organization. Leftist social-democratic corporatist governments have compromised with the strong labor unions to prevent wages and welfare from exceeding productivity growth (Hicks 1988). In Japan, rightist or business corporatism with firm specific "company unions" had similar success (Boswell 1987).

Finally, the formal separation of state and civil society under capitalism disperses economic class conflict among firms, industries, and regions. Workers and capitalists both find it difficult (although certainly not impossible) to translate their dispersed economic interests into unified political ones. That is, they rarely remain unified for long as conscious class actors. Instead, both tend to break into competing interest groups, producing coalition political parties and relatively autonomous states (Poulantzas 1973). Relative autonomy and some electoral responsiveness to the lower classes of politically democratic capitalist states are a central source of their high resilience against popular rebellion.

Centralized and militaristic, Stalinism was the exact opposite of flexible production. Rather than the harbinger of a communist future, state socialism was stuck in the 1940s. To restore growth and to try to achieve their self-conscious desire to lead or even equal the core economies, the socialist party/states began to restructure their economies.

The Hungarian model. The leader was the Hungarian CP, whose success by East European standards since 1968 had made it the model for the rest, including Poland and even China (Kolko 1988; Kornai 1989; Szelenyi 1989; Burawoy 1985). Hungary's "New Economic Mechanism" consisted of following two basic elements: (1) an increase in market control of secondary employment, wages, and (to a lesser extent) consumer prices; and (2) an opening to loans, investment, and technology from the core capitalist countries (Kolko 1988, p. 25). Market pricing raised the cost of consumer goods, providing internal capital and attracting foreign investment for their production, which would rise to meet the unfulfilled demand. Market wages, such as piece rates, increased both productivity and flexibility. Hungary borrowed heavily from the West and even joined the International Monetary Fund (IMF).

Despite its initial success in raising living standards, the Hungarian solution contained three critical risks. First, market pricing releases pent-up inflation if productivity does not rise faster than prices. Raising productivity by investment and innovation takes time, incurs debt, and requires involvement by the intelligentsia. Raising productivity by market wages, what Burawoy (1985) calls "market despotism," was faster, but increases worker discontent. Thus, the party/state increases its dependence on workers and intellectuals at the same time that it increases their animosity. Second, opening markets to the capitalist world economy contains the twin dangers of debt and trade dependency, especially during a world recession. Hungary's growth was debt-financed, resulting in the largest per capita debt burden among the socialist states. It also opens competition from lower-wage mass producers in the periphery. Opening to the West, moreover, invites envious socioeconomic and political comparisons. Third, as Kornai (1989) points out, the bureaucracies remained influential in all areas, especially pricing and credit, and retained control over the ultimate sanctions of "entry and exit." The result was "dual dependence" on markets and hierarchies, which sometimes produced both the supply shortages of hierarchical control and the insufficient demand and inequality of markets (Borocz 1992).

As we outline in the next section, the revolutions in Eastern Europe occurred despite initial success with the Hungarian model because all three risks were manifested in economic dislocation and political protest concentrated on the party/states.

Mass Production and Mass Revolt in Poland and China

Why did the party/states in Poland and China incite revolts by the class they purported to represent? We have proposed that most of the state-socialist countries were vulnerable to a revolution as world production shifted away from military-type organization and to more flexible and participatory forms. Whether or not any revolt occurs depends on a conjuncture of precipitating cultural and political events that is historically specific to each case. We will only outline the events that led to the 1989 rebellions in Poland and China, which prefigure subsequent events, then turn to brief comparisons with the other state-socialist societies.

The Worker Rebellions in Poland

In the 1970s, Poland seemed to have some initial success in going the route of foreign investment and loans. Production expanded with some degree of modernization as Poland borrowed heavily during the 1970s. Strike waves in 1970–1971 made foreign loans a politically attractive solution. With the rate of inflation increasing as the decade progressed, the early loans appeared to be bargains and the state continued to borrow Western capital even as interest rates climbed. But conservative governments in the United States, West Germany, and Britain were willing to sacrifice their workers to high unemployment in order to restore the integrity of the banking system. Combined with falling oil prices in the early 1980s, double-digit interest rates managed to stem the rise in inflation and to recoup the bargain loans of the early 1970s.

The 1975 and 1980 world recessions caught Poland heavily in debt and facing high interest rates. Per capita annual growth in GDP, which averaged 8.7 percent over 1970–1975, fell to 0.5 percent in 1975–1980, and declined an average −5.1 percent in 1980–1983 (United Nations 1983–1984, p. 152). In order to garner hard currency to repay its debt, the state had to cut internal consumption and reorient production and investment to increase exports. Price increases were a logical means to this end, but price riots, strikes, and protests soon followed in 1975–1976 from a working class long accustomed to subsidized living standards. The government responded with increased foreign borrowing to dole out renewed subsidies. This response backfired when the 1980 recession combined high interest rates and slack demand (the Volcker recession). Faced with declining living standards, inept leadership, and the national insult of "socialism" dependent on the capitalist West, the Polish workers revolted (Ash 1983). Even the delimited Stalinist promise of industrialization and social welfare rang false.

The combined economic and political character of the party/state unified all protest and made all protest political (Bunce 1989). That unity was reinforced and frequently organized by the Catholic Church. As a long opponent of CP rule, the Church was an obvious organizational and symbolic resource for the protesters to draw upon, especially after the ascension of a Polish pope. This was true regardless of the depth of their religious affiliation (Ash 1983; Bunce 1989). The Church also represented an enduring symbol of Polish nationalism, particularly in the face of Russian dominance. As an officially sanctioned event, the pope's visit in 1989 was an unparalleled organizing opportunity.

Polish workers have a long tradition of self-organization and protest, exemplified historically by waves of strikes in the 1930s, 1956, 1970–1971, and more or less from 1976 on, with peaks in 1979–1980 and 1988–1989. Intense centralization of mass production characteristic of state socialism also facilitated worker organization and made strategic strikes more potent than they would have been in a more decentralized economy—potent enough to bring down the government in 1980 and force the state to impose martial law.

Martial law froze political and labor relations in Poland. Unfortunately for General Jaruzelski, they froze at a depressed level of productivity. Bad turned to worse. The state raised prices 500 percent in 1982, 25 percent in 1983, and 18 percent in 1986. By that time, the incomes of nearly a third of all families were below what would be considered a poverty line in the West (Kolko 1988, pp. 35–36). Cut off from foreign credit and hobbled in Western markets, the Polish state could not borrow its way to appeasement as it had done in the past, nor could it internally generate adequate growth. Martial discipline could only garner reluctant productivity and low-quality goods from the industrial workers. This may have been sufficient for resumed growth in earlier decades, but now it could not compete with equally repressed but much cheaper labor in the newly industrializing countries.

Lifting martial law in 1983 did little to increase productivity. It did allow worker and intellectual groups to reorganize, again with the aid of the Church, along with foreign supporters such as the AFL-CIO and Polish émigrés. Strikes intensified in 1988 in response to another attempt to rapidly escalate prices. Recognizing that it could not restore productivity or access to Western capital and markets without Solidarity's cooperation, the "worker's state" took the extraordinary step of deciding to negotiate with the working class.

Most importantly, Solidarity gave the party/state a body with which to negotiate that could enforce a compromise and motivate productivity. It was the preeminent organization of both the working class and intellectuals, and was led by the charismatic Lech Walesa, whose popularity prevented a dispersion of authority. Moreover, the double role of Solidarity as a political party allowed the CP to spread the blame for the economic crises. This took its toll on Solidarity, resulting in a drop in working-class membership.

The Polish party/state was trapped between a pressing global economy and a stationary working class. Nevertheless, we do not wish to suggest that the material forces of production eliminate any variation in political forms. The Polish CP could have chosen (again) to chew off its working-class leg in order to stay in power. Two factors facilitated compromise: the moderation of Solidarity's rhetoric and the newly reformist bent of Mikhail Gorbachev in the USSR. Polish tanks may not have been backed up by Soviet tanks if another martial law had been enacted. Instead, the government let itself fall because not even the military continued to believe in the Stalinist model or wanted to rule over a resentful population and a deteriorating economy.

The revolution in Poland transformed the relations between state and civil society. The state structure in Poland underwent a rapid transformation in exactly the opposite direction than Skocpol's (1979, pp. 161–162) theory of revolution predicts. Rather than an increase in centralizing bureaucracies, the state is decentralizing, becoming less bureaucratic and more pluralistic, while civil society expands and incorporates voluntary organizations. According to Wallerstein (1998, p. 30), it is in this way that the revolutions of 1989 consolidated the world revolution of 1968.

The Urban Revolts in China

The major period of Chinese industrialization occurred only since the 1950s when the USSR transferred massive amounts of technology to their erstwhile ally. With the Sino-Soviet rift in the 1960s, Chinese technology and industry developed in isolation from an increasingly integrated world economy. The "Great Leap Forward," which even Mao admitted was a failure, proved that mass mobilization was a blunt and ineffective instrument for developing an industrial economy. In assessing the state of industry in 1981, the People's Daily reported, "The equipment of quite a few light industrial enterprises dates back to before the founding of the PRC or even to the 1920s and 1930s, while that of quite a few heavy industrial enterprises dates back to the 1940s and 1950s" (1981 [1986], p. 199).

If this was not a large enough burden, the repression of scholars and scientists following the "Hundred Flowers" period in the late 1950s, and during the Great Proletarian Cultural Revolution of 1966–1976, terrified and enervated the intelligentsia. The egalitarian intent of the Cultural Revolution was to produce revolutionary technocrats (both "red" and "expert"), where intellectuals would spend time in working-class jobs and prevent their ascension as a bureaucratic ruling elite). The reeducation campaigns and public degradation ceremonies only drove talent into hiding. By the late 1970s, state planners, managers, and workers were demanding economic changes to rehabilitate an antiquated economy stuck in the technological past. As the absolutist style of the Chinese CP (or CCP) brooked no external alternatives, the Party returned to power the old guard that had been ousted in the Cultural Revolution led by "capitalist roader," Deng Xiaoping.

In 1978 the Party, now led by Deng, replaced "class struggle" as the "key link" in ideology with "socialist modernization" (Burns and Rosen 1986, p. 368). Zhou Enlai's "Four Modernizations," embarked on in 1975 to modernize industry, agriculture, science, and the military, became the guiding principle of state policy. In the hands of Deng's "new economic group," the changes essentially consisted of the following:

- A return to family farming in agriculture
- An opening to the world market and the establishment of profit-oriented "enterprises" in industry
- A huge expansion of scientific and technical education
- A professionalization of the state apparatus based on technical merit along with a major reduction in the military

These innovations were intended to reorganize production in order to renew economic expansion, and for this purpose they were quite successful. Of the four, changes in the countryside were the most important. The communal system was dismantled in favor of a return to family farms and market pricing. This unleashed a massive increase in agricultural production, along with a growing unequal accumulation of wealth and proletarianization of propertyless peasants. From 1978 to 1983, average per capita income for peasants grew 130 percent (Shirk 1989, p. 328). The second step was to tap this capital and cheap labor by instituting a program of rural industrialization in the form of light-manufacturing "enterprises." This too was quite successful in increasing production, but it also hastened the pace of proletarianization and exploitation, sending a flood of former communal peasants to the already crowded urban labor markets (Nee 1989).

Deng's rural market development was matched in the urban areas with intellectual and technical development. Investment and technology was imported, especially from Japan, paid for by exports from the buoyant rural economy, loans from the IMF and foreign banks, and cuts in military spending. The army lost a million soldiers and pay was held low until only surplus agricultural labor still found enlistment attractive (Burns and Rosen 1986, p. 371). Deng also had to (re)develop a professional intellectual cadre to run the new technology and associated state infrastructure, especially if China were to become a world leader. A dramatic example occurred in 1979 when an oil rig capsized, killing seventy-two workers. According to Deng's supporters in the press, the laymen in charge ignored the advice of drilling experts and even failed to translate relevant literature on the imported rig (Ju 1980 [1986], p. 197). The petroleum minister was sacked and others in the heavy-industries ministries who had opposed increased control by scientific experts were discredited in the aftermath of this incident.

The universities rapidly expanded and reopened departments banned during the Cultural Revolution (such as sociology). Students were exported worldwide in a massive attempt to (re)create a modern intelligentsia in a single generation (including IMF economic training) (Kolko 1988, p. 36). The status of intellectuals was also raised from "the ninth and stinking class" it held during the Cultural Revolution to membership in the working class. Peasants and workers, who had been elevated to positions of authority in the state as "reds," were removed in favor of "experts" (although many "reds" retained their party posts).

In the cities, the combination of market pricing and in-migration of redundant labor from the rural areas led to price inflation, but not wage increases. In addition, prices at the mainly urban state-owned mass-production factories were not allowed to rise as fast, in part because they were still under direct state management. Inflation reached 20 percent in 1988 and was running at 30 percent in 1989, during the same time when inflation in the core capitalist countries was less than a third that level. Like Poland, increased integration into the world market meant increased dependence on, and vulnerability to, market vagaries and price setting. The Chinese state could not rapidly increase wages to match prices if it were to continue to attract foreign capital investment because its main attraction was cheap labor.

Unlike Poland, China is a huge country with pretensions of being a world leader. Given its mainly peasant economy outside the major cities, continuing development of low-technology mass production using cheap labor is necessary as evidenced by the success of the rural enterprises. Despite relative isolation, many Chinese were aware of the comparison. In comparing industrial cities, one manual worker was quoted as saying, "Shanghai was once ahead of Singapore and Hong Kong, even Tokyo—now look how far it has fallen behind!" (quoted in Terrill 1989, p. 36). For China to escape the fate of other poor peripheral countries— for it to be the next South Korea—it would have to modernize its urban industry to a level comparable to the developed core of the world economy. This put the ultimate fate of the country's modernization in the hands of the burgeoning intelligentsia.

Perhaps the real need for intellectual labor for the economy led students to take their role as national saviors seriously. As was true of the

Hundred Flowers period, students and intellectuals argued that political democracy would have to be added to the economic reforms in order for the citizenry (especially themselves) to actively participate in modernization. Western ideological influences were apparent, especially on those educated abroad. These are also the values more common in diverse urban settings than in the rural communities that formed a great part of the base of the CCP. In ways reminiscent of the Cultural Revolution, the students and intellectuals also condemned the rampant corruption, nepotism, and official privileges and elitism that had again become common practice by Party bureaucrats.

The CCP and government became riddled with nepotism. For instance, in 1989, at the time of the student revolt, Premier Li Peng was the adopted son of former Premier Zhou Enlai. Chi Haotian, chief of staff for the People's Liberation Army and likely director of the bloody repression, was the son-in-law of President Yang Shangkun. Offspring and relatives of other prominent officials filled important Party and military posts, including those of Deng Xiaoping and even reformist CCP ex–General Secretary Zhao Ziyang (Greenwald 1989, p. 23). Loyalty among in-laws is credited with a large part of the ability of Li Peng to enforce martial law. Widespread nepotism was also common in Eastern European CPs, especially in Romania (Sampson 1989).

Like the concentration of Polish shipyard and factory workers in huge enterprises, the concentration of students on large campuses and dormitories facilitated organization. Yet unlike factory workers, student strikes on campus have little immediate economic potency. As with past protests, they had to garner support from the urban population in order to be taken seriously. Most surprising was their support by industrial workers who have little tradition of mass protest, although worker support for the campaign against corruption and elitist privileges during the Cultural Revolution was also strong and the rampant inflation was squeezing the entire urban population. A Chinese "Solidarity" was supposedly one of the worst fears of the Party (Kolko 1988, p. 38).

Chinese students have a long and revered tradition of national protest: the May 1919 student protests were an icon in official CCP history and the 1966–1976 protests were an important legacy despite the reversed evaluation in more recent official history. In April 1976, students and other protesters occupied Tiananmen Square to commemorate the late Premier Zhou Enlai. The protest and ensuing riots were a deliberate affront to the then dominant ultraleft faction of the CCP who declared the protesters to be "counterrevolutionaries" and ordered mass arrests. Also dismissed was their most prominent supporter, Deng Xiaoping. Two years later, after the arrest of the Gang of Four and the rehabilitation of Deng, these protests were declared an honored revolutionary act (Burns and Rosen 1986, pp. 7–9). In 1989, a commemoration was planned for the late liberal Premier Hu Yaobang. Hu had been demoted for supporting free expression and dealing lightly with student protesters in 1987. It was with ample precedent that the student leaders in April 1989 chose to mimic the 1976 events by using the commemoration of Premier Hu Yaobang as a rallying call to again occupy Tiananmen Square.

At first, the student leaders took pains to define the movement as "patriotic," including opposition to the growing dependence on Japan. Like the pope coming to Poland, Gorbachev's visit symbolically galvanized support for a more democratic path, although one that recognized the leadership of the CCP. Not until the involvement of unions and the demonstration of massive support of the working class, a million people in one demonstration, was talk of revolution heard. Although they made more modest demands than Solidarity, the students used deliberately more inflammatory rhetoric. They sang the "Internationale" and erected a Statue of Liberty–like "goddess of democracy" as symbolic measures of defiance. This was especially irritating to the CCP leaders who recognized *cultural* revolution as a particularly potent force.

Deng's old-guard leaders did what they may have wished they had done during the Cultural Revolution—crush the student movement before it had a chance to oust them. Deng also knew from his own experience in 1976 that he would need to thoroughly discredit the protesters as counterrevolutionary and to eliminate their Party supporters (such as Zhao Ziyang) to prevent their return to power. Few politicians get a second chance at power and fewer still a chance to relive their worst crisis situations. Given that scenario, perhaps it is not so surprising that Deng's clique was willing to use bloody force.

Martial law and purges recentralized Party authority. But market reforms continued, as has impressive economic growth despite the recent Asian financial crisis. The army, the bulk of the population, and the main part of CCP support are rural, and it was in the countryside where Deng's market mechanisms had achieved their first success. After a brief respite, foreign investment and trade also reappeared. In 1989, the United States and European Community suspended loans and military sales, and both the World Bank and Asian Development Bank suspended loans worth nearly $2 billion (Yang, Javetski, and Holstein 1989). Even though repression continues, foreign governments, banks, and capitalists actively resumed loans, investments, and trade. By the end of the recession in 1991, China had resumed its position as one of the world's fastest-growing and most lucrative markets. It survived

Deng's death with little protest, although forgoing a big commemoration in Tiananmen Square. Whether it will survive a sustained recession without substantial political change is another question.

Comparisons

The problems encountered by Poland and China in attempting to reform and expand their economies—particularly the Polish foreign debt burden and the Chinese failure to integrate a growing intelligentsia—directed upon both party/states an emerging resentment by large numbers of workers and intellectuals. The common factors involved, as well as some significant differences, are outlined below in three general categories: economic, political, and cultural.

Economically, both Poland and China had huge outdated mass-production complexes and both were seeking foreign investment and loans to modernize. China introduced more market mechanisms, focusing on decommunalization of agriculture (Polish agriculture, about 75 percent private, always included many small farms). China was also rapidly expanding education and sending students abroad. Prior to the revolts, both economies experienced expansive growth followed by economic contraction, suggesting classic "relative deprivation" (Davies 1962). However, the expansion in Poland was a short, debt-financed period, and the contraction was steep. China's expansion was much more robust, resulting primarily from reorganizing rural production, although foreign trade and investment were also important. The contraction was milder and concentrated in urban areas. In both cases, the contraction was manifested in the form of high inflation and trade imbalance, cutting dramatically into the standard of living. In Poland, price increases were an explicit state policy, while more extensive market control in China resulted in diffuse and uneven inflation. Both countries had negative trade balances throughout the 1970s, although this was much worse in Poland, which experienced a 12 percent drop in exports from 1975 to 1980 (United Nations 1983–1984, pp. 950, 957).

For these reasons, the revolt in Poland had a greater economic focus, although the political demands were of at least equal importance. In both cases, international economic and political sanctions followed repression of the revolts. The sanctions played no small role in restricting the options of the Polish state and added heavy pressure to negotiate when a rebellion resurfaced in 1989.

While our argument rests upon the significance of mass-production industrialization, we also note that the politics of Poland's and China's classes have a distinctively rural basis. Peasants constituted two-thirds of

Poland's population in the period between World Wars I and II. Only in 1974 did industry surpass agriculture as the largest source of employment. As late as 1980, some 40 percent of the population resided in the countryside. Poland's two generations of industrial workers have maintained ties to their peasant past, a heritage that includes traditional Eastern European rural values, particularly religious attachment to the Catholic Church and suspicion of state authorities. These values resonate against the regulation and regimentation of industrial work in Poland. Polish state authorities recognized the problems of the "countryside," even well into the 1980s, yet government policy toward agriculture enhanced rural dislike of official authority (Lepak 1988, pp. 104–134).

On the other hand, Chinese class politics rested upon a rural peasant foundation where more than 80 percent of China's population of over 1 billion reside (Selden 1988, p. 4). The Chinese CP came to power with roots deep in the countryside and pursued "pro-peasant" policies. Mao's political coalitions were generally negative toward urban elements (Andors 1977, p. 22; Selden 1988, p. 154). Post-Mao China continues to stress this prorural policy (Selden 1988, pp. 154–180). Thus, while both were urban rebellions, the rural population influenced each outcome. Peasants in Poland were relatively antagonistic toward the state, while the Chinese state enjoyed a comparatively supportive peasantry.

Another major difference is in the origin of the state-socialist regimes. In Poland, the Soviet model was imposed by the Red Army and so the regime was never legitimate despite repeated efforts to gain popular support. In China, there was a huge and victorious social revolution in which the peasantry was mobilized and included in the revolutionary state. This is the major factor accounting for the differences in the level of support for the Polish and Chinese state-socialist regimes.

Politically, both party/states suffered from the organizational weakness of transforming all protests into political ones and concentrating them onto the state. Relying on foreign debt and investment, the Polish party/state failed to either restructure the economy or to democratically incorporate disgruntled workers and intellectuals. In China, the relative success at restructuring was not matched with political incorporation of newly empowered intellectuals or political redress against growing inequities and corruption. As a result, both rebellions occurred after the level of central bureaucratic state control had moderately declined, especially in China, but without a commensurate increase in democracy. As Muller and Seligson (1987) point out, moderately repressive regimes tend to suffer the most rebellion because repression is not strong enough to disorganize protest, yet a lack of democracy forestalls institutional alternatives. The initial response by both states was martial law, although a second strike wave in Poland forced the state to accept power sharing with Solidarity and this eventually ended party control.

Leading and supporting political actors were reversed—workers led the rebellion supported by dissident intellectuals in Poland, while students led a revolt that workers joined in China. Both leading actors derived organizational strength from high spatial concentration either in factories or universities. But the ability of Solidarity to cripple systematically the already faltering Polish economy gave the Polish workers much more economic potency than did the student-led protest in China. The reasons for this difference in leadership include the greater economic crisis in Poland and the rapid expansion of the student population in China.

Culturally, it is clear that Western ideals of liberal-democratic pluralism influenced both rebellions. But the manner in which this influence was conditioned by each state's environing context was different. Obviously, Polish culture is "Western" in the broad sense of the term, while Western ideals can be labeled as both bourgeois and foreign in China. Beyond these broad differences were specific differences in party ideology. In China, the Party's precept that class struggle was continuous and that capitalism can reemerge under cultural guises made reference to Western ideals "counterrevolutionary" by definition. Proletarian values stress selflessness, politically displayed through conformity (Pye 1988, p. 168; Stavis 1974). The intensity of repression may partly reflect the importance of "cultural transformation" in Chinese political movements (Pye 1988, p. 119; Stavis 1974, p. 236).

In Poland and elsewhere in Eastern Europe, Bielasiak (1982) points out that party leaders expanded membership in the 1970s in an attempt to integrate more of the citizenry into the political system. Among other things, this reflected a new theoretical concern with "socialist democracy in developed socialist states." It required some formal recognition of "diversity" and "complexity" of social interests (Simon 1982), as opposed to the greater value placed on conformity in China. Yet institutional mechanisms for participation or for resolution of conflict were stymied in Poland by the continuing stress on the primacy of the party. The Polish CP was thus the major and most obvious impediment to realization of the values it rhetorically promoted.

In attempting to restore growth, the party/states in Poland and China borrowed heavily and squeezed urban workers with inflation in order to shift income from consumption to investment and loan repayment. Following the Hungarian model, they introduced capitalist markets and Western ideas, binding their fates to the world economy. But they failed to politically incorporate the workers and intellectuals whose participation they increasingly needed. Instead, all grievances continued to be politicized and focused on the state. Spatially concentrated in factories and universities, and emboldened by traditions of protest and a relaxation of Stalinism, workers in Poland and students in China were able to organize mass revolts.

In both cases, the principle triggers of mass protests were a surge in inflation and visits from icons of change in the form of the Catholic pope and the Soviet premier. Nationalist resentment against dependency was also expressed in both cases, against the USSR by the Poles and against Japan by the Chinese. Polish nationalism was a much more important rallying point, however, due to Poland's long historical subjection to foreign powers and its military domination by the USSR since World War II. Finally, both countries were visited by icons of social change whose sojourns were catalysts for organizing. Pope John Paul II symbolized Polish nationalism and religious freedom in opposition to the ruling CP, while Soviet Premier Gorbachev represented a ruling CP that was introducing greater political democracy. Two more ironic symbols of radical social change would have been difficult to find.

Comparisons to Other State-Socialist Societies

With the dramatic events in East Germany, Czechoslovakia, and Romania, and the traumatic ones in the former Yugoslavia, popular rebellions have swept away all of Europe's state-socialist societies. Bunce (1989) lists three conditions that appear to preconfigure the revolts: (1) an informal redistribution of power from state to civil society; (2) an economic and "governability" crisis; and (3) the party/state's introduction of formal measures to liberalize. In order for a state to adopt full substantive democracy, electoral and legislative procedures for the expression and mediation of political conflict needed to become regularized and certain, while their outcomes are guaranteed to be variable and uncertain.

Successful rebels inspired one another and each faced similar and interdependent political economies. Nevertheless, variance in the extent and timing of rebellion needs to be explained. We can only hint at an explanation here. The exact conjuncture of cultural and political events that precipitated rebellion was historically specific to each case. Our discussion is intended to highlight some particular differences.

In the USSR, the state was pursuing a policy of "revolution from above." Gorbachev's goal was "Bukharin socialism"—state factories for mass production, and cooperatives and petty-commodity producers for agriculture, retail, and services. The intelligentsia was openly courted, but unlike China, there was no pressing need to reinvent it. It is possible that under more favorable global economic and political conditions,

Gorbachev could have succeeded in transforming the country from semiperipheral state socialism to a core-style social democracy. Even under the best of conditions, this would have been a tall order, however. In any case, the failed 1991 coup and the subsequent breakup of the USSR into national states derailed Gorbachev's effort.

In Hungary, the 1968 reforms put it ahead of the curve in terms of responding to the changes from the mass-production model. However, a huge debt burden slowed economic growth in the 1980s and the IMF imposed an austerity program usually reserved for Third World countries (Kolko 1988, pp. 30–35). Increased market despotism forced long hours at low pay (often at two jobs) on workers whose managers wielded tough and often arbitrary discipline (Burawoy 1985). Recognizing the depth of the problem, the party/state introduced from above the relatively free multiparty elections that rebellion from below won in Poland. By galvanizing political discontent, elections increased rather than decreased unrest. The result was a trouncing of the party.

The Czech revolt and the opening of the Wall in East Germany were dramatic examples of popular rebellion. Given their high levels of industrialization and urbanity, one might have expected Czechoslovakia and East Germany to have led rather than followed Poland or Hungary. Under Honecker, East Germany was the most politically rigid party/state in Eastern Europe, even banning several Soviet films (Larrabee 1989). Being on the front line of the Cold War had made military-style political discipline a more expected, if not a more legitimate, policy stance. Following the Stalinist model of economic development was a large part of the East German state's reason for existence. Soviet reform and de-escalation of the Cold War provided a prerequisite to a rapid delegitimation of an already unpopular state. Denied "voice," the people chose "exit," which was made possible by the newly opened Hungarian border. Berlin gave us the two most striking images of the 1989 world revolution—a night of frenzied shopping when Easterners claimed a bounty once the Berlin Wall opened and a joyful party as they tore the Wall down. Ironically, the opening of the Berlin Wall was intended to stem the flow of exit, as were the moves toward reform after Honecker's ouster. The response was huge demonstrations of voice that ousted the reform government, and hastened German reunification.

In the former Czechoslovakia, the Soviet invasion had been more recent than in Hungary and the residual effects were more potent in disorganizing protest. The reformists of 1968 were party leaders enacting changes that now seem prophetic of Gorbachev's, and the CP leaders who took power after the invasion owed their position to maintaining Stalinist orthodoxy. For them to promote glasnost from above would have been a humiliating self-effacement (Larrabee 1989). This put the party/state in a very awkward position because even a trickle of reform could open a flood of opposition. As in East Germany, reform in the USSR provided a prerequisite to negating the invasion's effect. Gorbachev even declared that his goal was "socialism with a human face" in an obvious (and successful) attempt to assure the Czech protesters. The rapidity by which workers and intellectuals organized protests and strikes in both states was nevertheless astounding, especially given the limitations on independent organization and resources.

Comparisons to the violent insurrection in Rumania are telling. In the 1980s, Rumania had become the economic basket case of Eastern Europe. Like Poland, a long-simmering conflict over consumer goods resulted in scattered strikes. Rumania borrowed heavily from the West in the 1970s with similar negative consequences for its economy. But unlike Poland, Ceausescu actually paid off the entire debt by promoting exports and cutting consumption. The resulting deprivation was astounding, especially since little of the sacrifice went to investment for future growth. Rumania was a tightly closed polity, even by Stalinist standards. Peaceful protesters inspired by events to the north were shot, including children deliberately placed in front in order to demonstrate their peaceful intentions. Disgusted military leaders refused to carry out further slaughter and they joined a swelling rebellion to topple the state.

Postcommunist Societies

In what turned out to be the last meeting of the Soviet Communist Party, Gorbachev in 1990 summed up the purpose and the failings of his ill-fated revolution from above in words eerily reminiscent of Sakarov's warning in 1968 quoted above. He stated that

> we were nearly one of the last to realize that in the age of information science, the most expensive assets are knowledge, breadth of mental outlook and creative imagination. To make up for lost time it is necessary today not to spare resources on science, education, culture and the arts—everything that elevates man and at the same time multiplies labor productivity. (Gorbachev 1990, p. 443)

State-centered theories explain why the internal contradictions of the Stalinist party/state transformed the socioeconomic protests of workers and intellectuals into political protests concentrated on the state. But they fail to explain why the political concentration of protests did not produce widespread revolts or widespread social change until 1989. The hypothesis of a world divide postulates that extended periods of stagnation result in crises that force firms and states to reorganize the socioeconomic structures of production. A divide occurs when innova-

tors resume expansion and the laggards fall behind. Workers, intellectuals, and other aggrieved parties increasingly interpret failures or
inequities during the divide as political questions that can be remedied
by radical action. The result was a series of potent rebellions with somewhat different consequences in different countries, but with the overall
result of further returning the counterhegemonic socialist states to the
fold of the world market and the interstate system of capitalist national
regimes.

By situating the party/states in the context of world historical development, we can explain both their past strengths and their eventual
weaknesses. The growing and innovative economic sector in the core
was changing from low-skill mass assembly run by military-type
bureaucracies to more flexible, high-skill batch production with decentralized control. This industrial divide in the world economy has forced
all countries to either match the innovations in accumulation or to be
satisfied with the low-technology industries cast off by the core. This is
why the Stalinist bureaucratic organization of mass production was successful at industrial development in the past and why it was abandoned
in 1989.

The prodigious sociological literature on postcommunism has
attempted to comprehend the social and organizational changes that
have occurred within these societies in terms of a hypothesized transition from socialism to capitalism. The implications of these changes are
obviously important theoretical issues in economic and institutional
sociology (Nee and Stark 1989; Nee and Liedka 1997; Keister 1998). This
literature has been quite fruitful for economic sociology, but with a few
noteworthy exceptions, there has been very little effort to place recent
developments in the postcommunist societies into world historical perspective.

The analysis of Chinese business groups within China and in the
Chinese diaspora has given new life to the study of economic networks
and social capital, as well as considerations of possible newly emergent
forms of capitalism that could serve as the organizational model for the
next epoch of global capitalism (Arrighi 1994). These topics have also
been interwoven with considerations of the possibility of an emergent
global hegemony of East Asia. The recent "crisis" there, and new, or
rather renewed, faultfinding about "crony capitalism," might seem to
have put the lid on all this. But the seers of an East Asian rise (e.g., Frank
1998) make much of the fact that a global economic crisis began in Asia
for the first time in centuries. Their argument is that, as in 1929, global
crises begin at the center, not in the periphery.

The best work on postcommunism that utilizes world-systems concepts has been done on Central and Eastern Europe (Borocz 1992, 1993, 1999; Borocz and Smith 1995). Jozsef Borocz's 1999 study is careful in the ways that it pays attention to the important differences as well as the analytic similarities of the processes of social change in the Central and Eastern European countries. His pithy characterization of the postcommunist Eastern European regimes as "auctioneer states" summarizes and compares the literature on emerging combinant property forms and class structures in these countries. The story of how the old elites have managed to become the new elites is a fascinating one.

Borocz argues that most of the Eastern European countries are downwardly mobile in the larger core-periphery hierarchy. Their former none-too-high situation of dual dependency between Soviet imperialism and dependence on Western finance capital is being replaced by an even greater degree of penetration by direct investment from global megacorporations. He also emphasizes that the breakup of many of the former states, which he argues was mainly motivated by hopes of early entry into the European Union, has increased the geopolitical volatility of the region and exacerbated the economic crisis. Borocz also cites comparative evidence on declines in life expectancy and the UN's Human Development Index that support his contention that Russia and the Central and Eastern European postcommunist societies are moving down in the core-periphery hierarchy.

We agree that most of the postcommunist states in Central and Eastern Europe and the ex–Soviet Union are likely to experience downward mobility, but we think that a few of these states may succeed in becoming incorporated into an expanded core region centered in the European Union in the next twenty years. This is certainly true of the former East Germany, likely for the Czech Republic, Hungary, and even Poland and Slovenia. Thus we predict a future bifurcation process in the development of the postcommunist states of Central and Eastern Europe with most experiencing peripheralization, but with a few managing to successfully move into the European core.

In Chapter 6, we outline some hypotheses about how citizens from these societies could figure in the next effort to transform the capitalist world-system. The intent of many of the 1989 rebels was to make it possible to catch up and join the core; this outcome is unlikely for most of these countries anytime soon. All semiperipheral countries are trying to find a profitable niche in the global market and the competition is fierce. While some have gained power and wealth in the postcommunist states, most of the masses and even many of the technocrats have fared poorly during the transition. Inequalities have risen sharply and even the most progressive change, democratization, has been undermined by massive corruption in what has become "crony capitalism," or in some places "Mafia markets." Such conditions are prime targets for organizing opposition.

Notes

1. This chapter is based in part on Boswell and Peters (1990). Their original paper was completed early in the summer of 1989, after the events in China and Poland, but before the governments in Eastern Europe had fallen. They predicted that protests and conflict, including ethnic conflict, would spread through the Soviet bloc, but were surprised by how rapidly the revolts spread and how easily states toppled. They revised the paper twice in prepublication in order to keep up with changing events, and we have revised it again here. However, the basic theoretical argument has remained the same throughout.

2. In addition to the sources cited in the text, the analysis of the Chinese and Polish cases drew on background information compiled from a variety of sources listed in Boswell and Peters (1990). We do not repeat the sources here to save space, except where needed to identify a particular point.

3. For instance, in the United States the average annual rate of productivity growth was 3.2 percent during the postwar expansion of 1948–1966, 2.3 percent in 1966–1973, 0.8 percent in 1973–1979, and 0.4 percent in 1979–1981 (Bowles, Gordon, and Weiskopf 1983, pp. 30–31).

4. Andrei Sakarov (1921–1989), the most prominent physicist and most prominent dissident in the Soviet Union, was rehabilitated in 1986 by Premier Gorbachev.

4

The Spiral of Capitalism and Socialism

The world revolution of 1989 that we analyzed in Chapter 3 led to proclamations about the end of history based on the final and complete victory of capitalist and liberal-democratic ideals (Fukuyama 1992; Kumar 1992). The current hegemony of neoclassical economics prescribes only one bromide for developing countries: accept "austerity" budgets and keep labor costs low in order to play ball with the big firms and compete for the global markets. Alternative visions have come to sound hopelessly utopian or anachronistic.

The world-systems perspective, as we have interpreted it, provides a different view of the long-term interaction between the expansion and deepening of capitalism, and of the efforts of people to protect themselves from exploitation and domination. The historical development of the socialist states is explained as part of a long-run spiraling interaction between expanding capitalism and socialist organizational forms. This chapter presents a further consideration of the developmental trajectories of the Soviet Union, Eastern Europe, and China in their world-system context. The socialist states were one manifestation of the counterhegemonic movements that have reacted to and transformed the capitalist world economy for five hundred years.

In Chapter 1, we presented a theoretical schema of the modern world-system. In that schema capitalism develops as a world-system, rather than as largely separate national societies. Both firms and states compete with one another within a global arena in which the core-periphery hierarchy is reproduced rather than eliminated. In this perspective imperialism is not a stage of capitalism, much less the highest stage, but is rather a recurring feature of the capitalist world-system. It is this larger world-system that develops, not national societies. What has been called national development is, in world-system theory, upward mobility in the core-periphery hierarchy. The history and developmen-

tal trajectory of the socialist states can be explained as counterhegemonic movements in the semiperiphery that attempted to transform the
basic logic of capitalism, but which ended up using socialist ideology to
mobilize industrialization for the purpose of catching up with core capitalism.

The spiraling interaction between capitalist development and
socialist movements can be seen in the history of labor movements,
socialist parties, and socialist states over the last two hundred years. This
long-run comparative perspective enables us to see the events of recent
decades in China, the Soviet Union, and Eastern Europe in a framework
that has important implications for the future of socialism. The
metaphor of the spiral means this: both capitalism and socialism affect
one another's growth and organizational forms. Capitalist exploitation
and domination spur socialist responses and socialist organizations spur
capitalism to expand market integration, to revolutionize technology,
and to reform politically. Class conflict oscillates along the spiral
between open struggle, managed compromise, and repressive domination. While class conflict of all types is omnipresent, open struggles proliferate in the semiperiphery, managed compromise is a hallmark of the
core, and repressive class domination plagues the periphery.
Additionally, the core-periphery hierarchy itself has been reorganized by
the spiraling interaction of expanding control and expanded resistance.

The capitalism referred to here is not only the phenomenon of capitalist firms producing commodities, but also of capitalist states and the
modern interstate system, which are the political backdrops for capitalist accumulation. The world-systems perspective has produced an
understanding of capitalism in which geopolitics and interstate conflict
are normal processes of capitalist political competition. Socialist movements are, defined broadly, those antisystemic political and organizational efforts in which people try to protect themselves from and to gain
control over market forces, capitalist exploitation, and state domination.
The series of industrial revolutions in which capitalism restructured
production and the control of labor have stimulated a succession of
political revolutions, movements, and institutions created by workers
and communities to protect their livelihoods. Skilled workers created
guilds and craft unions. Less-skilled workers created industrial unions.
Workers of all stripes participated in struggles for democracy. In many
countries, these coalesced into labor parties that played central roles in
the development of welfare states. In other regions, workers were less
politically successful, but managed at least to protect access to rural
areas or subsistence plots for a fallback or hedge against the insecurities
of employment in capitalist enterprises. This happened differently
under particular political and economic conditions in different parts of

the world-system, but viewed on a global historical scale we can see the commonalties and temporal relationships of these revolutions and movements.

The varying success of workers' organizations has had an impact back on the further development of capitalism. In some areas, workers or communities were successful at raising the wage bill or protecting the environment in ways that raised the costs of production for capital. When this happened, capitalists either employed more-productive technology or capital migrated to where fewer constraints allowed cheaper and more-profitable production. Where more-productive technology required more-skilled labor, living standards rose, setting a new and higher floor of social standards. The alternative of capital flight depends on whether the necessary technologies and skills are transferable to low-wage areas. The process of capital flight is not a new feature of the world-system. It has been an important force behind the uneven development of capitalism and the spreading scale of market integration for centuries. But like all facets of contemporary capitalism, the pace has quickened, particularly in the last thirty years. During the long post–World War II expansion, labor unions and socialist parties were able to obtain some power in certain states. Fordism—the employment of large numbers of assembly-line workers in centralized production locations—facilitated industrial organizing. Firm size increased and international markets became more and more important to successful capitalist competition. "Flexible accumulation" and global sourcing, a production strategy that makes traditional labor organization strategies much less viable, have supplanted Fordism. Just as the local craft unions of the 1890s were unable to organize the then-new assembly-line industries, national industrial unions in the 1990s are faltering in the face of global capitalism.

State Socialism in the World-System

Socialists were able to take state power in certain semiperipheral and peripheral states and they used this power to create political mechanisms of protection against competition with core capital. This was not a wholly new phenomenon. As discussed below, capitalist semiperipheral states had done, and were doing, similar things. But, the socialist states claimed a counterhegemonic ideology in which socialism was to be a superior system that would eventually replace capitalism. Ideological opposition is a phenomenon that the capitalist world economy has also seen before. The geopolitical and economic battles of the Thirty Years' War were fought in the name of Protestantism against

Catholicism, as we have discussed in Chapter 2. The content of the ideology makes important differences for the internal organization of states and parties, but every contender must be able to legitimate itself in the eyes and hearts of its cadre. The claim to represent a qualitatively different and superior socioeconomic system on the part of the socialist states is not evidence that they were indeed structurally autonomous from the capitalist world-system.

The socialist states severely restricted the access of core capitalist firms to their internal markets and raw materials. This constraint on the mobility of capital was an important force behind the post–World War II wave of the increasing scale of market integration and a new revolution of technology. In certain areas, capitalism was driven to further revolutionize technology or to improve living conditions for workers and peasants because of the demonstration effect of propinquity to a socialist state. U.S. support for state-led industrialization of South Korea (in contrast to U.S. policy in Latin America) is only understandable as a geopolitical response to the Chinese Revolution (Cumings 1987). The existence of "two superpowers"—one capitalist and one communist—in the period since World War II provided a fertile context for the success of international liberalism within the "capitalist" bloc (Wallerstein 1995). This was the political/military basis of the rapid growth of transnational corporations and the latest revolutionary "time-space compression" (Harvey 1989), a topic we return to in the next chapter. This technological revolution has once again restructured the international division of labor and created a new regime of labor regulation called "flexible accumulation." The processes by which the socialist states have become reintegrated into the capitalist world-system have been long, as described below. But the final phase of reintegration since 1989 was provoked by the inability to be competitive with the new forms of capitalist regulation as analyzed in Chapter 3. Thus, capitalism spurs socialism, which spurs capitalism, which spurs socialism again in a wheel that turns and turns while getting larger—the spiral.

In 1982, a collection of essays was published in which socialists debated the nature of the socialist states and their relationship with the capitalist world (Chase-Dunn 1982). In that collection, Chase-Dunn presented a world-systemic interpretation of the socialist states as territories in which movements with socialist intentions had taken state power, yet were not able to successfully introduce a self-reproducing socialist mode of production. The developmental trajectories of the socialist states are analytically similar to earlier, smaller-scale anticapitalist movements that attempted to create noncommodified relations of cooperation and that became encapsulated politically within organizations: cooperatives, worker-owned firms, unions, and socialist parties.

The market principle expands its scale in part to reincorporate these collectivities into the logic of capitalist competition within the larger world-system.

The socialist states were important experiments in the construction of socialist institutions, but they were perverted at birth by the necessities of survival and development in the context of the capitalist world market and the interstate system. Thus, they developed into forms of state capitalism that used socialist ideology to legitimate the state and to accumulate capital for industrialization. Even where initially successful at development, they became locked into a bureaucratic mass-production economic model that eventually became a fetter on further development (as we argued in Chapter 3).

Socialist revolutions did not take state power in the core, but rather in semiperipheral and peripheral regions of the world-system. The socialist states failed to institutionalize a self-reproducing socialist mode of production because of the strong threats and inducements emanating from the larger capitalist world-system. The conflictive interstate system and the direct threats from capitalist core states encouraged militarism, authoritarianism, and "defensive" imperialism. The existence of a dynamic and competitive world market encouraged corruption, consumerism, and political opportunism by the "new class" of technocrats and bureaucrats who could bolster their own positions by mediating the importation of sophisticated technology from the core.

In his contribution to the 1982 collection edited by Chase-Dunn, Albert Szymanski, one of the leading U.S. Marxist sociologists at the time, proposed a "domino theory" of the transition to world socialism. He based his idea on the large proportion of the world population then living in socialist states and the victories within recent decades of socialist national-liberation movements in Africa, Asia, and Latin America. Szymanski contended that the Soviet Union and Eastern Europe constituted a separate socialist world-system with its own autonomous logic of development and that world capitalism had been seriously weakened by the growing number of socialist states and their successes in building socialism.

World-systems analysts (e.g., Frank 1980) disputed this contention and saw the socialist states as having been significantly reincorporated into the capitalist world economy. Contrary to those who think that this reincorporation occurred only recently, the world-systems perspective on socialist states implies that these states never fully escaped the capitalist world economy. Their political and economic development can only be understood as a response to the threats and inducements of the larger environment. Thus, the political reincorporation of the Soviet Union began when it became apparent that the Bolshevik Revolution would have to survive within a hostile world and try to construct "socialism in one country." The realities of the interstate system demanded that the Soviet state create an apparatus that could defend against external political/military threats. Walter Goldfrank (1982) presented an insightful world-system account of "The Soviet Trajectory" from the October Revolution to the (then) emerging crisis of the Brezhnev era. Joan Sokolovski (1982) analyzed the dilemma that Maoist efforts at self-reliance posed and the class-based pressures for the reintegration of China into the larger world market, an analysis that can account for many of the developments that subsequently occurred in China in the last two decades.

Though distribution was more equal within the socialist states, it did not change substantially the competitive logic within which they interacted with other states. One of the most disconcerting features of the former socialist states was their most unsocialist behavior toward one another. This was a continuation of the same nationalism and interstate competition that is normal behavior in the capitalist world-system. Put simply, the big transformations that occurred in the Soviet Union and China after 1989 were part of a process that had long been under way since the 1970s. The big political changes were a classic example of the national "superstructure" catching up with the world economic "base." The democratization of these societies is, of course, a welcome trend, but democratic political forms do not automatically lead to a society without exploitation or domination. The outcomes of current political struggles are rather uncertain in most of the postcommunist countries. New types of authoritarian regimes with a shell of democratic rhetoric seem at least as likely as real democratization.

National economic planning, which was most highly developed and highly distorted in the socialist states, may be simply one peculiar expression of the trend toward state capitalism. There has been a secular trend toward greater state intervention in all areas of life for the last century (see Boli-Bennet 1980). Though the current ideological hegemony repeats over and over that state-owned firms and state regulation are not "efficient," state intervention was crucial to successful capitalist development in virtually every case, but especially so in those semiperipheral countries trying to move toward core status. Peter Evans (1995) has called these states "midwives" to describe their successful developmental policies. Consider, for instance, the success of state-led capitalism in South Korea, Taiwan, and Singapore. Evans's telling comparison of the electronics industry among would-be NICs in the 1970s–1980s shows how South Korea nourished and protected its industry up to the point where it became internationally competitive, then increasingly exposed its firms to the world market. Others failed by offering inadequate nourishment or overprotection. The socialist states represent cases in which state intervention went much further than in other semiperipheral countries, but the purpose of state-led development was the same. Rather than opposites, whether markets or hierarchies are most efficient depends on the circumstances and conditions of production (Williamson 1985). States, or other hierarchies, are most successful at governing an economy where markets fail—and vice versa. Historically, states intervene successfully when markets reach existing limits of fair competition. Corruption and cronyism flourish where markets are not very competitive or where states arbitrarily override fair competition. The most beneficial areas of state intervention fall into the following three categories: (1) public goods, social infrastructure, and basic needs; (2) "natural monopolies" where a lack of viable alternatives disallows fair competition; and (3) nascent or floundering businesses where temporary protection reaps long-term competitiveness. Markets, historically, flourished where innovative multiple buyers and sellers undermined monopolization, and where states could guarantee fair contracts. What works best changes over time. Successful states make for widely copied "miracles," which then rarely risk major change and are supplanted by the next miracle worker. The result is, once again, a spiral of ever-increasing state expansion and of market integration.

Trends from the 1970s to the 1990s show that austerity regimes, deregulation, and marketization within nearly all of the socialist states occurred during the same period as similar phenomena racked nonsocialist states. The simultaneity and broad similarities between Reagan/Thatcher deregulation and attack on the welfare state, austerity in most of the rest of the world, and increasing pressures for marketization are all related to the B-phase downturn of the Kondratieff wave. The trend toward privatization, deregulation, and market-based solutions among parties of the left in almost every country is thoroughly documented by Lipset (1991). Nearly all socialists with access to political power have abandoned the idea of doing more than polishing the rough edges off of capitalism. The ways in which the pressures of a highly integrated and competitive world economy impact upon national policies certainly vary from country to country, but the ability of any single national society to construct collective rationality is limited by its interaction within the larger system. The most recent increase in the pace of capitalist integration, termed "globalization," has made autarchic national economic planning seem anachronistic. Compare how different was the response during the last K-wave downturn in the 1930s, when welfare-state provisions were greatly expanded, as were increasingly hostile nationalism and imperialism.

Lipset (1991) documents a nearly universal swing toward the market among socialist politicians. He stresses the impact of the failure of

Leninism in the socialist states, the apparently self-evident inefficiency of government intervention and state-owned firms, and the rise of "postmaterialist" issues from the 1968 New Left, such as racism, gender inequality, environmentalism, and "freedom" in general. This last factor, the New Left, he explains, is the result of changes in the composition of the work force away from industrial workers toward educated professionals and service workers. Lipset largely ignores the world-system aspects of the phenomenon he is analyzing, although he does mention the shift from the period of sustained economic expansion to the period of relative stagnation as a factor. His work-force explanation may explain some of the shift within core countries, but it can explain little in peripheral and semiperipheral countries where work-force trends have been very different.

The restructuring of the international division of labor has been an important causal element in the shift toward the right. Globalization has accelerated the internationalization of capital to an extent that is considerably greater than ever before. The size of transnational firms and their policies of global sourcing have made national-level labor organizations increasingly ineffective, and until recently, there have been few efforts to create new transnational labor organizations. The phenomenon of capital flight has long been an important feature of the struggle between capital and labor, but the increased integration of the global market for labor and goods makes capital flight even more important in the current era (Ross and Trachte 1990). In addition, the revolution of technology is perhaps capitalism's most progressive feature. Though technological revolution is not without its costs, the effect of the most recent burst of new lead industries (computerization, biotechnology) has been to revitalize the glorification of markets and private entrepreneurship.

Comparative and Global Development

The world-systems perspective suggests that we should compare the socialist states with other semiperipheral countries, particularly in terms of national development (Comisso and Tyson 1986, pp. 401–422).[1] The economic reincorporation of the socialist states into the capitalist world economy did not occur recently and suddenly. It began with the mobilization toward autarchic industrialization using socialist ideology, an effort that initially was in ways successful in terms of standard measures of economic development. Most of the socialist states were increasing their percentage of world product and energy consumption up until the 1980s. Table 4.1 compares socialist states with the United States and with those countries with 60 percent of world population who have

Table 4.1   Socialist States in the World-System

	1950	1960	1970	N
Proportion of gross world product going to:				
13 socialist states	12.4%	18.1%	23.2%	
middle countries on GNP per capita				
with 60% of world population	23.4%	27.8%	28.6%	129
United States	41.9%	35.8%	30.4%	
Proportion of world electrical energy consumed by:				
9 socialist states	15.0%	19.1%	21.8%	
middle countries in KWH per capita with				
60% of world population	32.9%	34.4%	39.3%	75
United States	42.0%	38.5%	30.4%	
Proportion of world nonagricultural labor force living in:				
14 socialist states	22.4%	28.5%		
the middle countries on % nonagricultural				
work force with 60% of world population	48.4%	50.5%		138
United States	15.2%	13.6%		
Proportion of world primary students enrolled in:				
13 socialist states	37.3%	42.7%	40.0%	
middle countries on % primary students				
enrolled with 60% of world population	63.9%	65.5%	62.4%	91
United States	15.9%	14.7%	12.1%	
Proportion of world secondary students enrolled in:				
9 socialist states	13.4%	11.5%	14.3%	
middle countries on % secondary students				
enrolled with 60% world population	42.6%	50.4%	51.3%	91
United States	20.3%	18.0%	21.1%	
Proportion of world tertiary students enrolled in:				
8 socialists states	26.6%	28.8%	24.5%	
middle countries on % tertiary students enrolled				
with 60% of world population	38.9%	42.8%	42.8%	83
United States	38.8%	34.8%	34.9%	
Proportion of world city dwellers living in:				
14 socialist states	23.9%	25.5%		
middle countries on % urbanization with				
60% world population	44.7%	47.8%		133
United States	16.7%	15.7%		

Source: Table 2 in Meyer, Boli-Bennet, and Chase-Dunn (1975).

intermediate levels of the various resources and structural features studied in the table. This "middle level" category contains semiperipheral and some peripheral countries. Looking at the first set of percentages in Table 4.1, we see that a group of thirteen socialist states nearly doubled their percentage of gross world product between 1950 and 1970. During this same period, the United States' percentage of world product declined from 41.9 percent to 30.4 percent while the middle-level countries increased their percentage from 23.4 percent to 28.6 percent. Socialist states also increased their percentages of world electrical energy consumed during this period. Until the end of the 1960s, the Stalinist model of mobilization successfully urbanized and industrialized the Soviet Union and much of Eastern Europe. Moreover, the socialist states provided a much better physical quality of life than other semiperipheral countries at similar levels of economic development (Cereseto and Waitzkin 1986).

The economic reincorporation of the socialist states moved to a new stage of integration with the world market and foreign firms in the 1970s. Andre Gunder Frank (1980) documented a trend toward reintegration in which the socialist states increased their exports for sale on the world market, increased imports from the avowedly capitalist countries, and made deals with transnational firms for investments within their borders. The economic crisis in Eastern Europe and the Soviet Union was not much worse than the economic crisis in the rest of the world during the global economic downturn that began in the late 1960s (which we examined in Chapter 3). Data presented by World Bank analysts indicates that GDP growth rates were positive in most of the "historically planned economies" in Europe until 1989 or 1990 (Marer et al. 1991, table 7a). Table 4.2 compares individual socialist states with the United States and with the group of middle-level countries for the period between 1960 and 1980.

China, Hungary, and Yugoslavia (the only cases for which we have data on GNP for this period) continued to increase their relative shares of gross world product between 1960 and 1980. During this same period both the United States and the group of middle-level countries experienced decline in their shares of gross world product. When we examine shares of energy consumption, six of the socialist countries experienced increases while three (Czechoslovakia, East Germany, and Poland) experienced decline. The U.S. share of world energy consumption declined, but the middle-level countries increased dramatically, especially in the period from 1970 to 1980. The increase in the percentage of world energy consumed by the middle-level countries is due to the movement of heavy industry and other industrial production to certain semiperipheral countries. Note that this was not accompanied by an increase in the percentage of world income in the middle-level countries.

Table 4.2 demonstrates that the socialist states were relatively successful in industrializing and increasing their shares of world income and resources until rather recently, despite all the talk about the insufficiencies of the command economy. Their growth rates were very

Table 4.2   World Percentages Held by Socialist States, Middle-Level Countries, and the United States, 1960–1980

Country	GNP 1960	1970	1980	Energy Consumption 1960	1970	1980
USSR				14.7	15.0	17.6
China	2.67	2.44	2.92	5.5	5.0	6.3
Bulgaria				.3	.5	.5
Czechoslovakia				1.3	1.1	1.1
East Germany				1.9	1.4	1.3
Hungary	.15	.16	.22	.4	.4	.5
Poland				2.2	2.0	2.1
Rumania				.7	.9	1.1
Yugoslavia	.51	.55	.68	.4	.4	.6
United States	32.08	28.52	26.99	36.0	32.3	27.8
Middle countries (on GNP and energy usage) with 60% world population	19.4	18.9	18.1	16.1	18.8	29.1
Number of countries		112			126	

Sources: Energy Consumed—World Bank (I.B.R.D.), *World Tables,* 1983. GNP—World Bank (I.B.R.D), Economic Analysis and Projections Department, 1980.

high, and higher than other semiperipheral countries during the world economic expansion in the 1950s and 1960s. During the 1970s and 1980s they slowed down, as did almost all other countries, but even then most of them did not stagnate to a much greater extent than either core countries or most semiperipheral countries until the 1980s. Prior to the 1970s, both socialist and nonsocialist semiperipheral states pursued a policy of import-substitution industrialization in which they tried to protect themselves from competition with core imports and to sponsor the domestic production of industrial products. The effort of the socialist states to mobilize import substitution differed in form and extent from the strategies employed by other semiperipheral countries (e.g., Brazil and Mexico). But all the developing semiperipheral countries shared certain broad features in common, particularly the following[2]:

1. State power was used to try to catch up with core capitalism.
2. Protectionism was used to reserve the home economy for certain sectors, especially heavy industry and agriculture.
3. State firms were created in key sectors.
4. The stage of import-substitution industrialization was followed by a crisis in which this type of development reached its limits

and needed to be replaced by a new type of economic policy (Nee and Stark 1989, pp. 208–232).

The differences between the strategies of the socialist and nonsocialist semiperipheral states need to be spelled out. The extent of state intervention in the socialist states was much greater than in the nonsocialist semiperiphery and qualitatively different in select areas. State-owned firms carried out a greater proportion of all production and the concentration of these firms was usually greater in the socialist states. Capital investment and pricing were administrated, and this was the most important difference. But even here, currency and investment in the socialist states were never completely autonomous from international market and geopolitical forces. These forces became ever more constricting where they sought foreign investment and loans. The involvement of foreign capital was much greater in the nonsocialist semiperiphery from the start. These differences affected the way in which the exhaustion of import-substitution industrialization came about, and the options for restructuring.

In the nonsocialist semiperiphery, import substitution faced a problem of limited demand. Large-scale production for the home market soon saturated demand among a largely poor population. This could be resolved in two fundamentally different ways: either the home market could be broadened by increasing wages and consumption, or export promotion for the world market could be combined with continued low wages. The first way produced incessant inflation while the second offered continued deprivation. Political oscillations between populism and authoritarianism in the nonsocialist semiperipheral states partly reflected the tension between these very different possible paths of development.

In the socialist states, the options were somewhat different. Import substitution in the command economies did not produce a situation of weak demand because the "soft budget constraints" on state-owned firms in these economies ensured high demand for industrial outputs. Long lines and longer waits replaced the incessant inflation in the nonsocialist counterpart. But this demand was created by the state and there was an underlying problem similar to the nonsocialist equivalents. The development alternatives for resolving the exhaustion of import-substitution industrialization are analytically somewhat similar for both socialist and nonsocialist semiperipheral states. Both turned to massive Western loans and to export promotion (although the oil-rich USSR was only involved indirectly through its trading partners). Debt crises and increased exploitation, along with strikes and other social upheavals, spared few semiperipheral states regardless of their Cold War affiliation.

In the Soviet Union and Eastern Europe, the command economy could have been mobilized to produce greater variety and cheaper consumer goods, and indeed this was happening to some extent in the last decades. But the technocrats and bureaucrats of the Soviet Union and China, like the capitalists and technocrats of the nonsocialist semiperiphery, did not want to redistribute investment. To do so would have precluded their ability to import more expensive and elaborate technologies (and luxuries) from the core capitalist countries. These could only be financed by foreign debt and by selling commodities on the world market (for "hard" currency). Successful export promotion requires cheap skilled labor for the production of goods that can find a niche in the world market as well as politically negotiated access to the markets and banks of capitalist core powers. This requires reducing subsidies on consumption goods and tightening market discipline over labor. It also meant abandoning many ideological and political disputes with core powers in order to obtain "most favorable nation" trading status.

Both socialist and nonsocialist semiperipheral countries faced a situation in which they had successfully mobilized industrialization and created a type of production that was formerly the leading edge of production in the core. The effort to catch up with core capitalism was frustrated for most of these countries, however, because the core had, in the meantime, developed new industries and new modes of regulation. Heavy industry was sloughed off to semiperipheral producers and the highest rates of profit are now to be had in new lead industries and services. Thus most of the semiperipheral countries were and are running fast to stand still. Those that did succeed in the 1970s and 1980s, the East Asian NICs, have suffered their own currency and investment crises in the late 1990s. The economic consequences are again similar—higher foreign debt, increased exploitation, and greater export promotion. Social consequences, in the form of labor strikes and civic movements, especially where democracy is lacking, are also similar. The revolution in Indonesia is a case in point.

A final feature shared by both socialist and nonsocialist semiperipheral states in their rush to develop is the largely unmitigated rape of the natural environment by large-scale resource destruction and negligent pollution. The combination of militaristic secrecy and antiquated technology probably made industrial pollution worse in Eastern Europe than elsewhere (but see Gille, forthcoming), although countries like Brazil and Indonesia cannot be far behind. In addition, the rapid population growth and urbanization in the East Asian NICs have given them some of the world's most congested and polluted cities. Many other comparisons could be made, but determining the exact balance is less important than recognizing the common problems. The disastrous environmental practices of most of the semiperipheral states are a global problem with consequences that will extend into the future. Although the biggest polluters have been and continue to be the core states, democratic political pressures and higher economic development provide core environmental movements with much greater opportunities and resources for protecting the environment. The importance of democracy for global environmental protection is an issue to which we will return.

After the Fall

We have contended (Chapter 3) that the Stalinist command economy of the socialist states was incapable of crossing the "new industrial divide" from Fordism to flexible specialization. Our analysis contends that this created an economic crisis within the socialist states. Although "flexible specialization" is undoubtedly occurring in some sectors within core countries and the NICs, other areas, especially in the semiperiphery, are experiencing an expansion of Fordism, that is, large-scale industry with huge concentrations of workers. In most cases, the other side of Fordism, expansion of the purchasing power of primary-sector workers, has not emerged because much of the new semiperipheral industrial production is for export, not for domestic consumption. Thus, Fordism in the semiperiphery can be expected to have different political results from those it had in the core. We supplement this argument with a focus on class struggles within socialist countries, conflicts that are affected by the changing international context. The decision of which development policy to pursue is one that has different implications and consequences for different groups of people. Workers and peasants in the Soviet Union and China expected at least the mass-produced consumer goods that a command economy could have produced. It is the semiperipheral technocrats, bureaucrats, and capitalists who have benefited the most from the policy of export promotion.

The recent expansion of the scale of market interactions and firms has been accompanied by a new wave of "time-space compression" (Harvey 1989)—the reduction of transportation and communications costs—which has been one of the most dramatic consequences of recent capitalist development. The latest revolution in technology and the changes that this is causing in organizational forms have had important consequences for state socialism, as we argued in the last chapter. Some of that impact was also at the level of *ideology*. Capitalism had performed a miracle in the provision of low-cost electronic, computation, and communications goods. The spread of these goods has made those who do not have easy access envious of those who do. The importance of this factor in strengthening political discontent among the tech-nocrats and bureaucrats of the formerly socialist states should not be underestimated as a factor that produced the final abandonment of socialist ideology and its formal legal and political forms, as we argued in the last chapter. We argue in the next chapter that it also shapes the possibilities of new organizational forms that socialism might take in the future.

The aptness of the above comparison between socialist and nonso-cialist semiperipheral states was demonstrated, in a most ironic fashion, during Gorbachev's failed attempts at reform when Yuri A. Profkofiev, a top Communist Party associate, declared that Pinochet's Chile provided a model that the Soviet Union should emulate. During the 1980s, Pinochet applied the Chicago-school economic policies of state privati-zation, market deregulation, labor demobilization, and export promo-tion. Chile enjoyed rapid industrial growth at the expense of a marked increase in inequality and decline in labor standards (Goldfrank 1989). Chile became the poster child of neoliberalism, and neoliberalism had, until the Asia crisis, become the dominant ideology of the global policy-makers. Countries as diverse as New Zealand and El Salvador have adopted similar policies.

Perhaps neoliberalism did not reflect Gorbachev's own thinking, as he professed to favor some form of social democracy, but it does resem-ble Yeltsin's strategy. The Russian Constitution of 1993 enshrined mar-ketization and privatization in the context of a strong and potentially repressive state that can control nationalist and labor resistance—pere-stroika without so much glasnost. The goal would seem to be to pair Milton Friedman's economics with the politics of Louis Bonaparte. While unpopular domestically, global policymakers and the Russian intelligentsia have largely supported Yeltsin and his successors, as they see no other viable alternative. The failed coup by reactionary *appa-ratchiks* in August 1991 demonstrated the utter lack of a statist alterna-tive. The neofascist nationalists only offered a nostalgic cover for repres-sion. Even many of the self-proclaimed democrats are apparently quite willing to utilize authoritarian and corrupt means to accumulate capital, however primitively (Offe 1991).

There are of course important differences among the former state-socialist countries that we have not fully discussed. The biggest differ-ence was in the level of legitimacy of the party/state. The states of Eastern Europe, dominated by the Soviet Union, were never fully legitimate because the regimes were imposed by Red Army conquest. Much of the political upheaval in Eastern Europe was a nationalist reaction to Soviet domination and has led to their understandable rejection of socialist ideology as an externally imposed state religion.

This makes them vulnerable to unmitigated exploitation by the capitalist core. Politics in Eastern Europe needs to be understood in terms of shifts in a structure of "dual dependency" (see Borocz 1992) in which economic exploitation and political domination by both the Soviet Union and the Western capitalist countries have taken different forms over time.

There are also critical differences within Eastern Europe. As noted earlier, some of the former satellites have at least a chance of finding a niche in the next wave of capitalist expansion—certainly eastern Germany, and perhaps the Czech Republic and Hungary. Poland has seen some of the highest growth rates, but started from a lower base of development and has a larger agricultural sector. Hopes dim as one moves south and east. Even aside from the tragic conflict in the former Yugoslavia, the best hope for Balkan entrepreneurs is to convert the domestic economies into semiperipheral backyards of core capital, providing cheap skilled labor to transnational firms. The Caucasus and west Asian areas seek Western investment to become raw-material export economies. The only worse fate under capitalism, to paraphrase Rosa Luxemburg, would be for them to not be exploited by core capital.

Unlike Eastern Europe, China, Cuba, and Vietnam shared the feature that the socialist state derived its legitimacy from indigenous revolutions. Thus, the crisis of state socialism in these countries was far less influenced by geopolitics and nationalism than was the case in Eastern Europe. In these countries, communist movements took state power and mobilized immense political forces in an effort to build a socialist mode of production. Their failure to construct a self-sustaining socialist system was not due to the limitations of human nature, but rather to the constraints, both "internal" and "external," under which they labored (Chase-Dunn 1982). The USSR was somewhere in between. While the revolution and CP rule was indigenous to Russia, the same cannot be said for the other republics that made up the Soviet Union. Ultimately, it was geopolitics and nationalism that brought down the USSR. The failed coup of 1991, which lead to the dismantling of the USSR, was launched in order to prevent it.

Several differences between the Soviet Union and China help explain why the Party survived in China, and not in the Soviet Union, and why the CCP could introduce "market socialism" without undermining its own legitimacy. The comparison is also relevant for understanding the problems of semiperipheral socialism more generally. To start, a more recent revolution in China strengthened the grip of the Chinese Communist Party. In China, the level of cynicism about the Party and the state is somewhat lower than what was true of the Soviet Union. We discussed how the generation that fought the revolution was still in power and willing to use heavy violence to defend the Party during the Tiananmen Square uprising in 1989. Other differences include the role of the peasantry in the revolutions, which continues to have important political effects. In the former Soviet Union, the Party was not as popular in the countryside or in the provinces far from Russia. As we note above, most importantly, the Soviet Union was a barely transformed Russian Empire, with a multinational population. The problem of subnations is present in China, most obviously in the case of Tibet, but about 90 percent of the population are Han Chinese and nationalism is much less threatening to the integrity of the central state.

The timing and sequencing of reforms also differed between the two party/states in ways that produced different outcomes. In China, marketization was started earlier and in largely rural areas where the benefits were easiest to realize. Despite significant industrialization of some regions, China still remains a largely agricultural country while much more of the Soviet Union was urbanized and industrialized. While market reform continues, political reform in China has been halted for now and even reversed by the reactionary gerontocracy, though this is likely to be temporary. In the former Soviet Union, openings toward political decentralization and glasnost were implemented first, though the destabilizing nature of these openings led to the reactionary crackdown of 1991. The reaction to the reaction proved fatal. Had the coup been avoided, could Gorbachev have succeeded in building a social-democratic state? Quite likely yes, we think, but only in Russia and not for the USSR as an imperial whole. Even if Gorbachev was not fated to fail, the Soviet Union was doomed.

The Third Way: Social Democracy

Disillusioned with state socialism and disappointed with capitalism, discussion inevitably turns to the "third way" of social-democratic "mixed economies" for the former state-socialist and other semiperipheral countries. The topic usually proceeds from the assumption that bureaucracies are inherently inefficient and need to be subjected to market forces. This characterization of the problem fails to consider the nature of class relations under state socialism and the possibilities for democratic control of planning bureaucracies. Markets by themselves are not evil. Market socialism, we will contend in the next chapter, is the most viable and appropriate version of a socialist mode of production at the global level. However, the notion that the *only* antidote to bureaucratic inefficiency and oligarchic tendencies is marketization and privatization needs to be challenged. The question of efficiency is never either/or, but which form of economic governance best fits existing economic conditions and resources (Williamson 1985).

Small firms with rapidly changing technologies or with highly variable consumer demand, such as software designers or fine restaurants, suffer from the rigidities and sunk costs of bureaucratic hierarchies. This is a central reason why Soviet-style planning was notorious for its dismal service sectors and was constantly lagging in developing small-scale technology. On the other hand, large-scale projects with stable production lines, such as most traditional mass production, benefit from the planning and reliability of the bureaucratic form. This was a central source of Soviet success in the first half of the century.

What at one time is most efficiently organized by a bureaucracy, sometimes due to the bureaucracy's success, can better increase efficiency through marketization at a later point. Witness long-distance phone service in the United States, which was a natural monopoly in its origin to prevent incompatible systems. Once the system had been developed, however, monopoly was inefficient. The opposite is of course equally true. Computer chip production, once exotic, is now routine mass production. Markets and hierarchies, like capitalism and socialism, spiral in development.

Markets are often described as "horizontal" institutions that promote equality, while bureaucracies and central planning are described as "hierarchical" (e.g., Kornai 1989). Both characterizations are inaccurate. First, while competitive markets exchange commodities at their value, market exchange reproduces and multiplies inequalities in the ownership of productive assets. Unequal assets produce unequal exchange (exploitation) regardless of the merit, effort, time, or other sources of individual productivity of the producers. Variation in exploitation is most extreme at the global level, where the biggest asset inequalities in the capitalist world economy are between the core and the periphery.

Second, while bureaucracies have historically been modeled on armies (surely not paradigms of democratic equality), they need not be hierarchical or undemocratic. There is an extensive social science literature on participatory and democratic organizational forms (Rothschilde-Whitt 1979). Worker control in an otherwise capitalist firm tends to increase productivity and intrafirm equality. The trend among leading firms in the core countries has been to introduce partial elements of worker control, such as quality circles and employee stock ownership plans (ESOPs), in order to profit from the increased quality, productivity, and motivation they generate.

While such democratic organizational forms are important for redressing hierarchy and exploitation within the productive enterprise (a necessary element of socialism), they do not reduce the unequal exchange that results from differential access to capital in the first place. Even neoclassical theorists hold that, in principle, labor could "employ" capital with the same (we think better) productive efficiency with which capital employs labor. The cost and availability of capital to workers would, however, vary dramatically across the world economy, and would remain in the hands of bankers, brokers, and billionaires. As a result, attempts to build "socialist" firms within capitalist markets have proven less sanguine. A common problem, confirmed by the current crisis of Israeli kibbutzim, is that these institutions (like the socialist states) tend to revert back to the standard organizational characteristics of capitalist firms (private ownership, market-determined wages, etc.) when the larger context of expanding capitalism exposes them to financial crises or individualist opportunities. Some benefits remain, in terms of quality, productivity, and motivation, along the lines of those derived from the partial worker control instituted by leading capitalist firms. These are real accomplishments that socialist movements should embrace, but in terms of reducing societal inequality and exploitation, they are incomplete without democratic control of investment.

Can central planning agencies be controlled by institutionalized democratic structures? The history of Soviet-style socialism does not bode well for a positive answer.[3] However, a fully democratic institutional option was not tried in any of the former or current socialist states. Socialist democracy could be structured in the form of a popularly elected government that oversees the process of economic planning and investment. In such a state, the tradeoff between efficiency and equality could be decided democratically. Some may question if this is optimal for success in the capitalist world economy, but few would question that it could easily provide a good living for all citizens and a political situation free from repression. While Soviet planning failed the test of democracy or of enduring economic success, democratic state oversight of planning and investment does partially exist in social-democratic core states. The successes of social democracy, both regarding economic development and in developing democratic institutions, should give pause to the purveyors of the Chicago school of neoliberalism.

The research on social democracy reaches a consistent conclusion. Compared to other core industrial democracies, the social-democratic states have proven to have both high growth rates and the highest social equality (e.g., Hicks 1988). Public investment in infrastructure and human capital is part of the reason. The return on these social investments benefits all of society, starting with the working class. But the main benefit of social democracy is the social peace in the class struggle won by egalitarian redistribution and democratic participation. The state, governed by worker-run parties in cooperation with strong unions, guarantees the social contract wherein workers receive a share of the increased growth generated by labor peace (Przeworski 1985).

We should note here that conservative governments in core states that are able to exclude or repress weak unions—as in the aforementioned case of Chile—have also produced high growth rates, although without the equality and social welfare found in social-democratic states. The worst performance has occurred in states that are in between, where neither class cooperation nor domination can be consistently pursued.[4] The comparison demonstrates the benefits of social democracy. Where conservative governments face strong unions, or where leftist governments lack strong unions, strikes and inflation proliferate. Without a state-enforced guarantee, strong unions often seek immediate wage increases at the expense of capital accumulation because they have no surety that labor will benefit in the future from heightened investment now. Investment is deterred and wage increases outstrip productivity increases, resulting in inflation. Further, where leftist governments lack the coincidence of strong nationwide unions, a coordinated social contract falls prey to special-interest politics. Expectations for increased wages and social welfare soar with leftist electoral victories, which cannot be restrained without the long-term vantage of strong central unions. Capitalist investors also "strike" where labor cannot be restrained, once again producing inflation when productivity increases lag behind wages and social spending.

The term "labor restraint" may sound repressive, but it is used to indicate worker support for long-term growth, rather than demands for immediate, but inflationary, wage increases. The political question is the *source* of restraint. Conservative governments facing weak unions "restrain" labor by disorganizing, excluding, and repressing workers to hold down wages. Social-democratic states "restrain" short-term inflationary demands of strong unions by guaranteeing greater benefits from investment in long-term growth rather than from immediate redistribution.

Social democracy appears to have solved, at least in part, the trade-off between growth and equality, fostering the former by guaranteeing the latter. As we demonstrated in the introductory chapter, social-democratic countries in the industrial core such as Sweden or Austria have come closer to Marx's ideal of socialism than did any of the avowedly Marxist state-socialist countries.

Global Limits to Social Solutions

Social democracy faces its own class and global limitations. As noted earlier, electoral victories require a base of support that exceeds narrow class interests. As such, social democracy limits the options of electoral socialism regarding questions of property rights. More importantly, the social-democratic wage, welfare, and democratic guarantees stop at state borders. Most social-democratic governments have been coalitions (even in Sweden) and have been thrown out when the world economy stagnated. However humanitarian, social policies that do not ultimately pay for themselves by raising productivity are costs that raise prices in international competition. Capital flight across international borders, coupled with capital-investment "strikes" within them, have long been recognized as the impenetrable fortress that ultimately repels any non-revolutionary assault on capitalist property rights. If capital escapes payment through flight or failure, those costs drive a wedge within the social-democratic coalition, particularly between the traditional industrial proletariat versus immigrant workers and the dependent poor. Results include "blue collar" conservatives who sour on all forms of social welfare.

As we enter the information age, capital flight and strike have taken on dramatic new powers. Physical, mechanical, and location-specific forms of capital (such as those associated with Fordism) decline daily in value relative to the more liquid capital assets of conceptual technologies. At the other end, cheap imports of mass-produced consumer goods from the semiperiphery undermine the remaining value of large-scale fixed investments in the core. It is daunting to realize how much the living standards of the working class in places like Belgium and Sweden were held up by tariffs and other trade restrictions. These twin global processes of increasing capital liquidity and decreasing costs of imports have scissored holes in the protective legislation and progressive social welfare of Western European social-democratic states. These are the same processes that cut Eastern European socialist states to pieces.

We will return to the destructive processes of the world market on national efforts to construct socialism or even social democracy, and to their global solutions, in subsequent chapters. But first, we need to note that these efforts have largely been core or semiperipheral. This leads to the question: Is there a "third way" for the Third World?

Many in the New Left once looked upon Mao's Cultural Revolution to be an alternative method of attacking bureaucratic oligarchy. As we elaborated in earlier chapters, the Cultural Revolution coincided with and stimulated worldwide revolution against bureaucratic, ethnic, gender, and other repressive hierarchies. This was the New Left attack on inegalitarian and undemocratic Old Left institutions (communist and socialist parties, trade unions, welfare states, and other legacies of the 1848 world revolution) (Arrighi, Hopkins, and Wallerstein 1989b). Mao mobilized the Cultural Revolution in order to combat the formation of a new mandarinate in the Party and the state. This was a laudable goal, but Mao's efforts failed. The extremism of the Red Guards soon became more repressive than the oligarchy they attacked. Mass mobilization by a charismatic leadership was too dependent on the leadership itself to provide a stable solution to the problem of oligarchy formation.

The reasons why socialist states in the semiperiphery and periphery have not been able to sustain democratic socialist institutions are similar to the reasons why democracies have been so scarce in the semiperiphery and periphery generally. Only core states in the capitalist world-system have been able to sustain fairly permanent democratic institutions, and even these are subject to periodic challenges when wars break out among core states. As a general principle, states subjected to external threats and internal inequality are much less able to sustain democratic regimes. Most peripheral and semiperipheral states have extraordinary internal inequality as a legacy of colonialism and the ongoing process of dependent development. They are more exposed to strong external forces (both military and economic) than are core states. As a result, democracy has historically been much more difficult to sustain (see Chase-Dunn 1998, chapter 6).

The current wave of democratization in the periphery and semiperiphery is dependent on external peace. The Cold War's demise has meant that peripheral conflicts no longer become proxy wars for jockeying superpowers. Unfortunately, internal structural conditions that have undermined peripheral democracies in the past have not yet substantially changed. So, while conflicts are more frequent, their scope is more geopolitically limited. The dissolution of Yugoslavia, while horrible in its cruelty, has not spread beyond its former borders and the core powers have agreed to keep it that way. U.S. military dominance, at a new relative high with the fall of the Soviet Union, means that a quick return of proxy wars is unlikely. But, the present imbalance between military and economic power in the interstate system is not stable because the costs of the United States serving as the world's policeman are no longer paid by relatively greater profits. Thus it is likely military multipolarity will return to the interstate system in the next thirty years. The attendant specter of multiple arms races, proxy wars, and client states may again plague the periphery. Multipolarity has consistently led to world wars in the past five hundred years, a topic we return to in the last chapter.

If international peace is necessary for democracy, so is peace in the internal class war. Class relations are governed by an array of actual and implied contracts, from wage contracts to health and safety contracts, to social welfare contracts. However exploited, workers benefit from entering social contracts with capital, as long as relations remain capitalist and the contracts are enforced. Quite simply, workers benefit more from work than from unemployment. How much more depends on the power of the working class, both to garner high wages and living conditions, and to ensure that the state enforces the contracts. Democracy is the regime structure that allows for classes to negotiate and to enforce social contracts. Political democracy is the *consequence* of class compromise (Przeworski 1985). States and capitalists in the (semi)periphery face a tremendous and continual pressure to "cheat" on any social contract. Export promotion, in particular, reduces the negative internal consequences of low wages for consumption, taxes, and profits in dependent countries. Yet at the same time, industrial development is undermining the political power of the landlord class, traditionally the most anti-democratic, it is increasing the size and strength of the industrial working class, the historical source of democracy in most states. The choice in the semi-industrialized semiperiphery is increasingly democracy by acquiescence or by revolution. South Africa is emblematic of this choice, when after decades of trying to suppress a democratic revolution, whites acquiesced to democracy in a 1992 plebiscite.

The Spiral of Capitalism and Socialism

State socialism grew from a single multinational state in 1917 to as many as twenty-six allied states in 1988 with a third of the world's area and population and a fourth of its total production (Kornai 1989). Yet it did not, in the end, weaken the logic of world capitalism. Rather, the political constraints on the free mobility of capital that these states created were one of the elements that pushed capitalist firms and states to further expand the scale of organizations and markets. This extensive expansion was accompanied by intensive expansion—the conversion of ever more aspects of life to the commodity form and the expansion of profitmaking opportunities in the provision of everything from fast-food breakfasts to organ transplants. The potential for further commodification is great, especially in the periphery, where a substantial terrain of production and consumption for use remains.

Increases in the availability of undiscovered and easily commodified resources, including human resources, must eventually be exhausted, however. The major source of low-cost labor throughout history has been the movement of peasants and others in less commodified rural areas to wage-work in industrial areas. This movement has often been forced, either directly or indirectly, through the loss of access to arable land. Antisystemic movements increasingly limited the forced commodification of people and of the environment. The most important antisystemic movement in capitalist world history to date, the abolitionist movement, has been almost completely successful. Slavery, serfdom, and peonage, once the fate of millions and the outside brake that slowed the progress of wage-workers, have been all but eliminated. Additionally, within the global establishment of free labor, forces were set in motion to end colonialism worldwide. By 1960, the world order had shifted to such an extent that formal colonialism was an illegitimate interstate relation that most of the core would unite in condemning. To be sure, neocolonialism and coercive labor forms remain, especially against women. But, as we explored in earlier chapters, current antisystemic movements build upon the success of past ones such that the locus of struggle has shifted to equal citizenship rights for each nationality (or ethnic or racial group), women's rights, and environmental problems.

The seesawing, back-and-forth motion of capital expansion and antisystemic progress generates consciousness and coordination among groups who have an interest in collective rationality at the world-system level. Capital flight has pitted workers from different areas against one another for five hundred years, but the growing industrialization and expanding political claims of labor in the semiperiphery will eventually decrease their relative difference with the core. Equalization of profit rates across different regions of the world-system would decrease the incentive for capital flight. The periodic crises that accompany the K-wave, uneven development, and the expansion of commodification continue to stimulate new forms of political organization on the part of the exploited. As these new forms become coordinated on a world scale, the periodic crises may eventually develop into an overall systemic crisis. This will involve the possibility of creating democratic and collectively rational control over investment decisions in a context in which "private" wealth no longer has the power or the motivation to continue directing the production process.

The growth of social democracy, welfare states, decolonization of the periphery, and the emergence of states in which socialist parties control state power should be understood in this light. Despite the failure of these movements and states to fundamentally alter the capitalist logic of the world-system, new developments that manage to coordinate their efforts on a global scale can indeed transform that logic.

Post-1989

Given this context, let us return to the framework of world divides and revolutions to ask what the events surrounding 1989 mean for the future of the system. If this was a world revolution, comparable to prior events we have given the same name, then we should expect two consequences of global importance. We would want to know what initiatives from past world revolutions this one institutionalized, and what new initiatives were launched in its aftermath.

The first issue is the more obvious. Democracy is the first achievement most will ascribe to this revolution. Civil rights will likely follow in tandem, as the inseparability of the two is now taken for granted (another achievement, at least in part, of 1968). To be sure, these are significant achievements that provide real political progress for millions of people east of the Elbe. The significance is even greater when viewed globally, as the democratization in Eastern Europe was only one part of a huge wave that included nearly all of Latin America, parts of Africa (notably South Africa), and most of the East Asian NICs to varying degrees. Democratic states represent the majority of the world population for the first time in history.

In terms of democracy, 1989 may seem to be the final institutionalization of the world revolution of 1789. This is so, but it was also the institutionalization of 1848 working-class democracy, of 1917 women's suffrage and self-determination of core states, of 1949 national liberation in the periphery, and of 1968 civil rights. Given that the former socialist states were immediately embroiled in bloody national independence struggles, the 1917 legacy of self-determination in Europe has been the hardest-fought victory of the revolution.

But what of the 1968 New Left that was institutionalized during 1989? One can easily trace the leaders and intellectuals of 1989, along with the ideas they promoted, back to the student and civil protests of 1968. Alexander Dubcek, deposed as Czechoslovakian leader in 1968 and elected parliament chair in 1989, is the most obvious example. His president in 1989, Vaclav Havel, is perhaps equally obvious, as is the involvement in 1989 of other Czechoslovakian intellectuals who had been banned in 1968. In an article on the origins of Solidarity, Adam Michnik (1990) notes how state repression of the 1968 student uprising in Poland was important for creating a similar cadre of dissident intellectuals (including himself). The connection is less obvious than the Czechoslovakian case where the party/state itself was repressed and does not much apply to the labor movement, except in generational terms (i.e., for workers age thirty to forty-five, 1968 would have been an important formative event).

However obvious, the impact of Dubcek's "communism with a human face" during the Prague Spring of 1968 on the design of glasnost should not be underestimated. Gorbachev was quite self-consciously attempting to introduce a similar set of reforms, even accepting political pluralism at the end (1990), which was the reform of Dubcek's that triggered the invasion. As Havel's émigré publisher put it, Czechoslovakia in 1968 "appears to have been a sort of off-Broadway preview for Mikhail S. Gorbachev" (Skvorecky 1990, p. 254).

Given the lineage of leaders and ideas, it is not surprising that

Arrighi, Hopkins, and Wallerstein (1992) consider 1989 "the continuation of 1968." They see 1989 as the victory of the New Left over the Old Left. If for no other reason, the New Left movements succeeded because the Old Left disintegrated. For labor and civic movements, it was a victory of antibureaucratic and democratic organization over centralized and authoritarian forms. Most telling is that it was a victory for civil society. Lipset (1991) documents the rise of what he (unfortunately) calls "postmaterialist" issues in the Soviet bloc, such as racism, gender inequality, environmentalism, and human rights in general. He explains the New Left movements as the result of changes in the composition of the work force away from industrial workers and toward educated professionals and service workers.

Rather than "postmaterialist," these issues were actually closely intertwined with materialist concerns over the long-stagnant economy. Economic progress would require more-educated workers with far more flexibility and autonomy, and far less gender, ethnic, and bureaucratic strictures. Environmentalism was also far more than just a postmaterialist aesthetic issue as the gigantic scale and production quota emphasis of the Soviet model was ruining its environmental resources. Without restating or overstating our prior discussion of how flexible production and the information age produces movements against Fordism and centralism, the political connections between what began in 1968 and ended in 1989 should be clear.

The question remains, what initiatives and movements were generated as a result? Arrighi, Hopkins, and Wallerstein (1992) claim the events surrounding 1989 were only a continuation of 1968, much the way the Paris Commune of 1871 was only a continuation of 1848. If so, then we would have to await the next global upheaval to recognize what social movements and struggles offer the possibility to raise global standards to a new level of progress. In some respects, they appear to be right. In what has come to coalesce around the term "postmodernism," the New Left movements seem stuck at only criticizing modern society (mainly the Fordist version) without offering any alternative arrangements. Getting past this post is the subject of the next chapter.

Notes

1. While we emphasize the similarities more than the differences, Ellen Comisso's (1986) comparison between CMEA (COMECON) countries and NICs is an excellent presentation that emphasizes the differences while exploring the similarities.

2. In Eastern Europe and the Soviet Union, this crisis was described as the need to move from "extensive" to "intensive" economic development. Ivan

Szelenyi's (1989) excellent discussion of Eastern European reforms utilizes a comparative frame of reference that takes account of geopolitics and dependency relationships.

3. Another alternative would be to decentralize economic planning itself. It is theoretically possible for all investment, production, and distribution decisions to be made by direct popular vote. This would be absurd, of course, but our point is that the falling cost of communications makes direct participatory economic democracy much more feasible than it has ever been. Most people would rather delegate day-to-day decisions to hired administrators while reserving the right to replace them if things go awry.

4. See the extensive review of the literature in Hicks (1988) on growth and inequality in industrialized democracies.

5

Getting Past the Post

We have entered another divide in world history. For the last thirty years, philosophers and social scientists have reveled in the unraveling of the mass-production bureaucratic model that dominated the world's core for the previous hundred years. U.S. hegemony, which rose with American innovation of that model, has also been declining. This has raised the possibility that the transition is more than just another K-wave reorganization of technological style. The massive structural bulwarks of global hegemony and bureaucratic efficiency would seem to be crumbling, making it ever easier for human agency to break free of traditional boundaries and ever harder for human agents to find their bearings in a world without boundaries.

These rapid changes in the scale of economic integration and the precipitous fall of transportation and communications costs are termed "time-space compression" by the Marxist geographer David Harvey. Harvey characterizes the current time-space compression as when "the time horizons of both private and public decision-making have shrunk, while satellite communications and declining transport costs have made it increasingly possible to spread those decisions immediately over an ever wider and variegated space" (Harvey 1989, p. 147).

Of course, transportation and communications costs have been falling for millennia, but Harvey finds that the recent geometric scale changes are related to reorganization of the nature of capitalist accumulation since around 1968–1969. These changes have had important consequences for the culture of capitalism. Harvey focuses, as we have, on the contrast between Fordist mass production and "flexible specialization" for the global market. He claims that "flexible accumulation" is much more revolutionary than was Fordism. Says Harvey,

It rests on flexibility with respect to labour processes, labour markets, products, and patterns of consumption. It is characterized by the emergence of entirely new sectors of production, new ways of providing financial services, new markets, and, above all, greatly intensified rates of commercial, technological and organizational innovation. (1989, p. 147)[1]

Harvey's main point is that flexible accumulation and the associated geometric rise in time-space compression account for the *cultural shift from modernism to postmodernity* in architecture, art, and literature.[2] He explains that the time-space compression of contemporary times has thrown together past and present cultural artifacts, both local and exotic, in constant juxtaposition. Rapid change makes every cultural juxtaposition seem a temporary fix.

We find a complementary argument in the work of cultural anthropologist Jonathan Friedman (1994). Friedman shows that the fall of ancient empires produced similar cultural phenomena to what we now call postmodernism. The identity aspects of current postmodern philosophy—the concern for the other and the multiple personalities of the self—are explained by Friedman (1994) as a consequence of the decline of U.S. hegemony. In all "post" periods, intellectuals of the times discover that something has passed and many new forms have arisen, but how the new forms and functions will develop is indecipherable with the old analytic tools and frames of reference. They are certain only at having left the old ways behind, not at which way to go next or even if they have a common direction.

Culturally, philosophically, and theoretically, we are stuck at the post. Postmodernism has become the reigning cultural idiom for describing current trends without explaining where these trends are going. The stability of modernity is easily recognized as now gone, but the instability of the present leaves no point that can garner a proper noun to easily characterize it. We are thus faced with a plethora of "posts": postmodernism (contingent juxtaposition of time and space such that interpretation depends on contextual viewpoint and no viewpoint is privileged); poststructuralism (de-centered structuralism); postcolonialism (oppression without an oppressing subject); post-Fordism (flexible production rather than long assembly lines); postindustrialism (contingent service work replacing stable manufacturing jobs); postliberalism (liberalism, and conservatism, as community empowerment rather than state expansion); postcommunism (socialists with "administrative" experience in former communist countries); and post-Marxism (analysis of inequality and injustice without a socialist project).

We should note that the reign of postmodernism has been in decline of late and can no longer claim to be a source of intellectual vitality.

Indeed, we are now more likely to hear defensive refrains about how critics have overemphasized its "foolish excesses" (Wallerstein 1997, p. 124) or how globalization is really what it meant all along (Smart 1994, pp. 151–152). Since the revolutions of 1989, a new realism crops up among postmodern pontificators, not because of the revolutions themselves, which were validations of anti-Fordism and antimodernization, but because of events since. Despite democratization, "normal" capitalism has brought the deterioration of public infrastructure and a rapid rise of inequality and poverty, particularly increased gender inequality and terrifying ethnic conflict.

National Liberalism

If the aftermath of 1989 has tempered postmodernism with a new realism, is not communism's fall a triumph of liberalism? Are we not now giving credence to the "end of ideology" thesis that we derided earlier wherein liberal citizenship is heralded as the only ideology acceptable in the international arena? Quite the contrary, liberalism too has reached its high mark and is in decline. This may sound odd coming from ones who have defined universal human rights and freedoms as integral to any conception of progress. We are not retreating from or retracting that conception at all, and true, this is what some call liberalism. But it is not liberalism as it has been practiced for the last two hundred years. This is Wallerstein's thesis in his provocative, and exasperating, *After Liberalism* (1995).

Wallerstein's point is worth repeating here as a prelude to our own conception because his critique of liberalism is, like the postmodernists, about what is passing rather than what should come. Liberalism and modernity are components of the same worldview, according to Wallerstein, a view that sees society as malleable to rational reform by the state. This worldview, what he calls a "geoculture," was ushered in by the French Revolution of 1789, which reset the parameters of "what is possible."[3] Social change became accepted as a normal response to modernization. Liberalism offered rights to individual citizens to reform themselves. Alongside liberal reformism, the same geoculture included conservatism, which sought to limit change, and after 1848, socialism, which sought to accelerate progressive change. Within this geoculture, it is easy to see why socialist ideology was popular in less developed countries. It is also easy to see why liberalism would become the hegemonic ideology of the most modern states, both defending modernism from landlord restraints and restraining the "dangerous classes" with the promise of reform. With U.S. hegemony following World War II, liberalism became the hegemonic ideology of the entire geoculture. Conservatives came to accept the welfare state and socialists pursued development to catch up with, rather than replace, the core liberal states.

Yet liberalism always contained within it a fundamental contradiction between the rights of individuals versus the rights of nations, or of people versus *peoples.* Individual rights were proclaimed universal, but they were established only for citizens of particular states. Citizenship defines a group—propertied white Christian males born in a core European state was an early definition—with rights and reforms denied to noncitizens. Without this distinction, citizenship had no meaning. Granting rights required denying rights. Recognizing this contradiction is not new, but Wallerstein points out that it came to a head in 1968 with national-liberation movements demanding a state for every nation and human-rights movements demanding equal rights for all peoples in every state. Facing a K-wave downturn (and bereft of their imperial props), liberal welfare states proved unable to pursue both profitable accumulation and continued social reform to an expanding citizenry. They reneged on the latter (as we have discussed earlier), eroding support for the liberal welfare state as the solution to social problems. The revolutions of 1989 sealed liberalism's fate by delegitimating even the most interventionist of national states as the (sole) agents of rational reform and economic development in a global economy.

What comes after liberalism? On this point, Wallerstein exasperates any reader expecting the theme of his book to match its title (although he does offer scenarios in a subsequent essay, discussed below). He stops just before answering the question and instead concludes that the paramount challenge of progressive forces is "the creation of a new Left ideology" (1995, p. 247). The closest he comes to suggesting any content for that ideology is in proclaiming its most potent weapon to be "taking the old liberal ideology literally and demanding its universal fulfillment" (p. 250). Claiming that after liberalism comes "real" liberalism reminds one of Oscar Levant's quips about Hollywood in which he said that once you strip away the fake tinsel you find the real tinsel. This is not an entirely fair comparison, as, however overstated, Wallerstein's insight is profound.

Unfortunately, the insight is hidden in his play on words that fails to distinguish what we would call "national liberalism" from the universal liberalism of the Enlightenment. Liberalism in practice has meant national states enforcing rights and reform for "respectable" citizens (i.e., those with enough power to make claims on the state). This "national liberalism" contrasts not just with the principle of universal liberalism, but also with any chance for universal fulfillment. National states cannot enforce global practices. His example is immigration—if liberal rights were universal then immigrants would have the same rights as citizens, making meaningless the distinction between citizens and noncitizens on which liberalism rests. While we agree with Wallerstein's insight, and with the importance of human rights, liberalism alone is woefully inadequate as an agenda for progressive movements.

The problem with liberalism, universal as well as national, is that it assumes what it must achieve—no discrimination or coercion, no subterfuge or opportunism, and the existence of perfect competition in completely free markets with equal access to capital and other scarce resources. Under these conditions individuals are the prime agents of history and their market exchange would be equal and without exploitation. Even the labor theory of value applies under these utopian conditions, because the combination of no discrimination, completely equal access to capital, and truly free markets means that the only variation in value would be due to individual differences in the inalienable qualities of human labor. Those qualities include the amount of talent, ability, effort, and ingenuity of the individual. This is a worthy goal, but the assumptions ignore history. Once individuals have accumulated vastly unequal amounts of capital and once states designate some people as national citizens and some as not, or some as less equal than others, then individuals have class positions and national identities. Assuming the existence of classless individuals will always prevent its actual achievement. Universal liberalism is thus not wrong, but it is always inadequate by its own standards. One cannot address those inadequacies within liberalism because the solutions cannot be found in the sacred individual, but are rather found in social and global institutions.

At the beginning of a new millennium, we face this world divide without a clear vision of what comes after liberalism or how to get past the postmodern condition. We observed in the beginning of this book that, with the revolutions of 1989, state-socialist visions of the future appeared to be trapped in futility. Despite the long-ago recognition by most Western leftists that the Soviet model was undemocratic and oppressive, its utter collapse brought a surprising conclusion that the entire system had long been unreformable. Democratization of state socialism by any number of would-be true socialists, we have argued, would have been of great benefit to the Soviet people, but could not have turned state socialism into world socialism.

This recognition is what leaves Marxism as a theory and socialism as a practice in a crisis of purpose. Just as socialists of the nineteenth century had to reformulate the cooperative commonwealth to apply to mass society of the twentieth century, socialist ideas now must reconcile with the advent of flexible production and globalization. We contend that this means the reconception and reorganization of social democracy into *global democracy.*

One place to begin is at the end, that is, at an alternative possibility of what could be. In the next chapter we present an estimation of what will likely happen to the world-system if the patterned cycles and trends of the past continue. We will also offer a vision of *what could happen* if progressive social movements organize to establish global democracy in the emerging world polity. Wallerstein calls this process "utopistics," that is, creating visions of possible futures, which he contrasts with "utopianism," which offers deceptive illusions of impossibilities. In a short book with that title (*Utopistics*, 1998), he offers a hellish scenario of the near future, one where continuing decline of national states unravels civil society. Crime, piracy, and corruption flourish. War looms. An alternative to this unsavory destiny is to transform the logic of the capitalist world-system to one where endless accumulation is not its central purpose. He suggests a world of nonprofit companies replacing corporate firms in an otherwise market environment as a viable model.

Utopistics being a brief essay, there is little point in going over the fine points of Wallerstein's judicious argument, except for one thing. Surprisingly, there is little discussion of the alternative as a *world-system.* He addresses class, but not uneven development or peripheral poverty. Most importantly, he mentions no world institutions nor does he offer any sense of how the world order would be transformed. Without a focus on global institutions, how to transform the restraints on societal change that undermined state socialism remains unresolved.

Let us turn to a more elaborate world-systemic vision of a possible future, that offered in W. Warren Wagar's 1992 utopian novel, *A Short History of the Future*. Wagar, a historian[4], has written a utopian vision from a deliberately world-systemic point of view. While we will contest some of his apparent assumptions and political prescriptions, we share a basic theoretical perspective and a programmatic agenda with Wagar. We then end this chapter with a beginning, discussing strategies for building global democracy.

Utopian Visions: World State, World War, and World Party

Utopian visions of possible world orders proliferate every fifty or so years with the long stagnation of the Kondratieff economic cycle, according to the research of Kiser and Drass (1987). They found that the instance of utopian novels as a percentage of all published novels is highest during the downturn (B-phase) of the K-wave, peaking during the period when economic conditions turn for the better after a long crisis. Hegemonic decline also amplifies this cultural response to the economy. Kiser and Drass use the publication of utopian novels as something of a temperature gauge of the prevailing cultural weather. The relationship between ideological and economic conditions is turbulent at best, but over the long term the cultural atmosphere surrounding economic conditions shifts with the seasonal pattern of economic stagnation and expansion, as well as with hegemonic stability and decline.

Utopian novels pose new answers to the ideological question of what is possible (Kiser and Drass 1987). Along with answers to what exists, and what is good, conceiving what is possible forms the basis for any worldview. As we have already mentioned, Goran Therborn's (1980) classic work on ideology explains that defining what is possible is the last defense of the status quo. While one may empirically demonstrate that exploitation exists and even that it is unfair, for instance, one cannot prove empirically that a better alternative is possible when that system does not yet exist. Conceiving what is possible is often an act of extrapolation from what exists. During a long stagnation, when the world economy has unmistakably failed to grow at a satisfying pace for a generation, people become convinced that the existing forms of organization must be discarded and they experiment with new ones to put in their place. Utopian visions, at that time, have a new resonance. They take advantage of the pliable economic conditions to stretch our conception of the possible.

A classic case of a utopian novel churning up new visions of a better world for progressives to pursue is Edward Bellamy's *Looking Backward* (1888; see discussion in Kiser 1985). The book was a huge success at the time and spawned hundreds of clubs dedicated to reading the novel and promoting its vision. Bellamy's success drew from opportune timing. It was published in 1888, just before the great depression of the 1890s generated widespread disillusionment with the reigning ideas of Social Darwinism. His was a first wedge in the crack that eventually shattered the belief that poverty was natural and inherent in human societies. Success also came from Bellamy's skill at using images of an attainable future to illustrate the failings of the present. In so doing, Bellamy made an alternative, and better, world seem possible. His vision of what is possible lacked explanations of *why* the system had failed working people or *how* they should fix it. That would come later, with the reformulation of socialist theory to accommodate the new accumulation regime of mass-production technology. Bellamy clubs would soon add Marx to their reading list.

Wagar's *A Short History of the Future* is the *Looking Backward* of the present.[5] The novel is a historian's extrapolation based on an explicit theory of how the world-system works. Long treatises on social change punctuate epistolary interludes in which individual characters are added to what is otherwise all plot. Wagar's style is inspired more by H. G. Wells than Bellamy, and while as a novelist Wagar may be no Bellamy or Wells, he is arguably a better social scientist. Judging a utopian novel simply as fiction misses its most important points. As a utopian vision based on world-systems theory, Wagar offers scenarios that begin to provide what we must have in order for the theory to be more than analysis of what exists. This is not to say that Wagar provides a prediction of what will actually happen. The first edition (1989) contained a Soviet Union that continued to exist for another fifty years. In revising the next edition, Wagar found, however, that replacing "Soviet Union" with "Russia" changed none of the logic of the plot. He had already assumed that the Soviet Union was no different from any other great power.

The purpose of a utopian novel is not to predict the future but rather to offer what Wagar calls an "array of possibilities" (1992, p. x). His particular array is at least probable, and it offers a vision of a world socialism that is not constrained by the now common conclusion that the demise of the Soviet Union proves that socialism is dead. Wagar's vision is feasible within known parameters of the world-system and, most importantly, it revitalizes the now nearly extinct idea that concerted action to change the system would be worthwhile.

Wagar actually offers two utopias and one dystopia. Each follows from and requires the previous one to create the conditions for its subsumption. The novel chronicles the history of the world from 1995 to 2200. It is organized into three "books," "Earth Inc.," "Red Earth," and "The House of Earth," modeled on the Christian eschatology of "Armageddon, Millennium, and New Jerusalem" (p. xiii). The dystopia comes first. It is an extrapolation from existing transnational corporate capitalism that includes a corporate world polity, the Global Trade Consortium (GTC). If this sounds like the World Trade Organization, you are getting the point. The GTC functions as world hegemon, enforcing a corporate world order through economic boycott rather than military dominance. Initially, the GTC is an enlightened despot, maintaining world peace and ushering in a renewed global prosperity at the price of undemocratic rule, uniform cultural commodification, growing inequality, environmental degradation, and individual alienation. Global capitalist expansion leads inevitably to overproduction and recession. Wagar plays out the next century with dates from the one now ending. Global recession in 2032 lasts until world war breaks out in the 2040s.

Drawing from the same theoretical fountain, Wagar's scenario begins somewhat similarly to Wallerstein's, but adds a necessary emphasis on the importance of world organizations. Wagar's prospect also continues the cycle of world wars. His future experiences a nuclear holocaust. We will contend in the next chapter that the cycle can be broken and that a global holocaust can be avoided by concerted global action that democratizes the world polity. Democracy is the single best deterrent to war and so a movement for global democracy is inherently also a movement to create world peace, and vice versa. But let us precis Wagar's story first.

The GTC never gets around to dismantling the military apparatus of the interstate system. The United States continues its economic decline. The rich get richer and the poor get poorer and eventually a populist is elected to the U.S. presidency. A Latina president wins a short civil war against domestic reactionaries and her populist regime befriends revolutionary regimes in the semiperiphery. The GTC interprets this as an unacceptable challenge and launches a preemptive nuclear strike against the United States. However, through a lucky premonition, the president had dispatched a fleet of subs. Washington and New York are incinerated, but the far-flung U.S. military apparatus fights on. Earth Inc. self-destructs.

From the ashes of war, Wagar tells in "Red Earth," comes the rise of states in the Southern Hemisphere. Far less devastated than the North, the South becomes the new core of the system. These southern states coalesce to form a new democratic world state led by the World Party. The idea of the World Party is the most interesting and important construction in Wagar's book. The new world is a global democracy that is organized to redress the problems of inequality and environmental degradation while also restoring peace and prosperity. The world state starts as a large coalition of the survivors of the war who understandably want to create an institutional basis for preventing such disasters in the future. This requires global security, and the world state must forcibly incorporate a few pockets of resistance. Global citizenship replaces national citizenship and the world is reorganized into macroregional administrative departments that each include multiple national groups.

The democratic world state succeeds perhaps a bit too easily, but Wagar also reminds us that even in a democratic socialist system resistance will occur against the rule of the majority. After the World Party attends to the main ecological and social problems, democratic politics leads to the emergence of the Small Party, an anarchist alliance seeking individual and cultural autonomy through community self-sufficiency. In the final and most amusing book, the Small Party wins an election and dissolves the world government. The second utopia is a world of self-governing communities small enough to practice direct democracy and enabled by advanced technology to be both self-sufficient and fully prosperous. All hierarchies are rejected and the material determination of the spirit is finally reversed. Hegel is righted again at last.

The World Party

While the particular scenarios that Wagar presents are built upon an increasing number of "what ifs," the World Party is based on a set of principles that are applicable in a wide array of scenarios. Those principles deserve discussion, regardless of the merits of Wagar's speculative scenarios. We agree with most, question some, and think a couple of his principles are mistaken, as discussed below. The principles for which the World Party stands, as we interpret them from various points in the text, are as follows:

1. A world socialist commonwealth, including a democratic world state with a monopoly of military power
2. Global democracy with direct elections of leaders for all offices, global and local, and universal human rights, including freedom of speech, religion, privacy, and assembly
3. Legal and programmatic provision for equal opportunity, including a worldwide assault on racism and sexism; and state provision of basic needs, including education, health care, child care, and retirement
4. Incomes based first on need, with an (after income tax) goal of no more than a 2:1 ratio among individuals for those employed (half share for those unwilling to work) and no more than 2:1 across geographic departments [see our critique below]
5. "Declaration of Human Sovereignty," in which the world state abolishes national sovereignty and eschews national and/or ethnic identities [see our critique below]
6. "Integral humanism," a philosophical order of public affairs based on rationality, including a secular state and official tolerance for individual beliefs (i.e., no legal enforcement of religious, national, ethnic, or other traditions), and disdain for commodity fetishism
7. A global plan for ecological restoration, renewable sources of energy supply, and population control
8. A critique of world capitalism as the source of world wars and as an oppressive world order. World socialism would consist of a democratic world state with public ownership of the transnational megacorporations, global provision for human needs, enforcement of human rights, ecological restoration, an end to war, and global political, social, and economic democracy.

9. A critique of Stalinist-style state socialism as oppressive and illegal, with guarantees for democracy and individual liberty. The commonwealth would only own the transnational megacorporations. All else would be privately owned (including cooperatives, worker-owned firms, and small businesses of all kinds).

10. A vanguard party strategy for setting up the world commonwealth, including revolution, elections, and even conquest of those few military or criminal holdout states that refuse to join

The World Party is modeled to some degree on the German Green Party, with a heavy dose of the original Second International and the added twist of being based on world-system theory, rather than on Marxism or Keynesianism. It carries a New Left imprint of being socialist and democratic, anticapitalist and antitotalitarian, as well as class and individually based. We share and support the idea of a world party and other institutions organizing a progressive movement at the global level. We offer a different vision below of the world socialist commonwealth, one that operates mainly through the world market by globalizing capital investment and establishing minimum social standards, rather than through public ownership and rigid income ratios. Prior to outlining that vision, we also differ on critical issues of process concerning "stages" and trade-offs of goals. This includes questioning the possible assumption (not made by Wagar) of the necessity of a world war before any fundamental progress is possible. We want to address how the movement for global democracy can act to prevent the kind of world war that Wagar's scenario envisions as a deus ex machina for transformation.

We can start with the critique offered by Wagar himself, by enunciating the principles of the Small Party. As Wagar is offering scenarios, not proscriptions, he ends by suggesting what might come after the World Party, correcting or superseding its limitations. His Small Party carries an imprint from the other major offspring of the 1968 world revolution, the New Age conceptions that redefined identity and spirituality. To many, New Age means hippie wannabes wearing crystals, sleeping under pyramids, and listening to whales sing. It is that, but it is also an umbrella term for a wide variety of lifestyle issues that share a concern for personal autonomy and self-awareness. The most prominent are feminist, "indigenist," and ethnonationalist conceptions of identity.

Given the anarchistic and spiritual character of the Small Party, its principles are deliberately vague. Perhaps only the following two principles are necessary and shared: elimination of the state or other central authority above the community; and complete autonomy and self-reliance of small communities. Self-reliance is premised on utopian technology that provides for abundant prosperity with little effort. Wagar suggests that most such communities would be governed by town hall–style direct democracy, although religious and other traditional orders may also proliferate.[6]

Wagar's Small Party's New Age critique of the World Party's "scientific socialism" is understood as an alternative set of goals, achievement of which is premised on utopian technology that guarantees material abundance. Let us offer below a series of contrasts, interpreted from the text, with the Small Party's goals listed first: spiritual versus rational; early Marx versus late Marx; spontaneous versus planned; gendered versus unisex; identity versus humanity; community versus society; autonomous versus organized; self-sufficient versus interdependent; negotiation versus law; variety versus standards; freedom versus equality; relativist versus universalist; folk versus classical; play versus work; and, anarchy versus democracy.

In *Short History*, a stage of rational-scientific world socialism produces the abundance that enables the emergence of a communal spiritual world. Working-class technocrats become communal hippies. One strength of Wagar's array of possibilities is that he takes account of the slow movement of global time. He lets about fifty years pass before one world order slips into the next. Each set of social relations that characterize a period is predicated on the developments that preceded it—the autonomous community utopia requires the attained equality and prosperity of a world socialism, which in turn was built on the charred framework of a capitalist world polity.

Are these stages necessary? Wagar's stage conception requires sacrificing spontaneity, identity, variety, autonomy, and some freedom, for some rather long period of time, in order to achieve these desiderata in a postponed future of glorious abundance. This is a fatal flaw for this scenario to serve as a positive model for the next world revolution and where our vision of a world party parts company with Wagar's scenario. While Wagar repeatedly asserts that his novelistic scenario is not a prediction of the future, the stages he proposes could be understood as a necessary sequence.

Stage theories are not new to revolutionary thought. The worst example is Stalin's justification of a tyrannical present as a necessary step to a never-achieved future utopia. Wagar is anti-Stalinist in his conception of party and politics (number 9 above), and the problems of transition he points to are real enough. The real problem is to construct a program that is realistic about what can be achieved in the middle and long run. We think Wagar's decision to postpone diversity is a mistake. He underestimates the potential fear of a monolithic world state and an overzealous world party that requires peoples to renounce their subgroup identities in favor of global citizenship. Our approach to the national question is different.

Wagar forthrightly insists that the World Party be for global democracy and for individual rights (number 8 above). Nevertheless, his proposal of a vanguard party strategy for setting up the world commonwealth (number 10) undermines the fundamental principle of democracy that is premised on individual and subgroup rights. Wagar contends that identity politics is a prime obstacle to forging global citizenship.[7] His approach leaves little room for scenarios that transform the current state of nationalist competition and conflict into a higher degree of global harmony without a revolution that imposes the new order on resisters.

Fear of an oppressive world government is, ironically, a major impediment to attempts to constrain oppressive "sovereign" states or even to democratize existing forms of global governance. Global democracy must be premised on national democracies, and global human identity must be premised on the complementarity of national and indigenous identities. Sacrificing national identities cannot create the conditions for global democracy. Sacrifice is only worthwhile when it is an investment, that is, where the sacrifice reaps a greater reward, not just a postponement. We, and we think most others, would not support a world state that denies the rights of individuals and groups to construct their own identities. The right of national self-determination is one of the values of the European Enlightenment and the philosophy of liberalism that needs to be defended, preserved, and actually implemented rather than used as a fig leaf for conquest and imperialism. We agree with those who value cultural diversity, multiculturalism, and the rights of individuals and groups to their own languages, lifestyles, religions, and philosophies as long as these do not interfere with the rights and livelihoods of others. In general, the greater the diversity and overlap of crosscutting identities, the greater the basis for tolerance. We will argue that the solution to nationalism is hundreds of nations, with the option of overlapping borders and multiple citizenship, and not any attempt to assimilate everyone into one identity.

The vision of global democracy and world socialism that we are proposing is one in which autonomy and community as well as freedom and equality are inherently intertwined. We take up the issue of national identity and global citizenship at greater length below. One source of our difference with Wagar is that we emphasize that the "stage" of a one-dimensional mass society has already passed. Centralized bureaucratic organization with standard operating procedures for all decisionmaking is already becoming obsolete in the capitalist world economy. We propose a far less centralized, more market-oriented and flexible system.

While he plays out the critique of modernism as the final stage of history, we want to move past both modernity and its critics now. New Left sensibilities are no longer very new and the Old Left political parties have mostly dissolved in any case, leaving a rather disorganized set of progressive organizations that nonetheless share ever more in common as globalization proceeds apace. As we discuss in the final chapter, green, feminist, and peace movements at the global level have become inseparable from labor politics, although the converse is still far from true.

Nationalism and International Governance

The contemporary popular response to state illegitimacy and neoliberal downsizing and the dismantling of welfare structures has been far from the Enlightenment ideal of human universalism. Instead, the most common populist response has been nationalist. The burst of new states in Central and Eastern Europe is but the most visible manifestation of a rise of nationalist fervor throughout the world. From Azerbaijan to Quebec, ethnic populations with identifiable territories (i.e., nations) increasingly seek their own separate states. The result has been a massive outpouring of nationalist sentiment and of ethnic separatism within what had previously been long-stable multination states.

The destruction of Sarajevo, a city that as recently as 1984 was a crowning symbol of ethnic integration and universalism, was perhaps the most telling indicator of this new wave of destructive nationalism. Highly nationalistic right-wing terrorists such as skinheads, militia members, and religious fundamentalists have replaced infantile leftists as the prime suspects in bombings and assassinations. While such extremists have long existed in various guises, they are now the fringes of a larger tide of nationalist parties and politicians. The relationship between extremists and mass organizations on the right resembles more the 1920s and 1930s than anything in the postwar period up until recently. Even prominent conservative intellectuals are no longer impeded by the memory of Nazi horrors from reviving ideologies of racial superiority, whether biological (*The Bell Curve*) or cultural (*The End of Racism*). Nor does refutation by reputable scientists or flagging by respected journalists seem to constrain the popularity of these racist theories.

The irony is that the surge in nationalism is driven in no small part by the very process of globalization that makes state power less potent. In the face of world integration, dominant ethnic groups demand reinforcement of their national identity, and the competitive advantage nationals have within it. Subordinate ethnic populations with identifiable territories more and more pursue the establishment of their own

sovereign states as they gain less from having a voice within increasingly
ineffective multination states.

Nationalism has always been a response to integration (Bukharin
1917; McNally 1990). It is not nationalism that has changed, but the
pace of global integration. The result has been a massive outpouring of
both xenophobia and of ethnic separatism within what had previously
been long-stable multination states. A further irony is that the breakdown into smaller sovereignties makes each more dependent upon the
world market and more permeable to world integration. Deepening
integration and neoliberal competition have thus engendered centrifugal processes of nationalism,[8] yet have also raised the demand for
regional and global interstate governance.

We take issue with Wagar and others who claim that global governance and nationalism are irreconcilable. Quite the contrary, we observe
that they are inexorably intertwined. The growth of single-nation states
is both a product and source of global organization. Rather than opposing ethnic identity, national liberation, or multiculturalism, supporters
of global governance must reassert self-determination as a central principle of interstate relations. Self-determination is a component of universal human rights, not an opposing axiom. The breakdown of multination states into multiple nation-states becomes a tragedy precisely
when self-determination and tolerance are denied. Sarajevo provides the
telling example in that its survival and that of Bosnia greatly depend on
the enforcement of interstate agreements by suprastate organizations
such as the United Nations and NATO.

This is not to deny the evils of national chauvinism, which are
unfortunately likely to continue to rise, but to assert national self-determination as a necessary and desirable part of the remedy. Certainly,
racism and imperialism are the enemies for our times. The human
tragedy from ethnic separatism in Yugoslavia, Sri Lanka, Tibet,
Lithuania, Rwanda, Northern Ireland, Kosovo, East Timor, and elsewhere cannot be denied. Yet which of the national minorities in each of
these cases should be denied self-determination? Would a world state
have decreed that Slovenia or Croatia, or even Bosnia, must remain fed-
erated with a Serb-dominated Yugoslavia? Or to take Wagar at his utopian best, should a world state strip Slovenians, Croatians, and Serbs of
their separate national identities and replace them with a mandatory
global citizenship?

We think the answer is that a global movement that fights imperialism and racism should do so by asserting the cultural autonomy of
nations and ethnic groups, not denying it. For oppressed peoples,
nationalism is often a source of resistance and sustenance. The new
strength of indigenous movements during recent decades is an impor-

tant part of the emerging challenge to the Eurocentric ways in which states and nations have been constructed in the past. Contrary to what might be assumed, indigenous movements have developed high degrees of global organization in which oppressed peoples from different continents help one another struggle for recognition within states and at the United Nations (Wilmer 1993).

Without respecting self-determination, few oppressed nationalities would support global governance and many might realistically fear a new form of imperialism. To be sure, self-determination must exclude those parts of any national heritage that legitimate imperialism or racism. That is, it must be a universal self-determination, not just for the more powerful group. To encourage and support universal self-determination requires global governance. These are thus mutually reinforcing rather than contradictory forces.

What is critical to recognize is that "sovereign" states and national identities have mainly been created by the interstate system. That system is the set of agreed-upon institutions, treaties, rules, and unwritten norms that govern relations between states, ranging from United Nations peacekeeping forces to proper diplomatic etiquette. The system was forged in Europe during the Thirty Years' War (1618–1648) and was spread worldwide by capitalist and colonial expansion. Whatever the origins of a state, whether ancient principality or recent ex-colony, its definition and survival as "sovereign" has depended upon recognition by other states as a legitimate member of the interstate system. Prior to 1945, admission was primarily limited to imperial states. Now entry is potentially open to any nation that can militarily control a territory. As a result, there has been a geometric increase in the number of states, first from decolonization and now from the breakup of multination states. There is also a rise in military contestation for control over territories.

Admission to the system as sovereign is now codified and institutionalized by the United Nations. In principle, this includes acceptance of the Universal Declaration of Human Rights. Some may scoff at how powerless the UN and international community is to enforce this standard. One might have said the same two hundred years ago about slavery, or one hundred years ago about colonialism, or even fifty years ago about legal racist segregation. The definition of a legitimate state now excludes all these, as even the powerful South Africa was finally forced to admit. National cultures are highly diverse, often inconsistent, and constantly evolving. They change in response to global capitalist and other processes without any necessary loss of identity. People can hold allegiance to both national and global solidarities, just as one can maintain loyalty to both family and nation.

Rather than impede internationalism, the combination of state proliferation and world economic integration increases dramatically the importance of *global governance*. Historically, core relations with the periphery fell under colonial governance while interimperial relations tended to be highly conflictive, except when a world order was backed up by a hegemon (Boswell and Chase-Dunn 1996). Colonialism is now defunct and U.S. hegemony is breaking down. In its place are the multistate formations, international organizations, and shared norms of neoliberalism. Of the multistates, most prominent are the regional blocs of the European Union and its American offspring, the North American Free Trade Agreement. As we discuss in the next chapter, these may be joined by Greater China as a future hegemonic contender. Most important is a rise in the number and influence of international organizations, both governmental and nongovernmental. As discussed in the next chapter, these organizations, along with other global actors and events, constitute and reflect the world polity (despite the absence of a world state). The basic point we make here is the following: the greater the number of states, the greater the need for international authorities to adjudicate conflicts, guarantee standards, and otherwise regulate exchanges.

Global Democracy and World Socialism

We have labored to critique Wallerstein's and Wagar's utopian visions, but such a critique is neither fair nor complete unless we offer some alternatives. We discuss what we think could happen and could be made to happen in the next chapter. Here, let us end this chapter by outlining our own vision of a future world socialism.

To start, we must note that the very term "world socialism" is an oxymoron. The "social" in socialism is usually thought of as a societal referent. Most discussions of socialism admit in the abstract that socialism would have to be a global system, but then go on to elaborate a societal restructuring. We too contend that in any world socialism there would be a multiplicity of different societies, some much more socialist in character than others. Thus, it is more precise to talk of two processes rather than one. *Global democracy* is a form of world governance based on the democratic consent of the governed, and designed to foster international peace, equal development, and rising global environmental and economic standards of human life. *World socialism* is the abolition of class exploitation and the promotion of equal opportunity in all societies worldwide. So far so good, except the two definitions sound like platitudes with little substance and the two processes are necessarily linked. Socialist societies cannot survive, much less flourish, without global democracy. That is the fundamental argument we have made throughout this book. One could call the combined process progressive "globalism," but that leaves the relationship between global democracy and world socialism unexamined.

Could global democracy obtain without world socialism? Possibly, although it would face serious trends toward unequal development and international war. Certainly a world government could operate without being democratic, and perhaps could even function to prevent most international war, enforce international contracts, and foster world trade (i.e., Wagar's "Earth Inc."). All of this is to the good and is already occurring to some limited extent. But such a world polity would not alter the fundamental capitalist dynamics of unequal development, nor would it likely redress global environmental and economic standards of life without being democratic in structure and in action.

If, as we contend, world socialism is inherently intertwined and dependent upon global democracy, then it also follows that a world governance cannot be a monolithic, centralized, or "totalitarian" state in order for there to be world socialism. Global democracy is premised on the democratic self-determination of nations, which a centralized and hierarchical world state would deny. Moreover, if the bureaucratic inefficiency of the former state-socialist societies were not deterrent enough, the prospect of a centralized world bureaucracy is truly daunting. An alternative is found by reexamining and reformulating an old concept—market socialism.

Market Socialism

The recent demise of the Eastern European and Soviet command economies combined with the increasing power and influence of global capitalism have forced socialists to reexamine their goals, priorities, strategies, and visions (Laibman 1995, p. 83). One product of socialists' self-examinations has been the reemergence of serious debate about market socialism. At the forefront of this renewed discussion has been a series of works by the famed Marxist economist John Roemer. We will focus on Roemer's model of market socialism as outlined in his book *A Future for Socialism* (1994a), and elaborated in later articles.[9] First, we briefly examine Roemer's reasons for endorsing market socialism and we summarize published criticisms of his proposals. Our own critique and praise for market socialism involves extending and reformulating the model to the world level, an extension that we contend is necessary for market socialism to work. We also contend that world socialism is only feasible as a market system.

What *is* market socialism? And why should socialists prefer market socialism to other alternatives? This model traces its modern origins to the works of Oskar Lange (1938). Essentially, it is a social organization that uses market mechanisms to distribute goods and services, and to allocate capital and labor according to socialist ends, ends that capitalist markets are incapable of attaining. Proponents of market socialism argue that the use of markets would allow socialist societies to overcome the problems of inefficiency and principal-agent conflict that under-mined the economic performance of the state-socialist economies (espe-cially in the 1970s and 1980s). For example,

> How to monitor the managers of public firms to maximize profits, to get them involved in competitive races for innovation, to discipline laxity, and how to separate political from economic criteria in decision making—these are central economic issues any model of market socialism must address. And on these counts the models of centralized market socialism are particularly deficient. (Bardhan and Roemer 1993b, p. 11)

In the state-socialist societies, the "soft budget constraints," wherein firm managers need not be concerned with poor budget performance, eventually posed a debilitating problem (Bardhan and Roemer 1993b). The soft budget constraint problem is a special case of a larger, more gen-eral principal-agent problem that has plagued command economies. Even though "society" was the "principal" that hired managers as its agents, the managers could ignore consumers and citizens. The solution is for princi-pals to "design incentives so that following the rules is in the best interest of the managers" (Roemer 1994a, p. 3; i.e., the theory of incentive com-patibility, p. 33). Market socialists argue that in a centralized economy, managers have no incentive to maximize efficiency; hence, by establishing some market mechanisms, socialist economies should be able to achieve far greater efficiency than existed in Eastern Europe or the Soviet Union.

Another deficiency found in state socialism that market socialism aims to overcome is a lack of innovation. Roemer notes that "growth in economic welfare [by the 1980s] depended much more on the ability of the economy to innovate, to adopt new technologies producing improved commodities" (1994a, p. 44). Without the competition that markets stimulate, no business enterprise is forced to innovate. While state socialism produced quality education systems, it fared poorly at consumer innovation and deficiencies there eventually affected all of society. Roemer posits such a lack of innovation as an important factor contributing to and explaining the timing of the failure of the Soviet economy (p. 44). The combination of heightened efficiency and innova-tion in market systems results in greater flexibility in adapting to a more rapidly changing world.[10]

However, if markets are used, how does this form of socialism differ from capitalism? The most important distinction between capitalism and market socialism revolves around the issue of *property rights*—that is, control over the investment process and distribution of surplus (i.e., profits) (Roemer 1994a). The fundamental difference between capitalism and market socialism is that in the latter, large enterprises are not privately owned (Bardhan and Roemer 1993b, p. 7). However, public firms need not be owned by the state, either. Rather, as we explicate later, stock in firms can be distributed among citizens in an egalitarian manner and investment decisions can be the subject of democratic oversight. Therefore, the entire population has input (however indirect it may be) over investment decisions and shares in corporate profits. Contrast this with the concentration of corporate control and income in capitalist economies (for instance, 1 percent of all U.S. families own 60 percent of the corporate stock and 30 percent of all assets—Braun 1997, p. 23). While it provides improvement in efficiency and innovation beyond that found in state-socialist command economies, market socialism also offers greater equality than can be found in capitalism.

Note, however, that most market socialists, including Roemer, qualify this statement. For the sake of innovation through entreprenuerialism, and to avoid the inertia and red tape of large bureaucracies, individuals would be allowed to own and control *small* businesses. How small is a subject of dispute. Yet proponents of market socialism agree that once enterprises reach a certain size, they need to be transferred into the public market. We will say more about this in our discussion of world market socialism below.

Is this enough to be called socialism? Roemer (1994a, 1994b) argues that not only is the answer yes, but that it is superior at reaching socialist goals than an administrated system. Roemer asks: What do socialists want? In answering, he offers three principles upon which socialism stands: "I believe that socialists want equality of opportunity for: (1) self-realization and welfare, (2) political influence, and (3) social status" (Roemer 1994a, p. 11).

By "self-realization," Roemer means the "development and application of an individual's talents in a way that gives meaning to life" (p. 11). And "welfare," of course, refers to material well-being. Equal opportunity for "political influence" is one way to define democracy; "social status" refers to preferred positions within society. Another way to put it is that socialists want to eliminate alienation, exploitation, poverty, tyranny, and discrimination. Roemer focuses his proposal on only the first principle, which is predicated to some extent on success in the other two. Equal opportunity, in all cases, means far more than the liberal employment slogan because it presumes equal access to resources, the most important of which is the means of production. Equal opportunity to employ capital is the antithesis of capitalism, which is predicated on private accumulation of capital. The "opportunity" qualifier to equality recognizes the responsibility of the individual to work in order to achieve self-realization and welfare, influence, and social status. As such, equal opportunity requires democratic control over the largest concentrations of capital, equitable distribution of profits, and elimination of class exploitation. It does not, however, imply complete individual equality as individuals differ in their talent, ability, and effort. Market socialism is an improvement over capitalism and a step toward socialism to the extent that it achieves these goals.

Market socialism is not "communism," in which the surplus is so large as to make rewarding individual productivity irrelevant. Quite the contrary, it is designed to ensure that the product of individual activity is returned to its producer. This would transform the logic of capitalism, but it would not suddenly dictate that everyone give up their desires for consumer goods, live in a commune, or only watch the Public Broadcasting System. It is axiomatic that the outcomes of self-realization and democracy cannot be predetermined. Administrating outcomes, however well-intentioned, undermines the goals of socialism.

Why not just concentrate on reforming capitalism, as social democrats and leftist liberals have attempted to do through the creation of the welfare state and social democracy? As discussed previously, social democracy is vulnerable to expedient changes or reversals in the state, especially during global economic downturns (Moene and Wallerstein 1993; Weisskopf 1993). Welfare states redistribute income through political mechanisms such as taxation and transfer payments. They are thus dependent on high growth rates and protection from foreign competition in order to prevent transfers from producing zero-sum political conflicts. Changes in political regimes can result in significant alterations in such redistribution. This is particularly clear in examining the politics of the Reagan-Thatcher-Kohl era. Further, as Roemer (1994a, pp. 53–54) notes, the successful social democracies in the Nordic countries occurred under rather particular, if not perhaps unique, social conditions, including homogeneous populations with high levels of collective solidarity. Social-democratic states by themselves cannot control issues that are global in nature.

In market socialism, property rights are different than in capitalism, but equally institutionalized and therefore not as easily subject to such political whims. Nor are the equal-opportunity aspects of market socialism dependent on high growth rates. This is a critical advantage of market socialism over social-democratic or welfare-state redistribution techniques: market socialism is integrated into the fabric of the economy.

Although Roemer does not elaborate on the "transition," we can add that by retaining the efficiency and innovation of market incentives, along with the institutionalization of egalitarian property rights, a transition to market socialism could very well avoid the "valley of transition" problem that has undermined other socialist movements (Przeworski 1985). That is, the short-run effect of socialist policies has often been an economic recession, due largely to capital flight to other countries. The result is lower living standards among workers and loss of political support, even if their long-term prospects could be far superior. Stuck in this valley, elected socialists may lose office and have their policies reversed before long-term benefits emerge, or may become authoritarian in order to retain power and continue to pursue the long-term benefit of their policies.

Roemer's Proposal

Roemer's proposal centers on a "coupon" stock market. This mechanism is crucial because it is what makes this market socialist. There are four significant elements in this model of market socialism: an informed citizenry, a sector of public firms and public banks, a set of mutual funds, and the state treasury (Roemer 1994b, p. 462).

As in capitalism, Roemer (1994a) would allocate labor through a market. Workers' income would consist of two parts. One part would be the direct income from their labor, in the form of wage or salary. Workers would derive the second part of their income from the coupon market. While this income would not be equal for all adults, the coupon share guarantees some level of income to all regardless of participation in the labor market.

The state treasury would issue each adult citizen "an equal endowment of coupons that can be used only to purchase shares of mutual funds" (1994b, p. 462). When an individual reaches a certain age, the state endows one with, say, 1,000 coupons. These coupons essentially represent resources to be allocated to firms (paid by the state). Individuals use these coupons to purchase shares of mutual funds, which then invest in a set of various enterprises. Individuals receive a portion of the profits from the firms in their mutual fund's portfolio. However, individuals *cannot* sell their coupons for money. Such restrictions are useful toward two ends. First, by prohibiting individuals from selling their coupons for money or goods, poorer persons will not be able to act on any potential desire or need to "get cash quick" by selling their coupons. If individuals could sell their coupons for money or goods, we would likely find that the rich would buy up the coupons of the poor rather quickly, leaving us with the same mechanism and concentration of wealth as in capitalism. This is exactly what happened to public distributions of stock in state enterprises in the former Soviet Union. State managers quickly became capitalists. Therefore, the restriction is somewhat paternalistic, but it guarantees that everyone will share in the profits (i.e., surplus) produced in society.

Second, as just touched on, the prohibition on selling coupons also prevents a small class from monopolizing influence over the means of production (1994a, pp. 74–75; 1994b, p. 462). Just as individuals cannot sell their coupons, neither can they buy coupons with money. Individuals will only ever own the number of coupons that the state treasury has granted them, but their value would vary depending on how well they are invested and how well firms perform. This type of choice, with corresponding differences in returns and yet minimized loss, is now common among investment and retirement plans for the middle and higher classes. Choices include not just the risk of investment plans, but also the social and environmental desirability of the firms, thereby exercising an indirect (and admittedly loose) social control over corporate behavior. Market socialism would extend the benefits and influence of controlling investment plans to the working and lower classes, and no class would hold a wildly disproportionate control over everyone else.

Profits would be distributed on the basis of equal opportunity rather than being concentrated in a small class of owners, as in capitalism.[11] All adult citizens would be guaranteed some level of income dependent not upon political regimes or personal ability, but on the economic performance of society and, more specifically, on the economic performance of the firms in which their mutual fund invests. These two ends represent the *socialism* of the market.

The Process Within the Model

The socialist outcomes of Roemer's model should now be clear, but how does the model actually operate? Start with the assumption that the state treasury grants all adult citizens an equal amount of coupons. Roemer (1994a, 1994b) uses the figure 1,000. With the above restrictions, these coupons guarantee all adults some form of income. Adults use these coupons to invest in mutual funds. All large corporations are publicly owned through such coupons. Yet individuals invest only indirectly in corporate ventures via mutual funds. Roemer states, "Prices of corporate shares and mutual funds . . . will oscillate depending on the supply of and demand for shares" (1994b, p. 462). Each adult invests in a mutual fund, of which many will compete for investors' coupons. These mutual funds then invest in a set of firms in the public sector.[12] Consequently, firms would derive some of their financing through the coupon stock market. Firms would exchange their coupons to the state treasury for investment funds (1994b, p. 462). Public firms would also gain a large proportion of their investment funds through bank loans, whose capital would come from savings.

Public firms would be monitored (for efficiency and profit maximization) primarily by public investment banks and, to a lesser and indirect extent, by the individual choices of mutual funds (and the coupon stock market). Banks would also be publicly owned, through coupons. A set of large banks would hold loan portfolios for groups of interdependent firms and their role in monitoring the firms would be similar to the Japanese *keiretsu*. Importantly, Roemer argues that these public banks should be independent of the state in order to avoid political pressures that existed in the former command economies. Roemer states, "A main bank would be primarily responsible for putting together a loan consortia to finance the operations of the firms in its group; it would, correlatively, be responsible for monitoring these firms" (1994a, p. 76). When mutual funds move coupons from a firm, and the firm's value or standing in the coupon stock market correspondingly dropped, the responsible bank would "investigate how well the firm is being managed. It has an incentive to monitor the firms in its group effectively because, by doing so, it keeps its firms profitable and thereby able to pay back their loans" (1994a, p. 76).

Roemer confesses that he has no solid answer to the question, who would monitor the banks to ensure that they adequately monitor public firms? This has since become an even more important question as the Asian economic malady of the late 1990s can in part be traced to insufficient bank supervision. Roemer offers several possible answers. One which we think is particularly applicable for market socialism is that banks' boards of directors could be chosen democratically by investors (as now exists in some credit unions). State regulation would undoubtedly also be important.

Note that Roemer does not call for any immediate redistribution of personal wealth or income. Therefore, a small, wealthy class would initially persist in Roemer's market socialism. Banks might likely cater—formally or informally—to the desires of these large investors to retain access to their sizable savings accounts. Hence, to be democratic, the selection of bank directors must be strictly one vote per investor.

We cannot help thinking that Roemer misses a good opportunity by not increasing the role of mutual funds. We feel that mutual funds could have a more significant role in the ownership and monitoring of public firms. Our view of the role of mutual funds goes further than Roemer's (1994a) and approaches the vision of Bardhan (1993).[13] If mutual funds also adhered to the *keiretsu* model, then a dual system of monitoring public firms would exist—through both banks and mutual funds. First, mutual funds could be a stronger intermediary between individuals and public firms. They might offer portfolios that consist of stock in a fairly constant set of public firms. Therefore, mutual funds would have an interest in monitoring the firms in their portfolio. If firms in a mutual funds portfolio performed poorly, the fund would attract few investors. Conversely, if the portfolio firms were profitable, the mutual fund would draw an increasing number of investors, thereby increasing its own worth and resources (perhaps to purchase profitable smaller firms and bring them into their portfolio). Funds could differ by social appeal as well (as some do now), such as investing only in environmentally friendly companies, thereby increasing the social control of firm behavior.

As should be obvious, Roemer's proposal does not increase workplace democracy. This is one of the primary weaknesses of his proposal, although this could be remedied as we explain below. Still, Roemer's proposal does achieve significant advances over a capitalist economy. Importantly, Roemer's model would gradually move toward greater egalitarianism. First, all adults would have access to profits, thereby possessing a guaranteed income, thus eliminating the most egregious forms of class exploitation and inequality. Coupon income could replace most welfare and social security. Presuming adequate safeguards (which admittedly, recent debates suggest, may not be an easy feat), this could greatly wither state authority and increase direct participation in running society. Coupon income would buffer individuals against recessions, although it would not protect inefficient firms against failure. This is critically important for the long-term viability of the system. Yet, coupon wealth would not be passed to heirs after death—that is, coupons are not inherited. Rather, when people die, their coupons are returned to the state treasury, and then are passed on to the next generation. Second, Roemer (1994b, p. 462) discusses the role of personal and corporate taxes as means of raising funds for the state treasury; presumably, these taxes would be progressive and therefore redistributive.

Roemer's model of market socialism is a clear advance over the former command economies of Eastern Europe and the Soviet Union. Competition among public firms and the presence of smaller, privately owned enterprises stimulate product innovation that was inadequately fostered in the former communist states. In particular, it aims to address the principal-agent problems that command economies cannot overcome. Market socialism provides sufficient monitoring mechanisms (here, banks and mutual funds) to ensure firms' efficiency. Coupon investors would still have to take risks and losses, and the range of earned income would still afford high rewards to rare individuals of extreme ability and talent. Baseball pitchers with 100-mph fastballs would still be millionaires, but their teams would not have billionaire owners.

Finally, Roemer (1994a, pp. 90–94) only briefly discusses the role of the state. He proposes that the state should have various welfare policies as exist today. For instance, in Roemer's model, labor would be allocated through a market; hence, unemployment would still exist. Therefore, one of the roles of the state would be to provide various safety-net programs for such macroeconomic shortcomings. Unlike most socialists, Roemer does not tie socialism to investment in public infrastructure (education, environment, urban renewal, etc.). As is true now, public investment would be determined in response to social activism and democratic politics. The difference, which he does not discuss but could presume, is that the political influence of a class of extremely wealthy owners would be eliminated. Given the extraordinary power of modern media to influence politics, and its extraordinary cost, this would be a move toward *restoring* democracy. In a society where political democracy is not compromised by media manipulation by the rich, majority interest in public investment is much more likely to prevail.

Market Socialism and the World Market

Roemer has put forth a fresh and innovative alternative to the capitalist economy. We think that his model is best on the issues of redistribution and efficiency-maximization (via his monitoring mechanisms). We applaud him here. Yet, there are some important criticisms to be made of his proposal. We will address criticisms, from others and our own, and offer solutions for a revised model. The most important critique, we think, is that Roemer apparently fails to recognize the character and impact of the world capitalist economy. Our revised model focuses on global issues, although we consider other related criticisms. We discuss four revisions that would enable global democracy and world socialism (or "globalism") to end unequal development and eliminate the core-periphery hierarchy. These four revisions are the following: (1) a federal world bank, (2) significant employee ownership requirements, (3) progressive interest rate plans for international development, and (4) global standardization policies.

Without a supportive global context, any market-socialist society would face the old foes of capital flight, international isolation, and militarized opposition. Further, and most telling, any coupon system limited to nationalized industries would, as has occurred in the past, cut a market-socialist society off from the global investment markets, and with it, from most of the world's technological developments. Simply translating Roemer's design to the global level would not work. A single world treasury would face the problems associated with state social-ism—bureaucratic inefficiency and high transaction costs that would likely make it unworkable. Moreover, distribution of coupons among billions of people would be likely to make them worthless.

The solution here, as with most global institutions, is a world feder-al system in which societal units participate because it is in their interest to do so. The global institution, in this case a socialist world bank, would only directly invest coupons in transnational corporations (TNCs, those large firms with significant investments in more than two countries). The coupons would be owned by mutual funds, and by the employees of each corporation (more on the latter below). Over half the world's trade is presently controlled by just the top six hundred TNCs, which makes the transaction costs quite feasible. Note that TNC coupons would be owned and traded on the market by societal mutual funds, not by a world state (TNC employees would also own shares, as discussed below). We have to start with the world as it exists, which means that mutual fund accounts would have to be backed up by hard currency. Ownership would at first be concentrated entirely in the core, and even there it would vary as it does now from one national society to the next. Peripheral states would of course organize their own funds, and get loans from the world bank to do so, but their initial capital would be small. Socialism is not charity. Neither is it a return to some romanti-cized self-sufficiency of self-depriving rural ascetics. Improving living standards of impoverished populations in the Third World will require huge investments that can only come from the core, and thus have to be in the mutual interests of core populations, a point to which we will return.

Limiting the world bank to TNCs also limits centralized control that might undermine individual entrepreneurship, artistic expression, or cultural diversity of small domestic business owners, artisans, and such. In fact, world bank and government policies would strongly support the expansion of local small businesses and cooperatives as these provide more employment per investment dollar and more flexibility in responding to the world market than do TNCs. In each society, the socialist investment bank would differ, perhaps greatly, from nation to nation in terms of size, policies, and plans. Some national states would have extensive social ownership and state involvement, others little, except where their companies and commodities cross borders. Their relation to the world bank would also all be the same, and again, similar to that of the present federal reserve system in the United States. The societal banks would be required to maintain a minimal level of invest-ment capital with the world bank and would borrow from the world

bank at specified interest rates. Those interest rates would set bench-
marks for rates worldwide, the importance of which leads to our next
criticism/revision.

Roemer does not put nearly enough stress on the point that his proposal is only part of a market-socialist society. As a result of this lack of
emphasis, Putterman (1994) criticizes Roemer for retaining the "anarchy" of the market instead of replacing this anarchic competition with
planning. This criticism is somewhat overstated. Putterman fails to realize that competition and planning are not mutually exclusive. Roemer
advocates that the public banks monitor public firms in a manner similar to the Japanese *keiretsu*. The *keiretsu* typically involve a heavy dose of
long-term industrial planning and interfirm coordination. German
investment banks have similar policies. The banks, including the world
bank, would in turn be supervised by an elected board, and monitored
by the mutual funds and by international organizations in order to prevent cronyism and sweetheart deals. Investment banks and mutual funds
tend to focus on long-term returns in part because their investments are
spread over a variety of industries and their returns are spread out over
a large variety of investors. No one can "get rich quick," making the
banks and funds more amenable to investments with long-term returns
and less inclined (but admittedly not immune) to activities with short-
term benefits but long-term costs, such as currency speculation or non-
renewable forestry. With market socialism, this long-term planning tendency is enhanced, as the coupon owners would be spread over large
populations.

Our conception of market socialism and planning differs in emphasis from Roemer's in that it depends more on "investment politics."
Coupon holders would select mutual funds and mutual funds would
select public investment banks based on criteria that would balance
short-term profit returns against other social concerns, such as environmental and social progress. Workers, community activists, environmentalists, and others could influence investment choices, making capital
less expensive for socially conscious companies. Although all would have
an interest in efficiency and growth, none would have huge *individual*
gains (or losses) from one choice or another, allowing nonprofit considerations to play a larger role in decisionmaking with limited individual
consequences. The so-called choice of high pollution and high growth
versus low pollution and low growth, for instance, would become a
democratic one such that the benefits of high growth are not limited to
capitalists while the costs of pollution are not limited to the local (or
global) community.

An important aspect of investment politics is that the workers in
any firm hold some significant portion of that firm's coupons. Roemer

argues against such a proposition and for the use of managers who act independently of workers, that is, managers are not responsible to workers. However, other models emphasize the importance of worker ownership and managers who are responsible to their employees (e.g., Schweickart 1996). Weisskopf (1993, p. 122) refers to Roemer's model as a "pure" model of market socialism, and the latter as a "self-managed" model where workers elect their managers and vote on major company decisions. Self-management would offer workers greater economic democracy and would reduce alienation in the workplace. It also offers an incentive for teamwork and peer monitoring that can boost individual productivity. Examples of self-management include cooperatives, but also professional firms that are owned as partnerships where the purpose of the manager is to coordinate the output of autonomous individuals or teams. However, this micro advantage in productivity can also be a disadvantage in terms of macro-level efficiency. The self-managed model suffers from a "soft budget constraint" problem if workers are the sole owners. Employee-owners would undoubtedly have trouble cutting back their own work force or wages. Also, employees in successful firms, especially older workers, would want to sell their business as their capital gains would far outstrip their profits during their lifetimes. This could create large inequities in wealth and income to which there is no easy solution. If worker-owners could not sell, then success is less attractive; if they can sell, then all firms cannot be entirely worker-owned.

The pure market-socialist model also has shortcomings as it fails to promote "more democracy (because it does not extend democratic self-governance to the workplace), and it does not promote greater community at the workplace" since the worker-management relation would likely be adversarial (Weisskopf 1993, p. 125). Consequently, Weisskopf proposes a "hybrid" model that separates ownership from control. Firms would be socially owned, but controlled by workers. Markets would determine wages, employment, and investment decisions, while shop or office managers would be elected by employees. Schweickart (1996) offers a similar model, but with investment coming from state taxes on assets.

Schweickart and Weisskopf have a point, in that self-management has a variety of benefits. But, in addition to Roemer's complaints about efficiency, we have another problem with their proposals—size. Cooperatives and partnerships work fine when communication and relations are direct, but in large corporations, especially transnational ones, there are many layers of management with the top far removed from line employees. Self-management that would reduce alienation occurs mainly at the lowest level, but control is at the top where overall

performance can be judged. Obvious principle-agent problems of coordination result if low-level managers are elected by their immediate
employees, but are responsible to higher-ups. This is even true if
employees elect top management, because in a large firm the top would
represent thousands of employees. Additionally, if only employees
selected management, there would be no board of directors to represent
the interests of coupon owners. Further, worker self-management without the workers owning part of the firm could make coordination problems worse, as the interests of owners and workers inherently diverge.

Basically, we face here a trade-off between greater democracy of
management within firms versus greater democracy of ownership of
firms. We lean in the latter direction, closer to Roemer than to
Schweickart. We suggest a different hybrid where TNC employees would
be guaranteed a certain number of nontransferable coupons (shares in
the large firm for which they work) per year of employment. The
coupons would be distributed to workers as part of their pay, with the
goal of firm profits from coupon ownership eventually making up a
third of an employee's income. Phased in over time, employee ownership would also eventually constitute a third of the total ownership of
the firm, with the other two-thirds being publicly owned and traded
coupons. Through their representatives and unions, workers could also
push for self-management at the level of the immediate supervisor or
office manager, but it would have to prove to be efficient and cooperative. As coupon owners, workers would be represented on the board of
directors through elections. They would be able to monitor management policy and exercise real influence on employee and community
issues, but would do so in conjunction with the public and state interests. This is a corporatist model that treats huge corporations as not just
the product of labor and capital, but also as an integral social product.

As Weitzman (1984) points out, shared ownership of this type
spreads the benefits of productivity increases to workers, giving them a
direct incentive to increase efficiency. Shared ownership can also have
the benefit of reducing unemployment if workers receive a significant
portion of their income as variable profit shares rather than fixed wages
(as occurs to some extent in Japan). Workers who received a portion of
their income as profits would first lose those profits before losing their
jobs to a layoff in a recession (i.e., income elasticity rather than job elasticity). Forced unemployment, with its associated community and family destruction, would be the last rather than the first step in lowering
costs during a recession.

Most important from a global perspective is that peripheral employees of TNCs would be guaranteed a share in the company and directly
benefit from high profits garnered in their homeland. As noted above,

TNC coupons owned by mutual funds would initially be concentrated in the core and peripheral ownership would start small. Requiring that TNCs provide employee coupon ownership hastens the spread of capital ownership and returns to the periphery. It would also give peripheral and core labor a common interest in organizing their vote and voice on the TNCs' boards of directors.

Additionally, but of crucial importance for Third World development, is that distributing coupons to employees raises the incomes of workers without raising their wages. Although our prime goal is to raise living standards in the periphery, if wages increase without commensurate increases in productivity, then TNCs will not invest there and wage increases will be soon lost to inflation. The only long-term solution to uneven development is to raise the *productivity* of Third World workers. Raising productivity requires capital investment, both in humans through education and training, and in production, through technology and public infrastructure. Investing in the periphery would benefit core populations who get a direct return on their coupons from high profits there, which as coupon holders, peripheral workers would share. Core investors would also benefit indirectly from raising wages there and from reducing the social ills of underdevelopment, which inevitably reflect back on core living standards in a highly integrated global economy. Capital investment would come in part from long-term planning by those who support more even and equitable development over the crises of wars, refugees, environmental destruction, and human suffering produced by underdevelopment.

While transforming the politics of investment so that core and peripheral labor have greater common interests is a necessary step, we recognize that it is insufficient by itself to reorder the core-periphery hierarchy. No matter how much people support and benefit from long-term goals, these will remain marginal to profit returns, because in the immediate present workers must provide for their own lives and families, and cannot be expected to do otherwise. As such, there need to be additional mechanisms for promoting global development beyond investors' long-term interests.

The third element in addition to *keiretsu*-style investment banks and worker ownership is that the state treasuries and the world bank would also manipulate interest rates. A fourth element involves establishing global standards and regulations, which we discuss below and in the next chapter. These first three, however, are the essentials of what makes property relations "socialist" at the global level in our model.

The manipulation of interest rates is mainly used now to raise rates in core economies as a way to fight inflation, but it could also be used to lower interest rates in order to increase investment in progressive social, environmental, and development projects. As such, corporations would finally be held accountable for their negative externalities, such as fostering pollution, disease, or inequality—problems much more acute in the periphery than in the core (Dixon and Boswell 1996a). In particular, the world bank would discount loans to TNCs that invest in the periphery in ways that link with domestic suppliers. Although not a panacea, this would help spread the benefits of investment and reduce the disarticulation between TNC and local sectors (Dixon and Boswell 1996b). Discounted loans to societal banks would also be designed to support long-term planned development and social progress, including loans to fund societal banks in the periphery. This would strongly encourage states to voluntarily set up societal versions of the socialist world bank and use it to pursue progressive goals.

Our socialist version of a world bank, tied to state versions and to TNCs, would have great influence over interest rates and could use them to foster investment in less developed countries. The first mechanism was the distribution of TNC coupons to their workers in the periphery and the corresponding development of investment politics. This affects the ownership and control of the means of production. More traditional socialists might see manipulating interest rates as an exceedingly indirect way to address unequal development that disparages the socialist principle of "production for use." They are half right.

Interest rate manipulation as a way to influence investments is deliberately indirect in order to make the social goals pursued conform to the interests of the investors (which are no longer capitalists, but whole populations). This avoids the problem of principal-agent incentive incompatibility found in direct forms of manipulating investments, such as in the former Soviet Union, which can undermine the intended positive effects. On a more abstract level, manipulating interest rates for planned social goals is controlling capital property in its purest form, without the administrative hierarchy of control that can become an exploiting class in its own right. In short, the global mechanisms we propose for pursuing world socialist goals are deliberately indirect and decentralized in order to prevent the mechanisms from obstructing pursuit of the socialist goals. This is nowhere more necessary than at the global level, where the enormity of the task makes principals and agents, world leaders and world citizens, the most distant and diverse that they can possibly be.

Market Socialism and World Government

Putterman (1994) criticizes Roemer's proposal for not redistributing wealth. Roemer proposes only that profit be redistributed. Over the generations, this would redistribute wealth, but great disparities across current classes and especially across countries would long remain. The politics of investment and interest rates we discussed above would slowly begin to address this problem, but we also stated that this is an indirect process and that a fourth mechanism would be needed in the form of a democratic world government that would pursue international peace and raise global living standards. Roemer (1994a, p. 90) acknowledges the need for a welfare state in conjunction with his market proposal, and he argues that the state treasury should be funded through personal and corporate taxation (1994b, p. 462). Hence, Roemer concedes quietly that his market-socialist proposal is not a comprehensive plan. He claims that market socialism is a *transitory* organization of society en route to even more complete egalitarianism. What this future society would be, how we would get there, and why we cannot go directly, is largely left unsaid. We reject the idea of socialism as a sort of purgatory. To be sure, once in place there would surely be ways to improve upon market socialism that are not now obvious. However, the point of socialism is to make a better world now, not to prepare the world for some future heaven.

A world government would serve three main functions: supporting international peacekeeping activities, providing certain public goods best delivered or coordinated globally, and enforcing global standards for human rights and environmental conditions. Of the three, the first gets the most attention, but the last is the most important. We outline all three here and discuss specific standards in the next chapter. In addition, any world government would require an independent tax base and we offer a few suggestions. Our goal, however, is to outline the necessary functions of a world government for building a socialist world-system, not to diagram its every branch and bureau.

Peacekeeping forces and a standing rapid-strike intervention force would act as "firefighters," intervening to prevent spiraling escalations of conflict. Assessing individual states, as is now done by the United Nations, would pay for these forces. States are the source of war making and should pay the cost of peace. We suggest a graduated levy for the strike force based on a national state's military budget. This could start with an expansion of what now exists in principle. But, the levy would grow to the point that national states would have a distinct financial incentive to cut military spending, which if followed, would also cut funds for the global force in proportion. The point is not to build a world-state leviathan, but to change those features of the world-system that produce cycles of warfare.

The systemic sources of war we have discussed are interimperial rivalry and the cycle of hegemonic contestation. Some combination of international governance and liberal tolerance has, since Hobbes, been proposed as the prerequisite for lasting world peace. The rare instances in which a hegemon provided this combination have proved the validity of the argument. The problem is that hegemons decline and imperialists compete to take advantage of dependent peoples. By pursuing more equitable and even global development, global democracy would break the hierarchy of dependency and the advantages from imperial rivalry. Colonialism has already been banned. Only democratic states are now fully legitimate in the existing world order and democratic states rarely fight each other (Russett 1994). As we elaborate in the next chapter, global democracy is the key political strategy to ensure that a hegemonic combination of international governance and liberal tolerance becomes permanent.

Much as the way state democracy shifts class struggle to the political arena, global democracy would shift international contests to world governmental forums. This includes the cycle of hegemony; with a world government setting global standards and enforcing international contracts, the struggle for hegemony would shift to a political fight among coalitions with different interests, rather than a military fight among allied states. To be sure, border disputes and ethnic or cultural differences would still result in wars, even vicious ones. One would want a strike force large enough to prevent the spread of such conflicts. While greater equity might reduce their prevalence, ethnic and cultural conflicts mainly spring from attempts, often imperial in nature, to suppress cultural diversity and identity. The only lasting solution is to encourage proliferation of identities and national sovereignties such that conflict is always limited to a small proportion that can be overwhelmed by the common desire for peace among the vast majority.

The main global institution for pursuing equity and even development would be the new world bank. It would be self-financing (and nonprofit) through holding coupons and through interest paid on loans. A world government would have its own administrative costs, including those of contract enforcement, but the main reason for independent taxes would be for social and health programs, such as greatly expanded versions of the World Health Organization and the United Nations International Children's Emergency Fund. These programs are *public goods* in that their benefits are widely shared and cannot be easily differentiated into individual costs. Certainly Americans, for instance, benefit from preventing the spread of deadly diseases in Africa, but it is nearly impossible to determine and divide such a benefit in order to charge people for it.

Socialists have long called for an expansion of public goods. Some public amenities that are now provided by national states would be more efficiently produced by a global government. Cost effectiveness should be a major factor determining which public goods should be produced globally as opposed to those that are provided by coordinating national state policies or by regulating TNC activities. We suspect that most public goods will remain as coordinated activities of national states, as the benefits of a single global administration may be lost to the high transaction costs of centralized bureaucracy. There are some obvious exceptions, such as the prevention of world war, the fight against infectious diseases, and the amelioration of certain environmental problems, which can only be addressed by global-scale action.

We do not advocate individual taxes at the global level. We have already mentioned the funding of collective security by taxation of national states. Other revenues for the world government should come from taxing those international transactions that the world government is charged to promote and protect. As such, the world government's revenue would be tied to its success in governing the world economy. There are a variety of tax possibilities with varying effects on growth and redistribution. One would be to tax large currency transactions, say at 1 percent, which would generate several billion dollars annually (Tobin 1996). This would be a progressive tax as small transactions done mainly by tourists would be exempt and it would select against currency speculators. It would also encourage the increased efficiency of currency unions, such as the euro, and perhaps a global currency at some point (which would then necessitate alternate income sources).

Finally, we turn to global standards of human rights and environmental protection. These may sound like the claim for "real" universal liberalism promulgated by Wallerstein, and so be it, they should. But we predicate our claim on the establishment of a socialist world-system, which we argued was a necessary assumption for equal rights to be universal rather than the rights of "national liberalism." Enforcing global standards is likewise necessary to making socialism global by preventing any state from using predatory competition based on oppressing or exploiting its own people or its environment. Minimum standards shift advantage to investments in human capital and productive innovation. Enacting common global standards, which would involve increasing world regulation of TNCs by a world bank and other institutions, would be a first step toward a socialist world-system. Raising labor and social standards worldwide, and requiring their worldwide enforcement, is thus the key strategy for building global democracy that we present in the next chapter.

More to the point of our discussion here, enforcing global standards also fills a central lacuna in Roemer's proposal—his inattention to problems associated with status discrimination by race, gender, age, sexual preference, or ethnicity (Folbre 1994). To be sure, we can assume that

Roemer would support universal human rights and environmental protection. But, enforcing standards by themselves could lock in high labor and social costs in underdeveloped countries, exacerbating uneven development and the hierarchy of dependency. Our solution of progressive investment and interest rate policies has a strong built-in preference for more even development. Although indirect and long term, this is fundamental in its consequences. The ultimate source of ethnic and racial conflict is uneven development itself, a process obscured by focusing on ethnic conflicts within a society but obvious from a world historical perspective (Bonacich et al. 1994; Boswell and Jorjani 1988). Ethnic minorities within a society often start as migrants from some poorer part of the world. Thus, reducing uneven and unequal development is the only real solution to ethnic and racial inequality. These policies would be most effective in encouraging investment in underdeveloped and low-income areas. As Wilson (1996) points out for the United States, decapitalization of poor minority neighborhoods is one of the primary causes of the widening disadvantage of the urban underclass. To be sure, such a process would be slow, but it would eventually produce a much more egalitarian multicultural world society.

What of gender inequality? Again, greater equality in ownership and profit distribution does not directly generate status equality, but it does provide resources to people in pursuit of that equality. Industrial development not only increases gender equality by opening economic and educational opportunities for women, but these in turn reduce fertility. High fertility is itself a reinforcing source (and consequence) of patriarchy. Reducing fertility results in raising living standards and increasing investment in human capital, and as such, greater gender equality globally is critically important for reducing uneven development. This is especially important for the worst aspect of gender inequality, the feminization of poverty. It is also of primary importance in addressing superexploitation of women workers on the global assembly line (Ward 1990). We take up some of these points again in the next chapter when addressing organizing strategies. While the egalitarian aspects of global democracy and world socialism are important for addressing economic aspects of gender inequality, they do not address gender per se, nor do they much affect other aspects of gender inequality, such as patriarchy within the family. Addressing these issues requires the attention of a broader political movement—the "new internationalism from below" proposed by Andre Drainville (1995).

Roemer provides no political strategy that would lead to the establishment of market socialism. He shrugs off the idea that socialist institutions should foster the growth of solidarity, what he calls "socialist man" (1994a, pp. 113–114). His theory is based on pursuing the rational interests of the working class, individually and as a whole, and thus he avoids (as do we) any reliance on self-sacrifice or charity. Both presume the same class inequalities he seeks to eliminate. Socialists should begin with markets because people are already adapted to market behavior and we should deal with people as they are, not based on what we want them to become.

At one point, however, Roemer acknowledges that social institutions play an important role in shaping individuals' behaviors and motives. People's interests are varied and what they pursue depends on what is salient and seems possible at the time. In order to move toward the long-term goal of human equality, socialists must construct institutions that foster the ideals of community and solidarity. Roemer himself repeatedly states that socialists need both long- and short-term visions. Consequently, in constructing markets for innovation and other mechanisms for monitoring efficiency, we need to take care not to allow divisive and competitive ideals to permeate market socialism as they do capitalism. It seems clear to us that he is mistaken if he thinks that market socialism can be achieved in the absence of a much broader global socialist movement. Market socialism, despite the kinship Roemer feels it has with current economies, must be part of a larger, mass-based movement that includes a movement for global democracy. Scattered small movements in that direction since 1968 and especially since 1989 have proliferated, although few if any have self-consciously advocated globalism of any sort. It will likely take a cluster of social upheavals, hopefully and probably with little violence, for the multiple movements to suddenly recognize their common visions and for world institutions to acquiesce to by-then dated demands for global living wages and other common standards. In retrospect, it will appear that a world revolution in global institutions and cognitive parameters had taken place.

Back to the Future

We have offered in this chapter a speculative discussion of where we should end, that is, a vision of a better future world-system that is both feasible and worth pursuing. Having glimpsed the end goal we return to the question, where to begin? What are the structural prospects of the system and what are the appropriate organizational strategies for those prospects? A utopian perspective is ill equipped to determine what we should do; it offers only scenarios of what could be. Wagar offers an alternative scenario to traditional party organizing. He has the World Party evolving out of study groups, salons, and other nonhierarchical interactions. The most important are discussion networks on the Internet. An analogy to the Bellamy clubs is obvious, but so are the limitations.

Historically, attempts to organize international parties have succeeded only up to the point of exercising real power. Power is located in states, which have societal constituencies and physical borders that frequently contradict global concerns. The nationalistic division of the Second International over World War I is the classic example of failure to organize globally. The subsumption of the Third International by Soviet foreign policy is another, albeit more complicated, example. Yet, ironically, the Internationals—First, Second, and even Third—remain the most successful historical examples of common forums for designing and coordinating progressive policies.

Despite globalization, international political parties and labor unions have not been among those international organizations on the rise. The fastest-rising type as a proportion of all international organizations is, instead, industry and trade organizations, that is, organizations of international capital rather than labor. Capital is laying the foundation for organizing labor globally, as it previously did industrially. If capitalists and states benefit from, and are rapidly pursuing, transnational organization, why not labor? Could a new global forum emerge that supersedes the national question, creating a true world party? In the next chapter, we examine the future of the world-system as a whole. We focus on the growth of international organization, consider the possibility of a multistate hegemony, and pursue the ability of progressive movements to transform it.

Notes

1. Harvey contributes an important specification of the institutional aspects of capitalism that have *not* changed with the transition from Fordism to flexible accumulation. He also points to the different ways in which Fordist and flexible-accumulation regimes respond to the contradictions of overaccumulation (Harvey 1989, pp. 179–188).

2. Harvey's discussion of modernism points out that it has always been composed of a dialectic between the eternal and the ephemeral. In this light, postmodernism is just the ephemeral phase that corresponds to the latest acceleration of time-space compression.

3. Oddly, despite his claim that the French Revolution was responsible for creating a geoculture for the capitalist world-system, and for establishing the three main ideologies within the geoculture, Wallerstein nevertheless does not consider 1789 to be a world revolution. Nor does he consider 1989 a world revolution, despite his contention that those events ended liberalism's ideological hegemony in the geoculture. He offers that designation only to 1848, which added socialism to the geoculture and to 1968, which challenged the limits of liberalism.

4. Wagar is a professor at the State University of New York at Binghamton, where he has long been a colleague of Immanuel Wallerstein and others in world-system studies.

5. Wagar's scenario and proposals are the focus of a special thematic issue in volume 2 of the *Journal of World-Systems Research* (http://csf.colorado.edu/ wsystems/jwsr.html), in which scholars from several disciplines and political activists provide comments and criticisms.

6. Wagar assumes that abundance would guarantee a general equality and eliminate any desire for hierarchy or conquest. A missing assumption, which we can add, is that the technology would have a diminishing return to scale, and perhaps even to hierarchy, which would make small egalitarian communities the optimal form. Unfortunately, this assumption makes the technological form, and thus the Small Party option, even more fantastic.

7. In a comment on our manuscript, Warren Wagar writes, "I regard identity politics as one of the supreme obstacles to the globalization of democracy, comparable to capitalism itself. If we do not get beyond identity politics, if we do not manage to evolve a sense of species humanness that *transcends* and to some extent *replaces* ethnic, racial, religious, national, gender, and sexual identity, there is absolutely no chance of a global socialism or a world state" (personal communication to the authors, March 18, 1998).

8. Keohane (1984) and others have also recognized the centrifugal potential and have suggested ways to build a collective world order.

9. See Roemer 1994a, 1994b; Bardhan and Roemer 1993a, 1993b; Roemer and Silvestre 1993. We also draw from Schweickart (1996, 1998). Although similar, his model places greater emphasis on the benefits of worker control and self-management, a point we share to some degree. However, the difference among these and other societal models of market socialism fades in importance when examined from a global perspective. We would expect (and desire) a wide variation in societal forms operating within the global framework.

10. We place greater emphasis on the flexibility of market socialism than Roemer, although he has implied this by his stress on innovation and efficiency.

11. Roemer proposes "equality of opportunity" rather than (absolute) "equality." In this specific proposal for market socialism, absolute equality would mean that everyone received the same portion or share of the part of the national income composed of profits (i.e., every adult would receive an equal portion of total profits). However, Roemer argues for equality of opportunity, meaning that every adult begins with the same amount of coupons and invests these coupons differently (i.e., some adults invest in this mutual fund, while others invest in that mutual fund). Consequently, "at the end of the day" some adults receive a greater income from profits than other adults do, because the former's mutual funds were more productive.

12. Roemer allows for the private ownership of smaller firms, but requires that, upon reaching a particular size, the firms are brought into the public sector and owned through coupons.

13. Roemer places more importance on mutual funds in his article (1994b) than in his earlier book (1994a). In his book, Roemer seems to propose that individuals invest their coupons directly into firms as in the current capitalist stock market. The version of his model with a greater role for mutual funds increases monitoring of firms (which is a major primary concern to Roemer). It also achieves a much higher degree of equality of profit distribution—which are the main socialist aspects of his proposal. Regarding the latter, if individuals can

invest coupons directly into firms as through the capitalist stock market, then those with the greatest access to information and understanding about the stock market (likely those who retained vast amounts of income from the earlier capitalist mode) would probably attain the greatest portion of profits. With a set combination of firms in mutual funds, a greater degree of equality could be created. All of the most profitable public firms would likely not be in the same mutual fund, but rather dispersed among various mutual funds. Hence, no small class could derive gargantuan amounts of income from profits.

6

The Future of the World-System

Political Implications of the World-Systems Perspective

A central question for any strategy of transformation is the question of *agency*. Who are the actors who will most vigorously and effectively resist capitalism and construct social progress? Where is the most favorable terrain, the weak links, where concerted action could bear the most fruit? There are many layers to the system—global hegemon, core, semiperiphery, periphery—and multiple efficacious actors within each layer—international organizations, states, firms, media, organized class, status, and interest groups, and so on. We have been arguing that change must take place at the global level and be institutionalized in the world order. That puts an emphasis on international organizations, both as actors and as sites of conflict and power; thus the conceptual importance of discussing a world party in the last chapter. We will add our perspective to international labor and social organizing below, and how the semiperiphery is the zone where such movements will likely find most fertile ground for planting revolutionary seeds.

The discussion of movements must first be tempered by the realities of power. A world order is constituted in the context of the international state system, which is dominated by the core states. While there is an emerging world civil society, on which we place great hopes, it emerges within the given world order and balance of power. As we have discussed throughout, the world order is set and enforced by the collective interests of core states, with the greatest unity and power occurring when one state is hegemonic over the system. The efficacy of global movements thus depends upon a world order that is both amply powerful in enforcing norms and standards, but at the same time is politically open and responsive to social pressure and conflict from below. Lest this seem daunting or overly complicated, the same is true for any societal movement. The opportunity to enact social change depends on effecting a normative and legal system that has enough power to enforce the change, particularly on capitalists and their corporations, but also must be democratic enough to allow organizing—or be vulnerable to social conflict and revolution (Tilly 1978).

Note that social change from below inevitably begins in civil society, not the state, and may only or mostly affect civil or market relations, such as gender and family relations or workplace conceptions of authority. This is especially true at the global level where there is no world state, but where it is also true that there is far less restraint on the naked exercise of power through war, imperialism, and repression. Thus, any conception of what international organizations or movements might accomplish depends upon the opportunity structure set by states, especially a hegemon. We start then with a discussion of the future of hegemony and the potential for a hegemonic world order, led by the European Union (EU), that would be most conducive to international organizing and most open or vulnerable to global changes that reset the world order.

To understand the future of the world-system, we needed first to explain how the system has developed in the past and how, if left unchanged, its cycles will likely repeat. The analytical theory and historical tables in Chapter 1 take us up through the maturation of U.S. hegemony in the postwar period. The model presented there explains the cyclical nature of world leadership as resulting from the interaction of three systemic trends—interstate political competition, world market integration, and uneven economic development. A world leader becomes hegemonic when the institutional order it enforces builds inertia into the otherwise chaotic movement of the system. Hegemony is a period of comparative peace and order in a system that is inherently competitive, dynamic, and uneven. Global cycles of leadership and hegemony have repeated since 1492, leaving to history Dutch, British, and now declining U.S. hegemonies. Theoretical models (Chase-Dunn and Rubinson 1977; Hopkins and Wallerstein 1979; Arrighi 1994), historical narratives (Wallerstein 1974, 1980, 1989; Kennedy 1987), and statistical analyses (Modelski and Thompson 1988; Boswell and Sweat 1991) reveal the cycle of hegemony as a fixed dynamic inherent to the world-system. Can we expect the future to be any different?

While discussing past cycles and trends, we have also introduced recent developments and trends that offer great potential for changing the system. A significant change has already taken place, one little noticed in previous theories because its sources are trends not previously important to understanding hegemony and war. Those trends are proletarianization, democratization, and decolonization, the cumulative effects of which are now weighing heavy on the transmissible machinations of the capitalist world-system. The interaction of these newer trends with older ones has the potential to fundamentally alter the basic processes of world-system development.

A repetition of global cycles as they have occurred for five hundred years will not come in any routine manner. Every cycle must be different because it builds upon past ones and because it occurs in conjuncture with other developments that do not necessarily follow the same pattern or any pattern. Contingent historical events and unintended consequences, as well as natural and biological ones, always interact with systemic processes in unpredictable ways. More importantly, social actors can influence changes in one direction or another, especially during world divides when the parameters of the world order become elastic. We are more likely to stretch those parameters in a progressive direction to the extent that we understand the system we are trying to change. At best, one can offer broad guidelines of what can happen so that actors can make reasonable choices. With such a license, we will make two types of speculations: one based on a simple, even mechanical, repetition of world-systemic cycles, and a contrasting second one that emphasizes new developments and feasible alternatives. The first scenario is based on mechanical continuities with past cycles and trends. It includes the following ten steps (to which we add some speculative dates):

1. Late 1990s–2010s: The United States remains the world's dominant power, but it continues its relative decline (recall Figure 1.2 in Chapter 1). Other powers rise and consolidate during a K-wave expansion.

2. 2010s–2020s: Increasing economic competition and rivalry among contending states leads to anarchic political conflicts, one of which escalates into a war among combatants with ample military resources accumulated during the K-wave upswing.[1]

3. 2020s: Peace resumes with a new world leader who emerges with a preponderance of military power.[2]

4. 2020s–2040s: War expenditures produce inflation despite declines in employment, which along with market saturation in the once leading, now decaying economic sectors results in a stagnant and erratic economy—another K-wave downturn. Serious economic recessions threaten political stability.

5. 2040s–2070s: Innovation in social and state structures jumps the system into a renewed K-wave expansion, concentrated in the new world leader.

6. 2040s–2050s: The variation in social and political structures shatters the common assumptions of the world order, leading to fundamental conflicts over the legitimacy of competing states.

Resources are again available for a political conflict to become a major war, which becomes a global war over hegemony as the world leader is drawn in.

7. 2050s: The victorious combatants agree to a common world order to govern global transactions, with enforcement and benefits falling first to the world leader.

8. 2050s–2080s: Dependence upon and institutionalization of the world order transforms the leader into a hegemon that manages a new golden age of peace and prosperity.

9. 2070s–2090s: The K-wave economic expansion dissipates due to emulation of innovations, infrastructural decline, and saturation of easy markets, which leads to a long stagnation.

10. 2080s–2090s: The hegemon declines relative to rising competitors who free-ride on the hegemon's enforcement of the world order and whose institutions are not fettered by concentration in the now-declining economic sectors—bringing us back to step 1 a hundred years hence.

The three past hegemonies (Dutch, British, and U.S.) have followed versions of these ten steps.[3] The systemic trends that produced the cycle have not diminished in importance or intensity. If there is an alternative future, it will come from trends, processes, or events that have not heretofore been crucial in structuring the history of global wars and world leaders. Such trends exist, we contend, in the following three processes: (1) proletarianization, (2) democratization, and (3) decolonization. None of the three processes are new to the capitalist world-system, but they have increased exponentially over the last fifty years.

The Rise of Nations and the Decline of States

To some extent, all three trends stem from the cumulative expansion of *commodification,* the transformation of human interactions into monetized market exchanges. Commodification, in interaction with state formation, has led to the rise in the number of sovereign nations, and since World War II, to the decline in size and imperial reach of states. This occurred because groups of people organized to counteract the negative effects of their exposure to market forces. Although market forces have become stronger and spatially more extensive, at the same time human collectivities have organized culturally and politically to protect themselves against and to gain control over threats to their identities and resources coming from the global market. This phenomenon did not begin in the twentieth century, but it has grown in scale because com-

modification and resistance to commodification have positively interacted. The interaction causes the *spiral* of market expansion and organized resistance on a larger and larger scale (see Chapter 4).

These movements, including workers' co-ops, labor unions, granges,
labor parties, anticolonial movements, women's movements, environmental movements, socialist parties, and communist states, are all
included in Immanuel Wallerstein's (1984b) rubric—"antisystemic
movements." The organizational forms and scale of these movements
have increased in interaction with the scale of capitalist firms, states, and
world market integration. Not all resistance is progressive. Attempts to
isolate people from commodification, rather than to control and transform it, often lead to xenophobia, racism, religious intolerance, and
other expressions of exclusion. While those suffering from market
degradations may be susceptible to the appeals, their oppositional or
lower class position will almost always incite a progressive, inclusive
alternative as well. Communist states—socialist movements that took
state power in the semiperiphery—challenged the capitalist system on a
global scale. Ironically, the communist challenge fueled U.S. hegemony.
Soviet and Chinese threats to capitalism and democracy legitimated the
key post–World War II policies of international liberalism, such as the
Marshall Plan, support of German and Japanese (and Korean and
Taiwanese) economic development, and military Keynesianism at home.
The success of these policies provided the political basis for a more
rapid expansion of the world market, now known as "globalization." The
recent wave of globalization has only now begun to spur organized com-
pensatory counteraction. Revolutionary technological changes that have
occurred in information and communications have created new and
easier ways to organize internationally, making global movements a nascent reality.[4] We can expect a spiraling increase in global movements,
some new ones and several revised versions of long-established movements.

Key differences with the past that we will detail are the following:
abolition of formal colonialism, disassembling of imperial multinational
states, proliferation of nation-states, and formal democratization of all
core states and many in the semiperiphery and periphery. Huge imperial
states have broken into literally hundreds of nations. The British Empire
broke apart in a series of steps in the 1940s and 1950s; the French
Empire dissolved in the 1960s; the Portuguese Empire ended in the
1970s; Yugoslavia and the Soviet Union unraveled in the 1990s. As a
result, imperial regulation of international exchange is being replaced by
"world polity" regulation, that is, by shared conceptions and rules of
appropriate international exchange. More precisely, the world order of
sovereign nation-states in the core has spread to the entire decolonized

periphery. As a result, a massive proliferation of international non-governmental organizations and a growing standardization of global exchanges are turning the world order into the early stages of a world polity. In analyzing data on the establishment of INGOs since 1875, Boli and Thomas (1997) find a linear increase interrupted only by war and depression which, after World War II, increased geometrically (there are three times as many INGOs in 1990 as in 1960). International organization, like commodification, is not a newcomer to the world-system, but again, the pace has accelerated. An upward trend in international regulation by means of normative and contractual agreements has been noticeable since the Concert of Europe following the Napoleonic Wars. The strength of "global governance" (Murphy 1994) has increased geometrically since World War II, however, as the strength of a globally oriented world bourgeoisie has increased vis-à-vis the nationally oriented fractions of capital.

The formation of a world polity opens the possibility of alternative paths to hegemony and even of a transformation of the system based on the rise of a world government. Of course, it is also possible, and perhaps probable, that these changes are temporary, and that the cycle of hegemonic rivalry and war will again repeat in devastating fashion. But the possibilities for fundamentally changing the system are greater now than in the previous century. We are soon to reach a bifurcation point in the path of world history.

Let us explore the trends and changes by tracing them in Figure 6.1, then return to the question of alternatives and possibilities. In Figure 6.1, we revise our world-system model specified in Chapter 1 to include recent changes in the cycle of hegemony and possible other future changes. The trends are repeated at the bottom of the new figure, which adds the new trends at the top and possible future developments to the far right. This figure includes the trends presented in Chapter 1, then adds new developments that we discuss in more detail throughout this final chapter. The additions start with commodification that, like the other trends of the world economy, results from the expanding accumulation process inherent to capitalism. The expansion of market relations overlaps with all the other trends. Market forces increase in strength and the spatial scale of market integration also increases. Not only are more and more aspects of life mediated by market interactions (e.g., fast foods for breakfast), but organization of the market is carried out on a global scale by transnational corporations (e.g., McDonald's in Beijing).

Commodification has particular effects that are usefully considered independently. The most important form of commodification has been proletarianization—the making of labor relations into wage relations.

Figure 6.1 Sources of a New World Polity: The Interaction of Global Trends

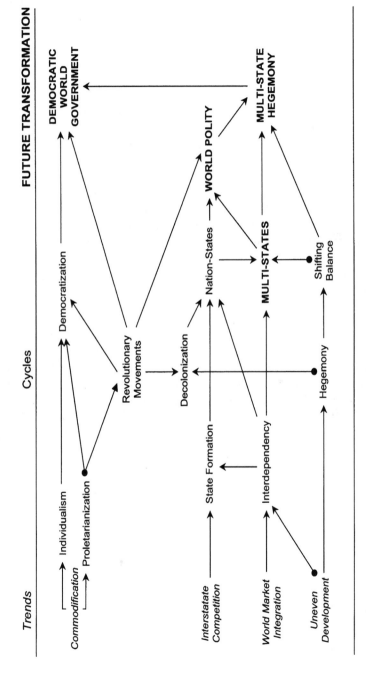

Trends   Cycles   **FUTURE TRANSFORMATION**

= Indicates that effects of K-waves are also important

BOLD/CAPS = Indicates future transformation

While labor markets have long existed, the proletariat has only included the bulk of the core population since the nineteenth century, and it does not yet constitute the majority of the work force in much of the periphery. Commodification has also transformed the nature of work and life for most of those individuals who are outside the formal labor market. The livelihood of peasants is linked in every country to production for local, national, and global markets even if they are not wage earners. The transformation of agriculture in response to world market forces has been, and continues to be, a major cause of peasant support for revolutionary movements.[5]

Another consequence of commodification is individualism. As Max Weber (1978) lamented, monetized markets undermine traditional authority, including religious, familial, noble, caste, ethnic, and other nonmonetary relations that regulate production and/or distribution. What remain are instrumental interactions of individuals. As market forces become ever more important in regulating production and legal exchange, normative and ideological institutions emerge that constitute the individual as the main locus of social meaning and immanent value. Commodification also undermines nonmarket relationships among individuals that interfere with "productive efficiency" as constructed by the world of commerce. Exceptions exist, of course, where the advantages of social capital (such as a family or clan) outweigh the losses from particularistic selection. But the trend is that individualism has become ever more institutionalized and central in the moral orders of core capitalism since the Reformation and Renaissance. Families, religions, cultures, and nations remain as consumption groups with common "tastes," in economic parlance, but not as production units. Paradoxically, market individualism in production may enhance "traditional" identities in consumption as consumer choice increasingly becomes one of individual taste.

Not all collective solidarities and authority are undermined by individualism. The main collective solidarity that has flourished in the modern world has been the nation. We define the term "nation" here as a multiclass group of people that identify with one another based on a common culture and language, and who claim sovereignty over a contiguous piece of territory. An ethnic group differs only in lacking the last criterion (territory).

National collectivities flourish despite the strong forces of commodification and individualization for three main reasons. First, nationalism is a collective solidarity that is peculiarly well fitted to an individualist culture because nations allow for much variation in individual and subgroup identities. Nationalism is not a total identity. It is a specialized identity with a goodly chunk of *gesellschaft* to go with its *gemeinschaft*. This is one important difference between a nation and a clan or tribe. Anyone who shares territory and culture can develop national allegiance. That humans grow loyal to the persistently familiar aspects of their lives is recognized by armies as well as by advertisers. National armies are huge organizations of individuals, which replaced small armies based on clan alliances. As such, they replace the latter or other competing allegiances as organizing units for states.

Second, nationalism is legitimated by the same ideological forces that promote individualism as a constitutive element of global culture— the capitalist core states. Nationalism is the prime ideological and organizational form for mobilizing soldiers to defend the property of their wealthier conationals, and for undermining working-class challenges to capitalism.[6] The ideological legitimization of nationalism within international liberalism has helped to sustain capitalist property and capitalist states.

Third, nationalism has defined politics in the semiperiphery and the periphery. As we elaborate in the next section on decolonization, national self-determination provided a powerful legitimization for anti-imperialist movements and for the construction of political mechanisms of control over or protection against global market forces. Nationalism legitimates resistance to imperialism across class lines. The most serious challenges to capitalism as a logic of social organization—the socialist revolutions and communist states in the semiperiphery—utilized nationalism as a mainstay of mobilization despite their ideological rhetoric of international class solidarity. Further, because nationalism is a strongly held value among core states, appeals to national self-determination in the periphery have won increasing core support, especially after socialist and civil-rights movements stripped away racist justifications for colonialism. Proliferating national, ethnic, and indigenous identities, while ostensibly asserting cultural differences among people, have become increasingly isomorphic with regard to the structure of their legitimating ideologies. Ironically, these convergences facilitate the further institutionalization of multiculturalism and the rights of minorities within many national societies and in the emerging global moral order of human rights.

So, the way it works is that individualism undermined traditional authority, but fueled national identity. Proletarianization fostered a growing working class with a common interest in political democracy. With industrial development, working-class resource mobilization became capable of implementing democracy through *revolutionary movements* (Boswell and Dixon 1990, 1993). We would not want to completely reduce revolutionary movements and democratization to these two trends (individualism and proletarianization), but they are key long-term causes operating on a global scale.

Revolutions have occurred throughout world history in many guises, shapes, and places. We have pointed out that, not surprisingly, revolts were concentrated during periods of economic crises and following major wars, which have recurred cyclically through history. But, they are also related to a variety of conjunctural and structural factors not easily predictable nor directly related to systemic cycles. The effects of revolutions have also varied. Their effects on the world-system vary with the stability of global cycles and trends. Revolutionary movements have their greatest effects, intentional and unintentional, when systemic properties are in flux, producing world revolutions of lasting importance. With both hegemony and K-waves in transition, the world-system has recently entered a divide of greater fluidity than it has seen in a hundred years. Three world revolutions in the last fifty years have successively expanded the possibilities of human progress. Each revolution was less violent than the last, yet each raised possibilities that the next might achieve. The next world revolution, perhaps a nonviolent one, thus has great potential to stretch the boundaries of the system, and perhaps even to break them.

Decolonization

Decolonization is also a process with numerous antecedents, but as we have discussed, one that includes the effects of global dynamics. Colonial conquest by expanding core states served to force commodification onto peoples who were previously external to the system. Colonization increased during K-wave downturns when states used coercive means to replace failing markets, and receded during expansions (Boswell 1989a). In turn, coercion adds less value as markets spread and expand. Also, industrialization makes traditional colonial production an increasingly smaller part of the global product. Colonization eventually became irrelevant for the purposes of labor extraction, and the vast unused labor reserves it forced into existence have instead become a drag on the world economy. Much of that drag was due to the revolutionary resistance of colonial populations to their subordination. Once the great source of "primitive accumulation," after World War II colonialism probably cost industrial core powers more in administrative and military spending than they received in coerced unequal exchange. To be sure, few imperialists gave up their empires without a fight, but neither did they suffer heavily from the loss.

Neocolonial dependency would produce high profits in the "free" market, making coerced exchange increasingly less remunerative.

Hegemons have historically supported decolonization (other than in their own colonies). With a comparative advantage in key industries, they profit most from trade unhindered by imperial regulation. The cyclical combination of U.S. hegemony and a massive K-wave economic expansion following World War II provided resources to national-liberation movements and made colonial wars increasingly costly. By 1960, decolonization became inevitable and irreversible, and was recognized as an important part of the world order by UN declaration. This is extraordinarily different from the prewar period, when the greatest number of colonies ever was in 1939 and political expansion by the core powers became a zero-sum struggle. The breakup of empires has continued with the dissolution of multination states. The United Kingdom, Canada, France, and Spain all suffer separatist movements of varying stripes and some of these will likely succeed. In the semiperiphery, India and China are possible candidates to break apart, and in the periphery the logic of maintaining colonial boundaries fades in relationship to the world market, meaning many states in sub-Saharan Africa might seek to change their borders.

With decolonization has come a marked upturn in the pace and degree of world economic and political integration. This is usually explained by reference to technological changes in transportation and communication, and these have undoubtedly played important roles. Decolonization has also been important in replacing administrative relations with market ones, and in dissolving imperial barriers to the world market. Capital mobility to the low-wage periphery, always a feature of capitalism, has accelerated as political impediments have been removed and technology has become more portable. Growing integration of the world economy has, in turn, a contradictory effect on states, encouraging states to both shrink and to expand at the same time. That is, older multi*nation* (imperial) states are shrinking down to nations just when new, larger multi*state* governments are emerging.

On the one hand, transnational capital shifts the political focus to international relations, where only sovereign states are recognized actors. This rule of the world order was originally established following the devastation of the Thirty Years' War. It only applied to a handful of core nation-states, which outside the core were, ironically, colonial empires. From about 1648 to 1948, the core and the periphery had strikingly different politics, what we might call nation-state politics versus class-nation politics. In the core, states were legitimated as representing nations, although many contained subordinate ethnic groups. Each state vied with other competing nation-states for leadership and hegemony over the system. Classes within those states fought over political power and economic distribution.

In the periphery, almost all nations were colonies. By defining themselves as nation-states, core states ruled their colonies in racist terms. As colonies of core imperialists, politics in the periphery often fused class and national conflicts over the issues of economic and political independence. While the class-nations of the colonial periphery largely won the conflict for political independence, thus becoming nation-states themselves, they mainly lost the struggle for economic independence. Ironically, though dependency theory has been largely dismissed by many establishment intellectuals in both the core and the periphery, the recent expansion of capitalist globalization has put most of the ex-colonial countries in a situation of greater economic dependence than when dependency theory was quite popular. Rather than dependence on the former imperial "mother" countries, they now face dependence on an unholy alliance of name-brand companies and anonymous investors. The alleged requirements of competitiveness in the world market would seem to preclude any action that might sour the business climate for the transnational firms.

The explosion of nations in the last decade has also been facilitated by the decline of U.S. hegemony.[7] The ideologies of the Cold War helped to restrain ethnic groups from national aspirations, as did the political and military power of the United States and the Soviet Union. With these Cold War forces now irrelevant, nationalism emerges unrestrained by the once daunting prospect of triggering a nuclear world war.

Globalization

As we have shown in Figure 1.1 in Chapter 1, economic globalization is both a long-term cumulative trend and a cycle of expanding and intensifying links. But the pace of this integrative process has accelerated markedly since the mid-1970s as a response, and a solution, to an uneven and stagnant world economy. The world economy has gone through long K-wave phases of stagnation, the solution to which has been new social structures of accumulation. Each solution has been different. The current phase involves a rapid increase in world integration in part because the concurrent culmination of U.S. hegemony and of decolonization eliminated vast political barriers to global competition and interpenetration.[8] The Soviet collapse was perhaps the most striking dissolution of political barriers. This has further hastened the pace of integration. In a cumulative process, even a small increase in growth rates soon has large effects. The result is a conspicuous qualitative shift in political structures within a single generation that accompanies the less perceptible ongoing changes. Adaptation to the process now elicits integral rather than incremental change. What is the result of a long-term process thus appears to contemporary observers as entirely novel.

States have long been subjected to international economic forces in the modern world-system. Starting with the Italian city-states in the fifteenth century, states have been both beneficiaries and victims of relying on international economic developments (Arrighi 1994). States appropriate income from raising their share of international trade and financial operations. They also appropriate income (and soldiers) from their own populations, especially in large territorial empires, which is an advantage in times of prolonged land wars. In times of peace, the advantage shifts to trading nations, and maintaining large imperial boundaries and large armies becomes increasingly costly. With fifty years passing since the last prolonged land war among core powers, and none in sight, most all states in the system are devoting their efforts to export promotion and the expanding international economic activities (Iraq and Iran are exceptions in several senses). As international transactions have become a greater proportion of all transactions, states increasingly orient their economic policies toward coping with, and trying to benefit from, the international economic environment. This further expands trade in a mutually reinforcing cycle. The cycle can be broken and reversed by war, such that the 1914 mark of trade globalization has only recently been surpassed (i.e., Figure 1.1).

The term "globalization" is used in social science and in popular discourse to mean quite a number of different things. We contend that it is important to distinguish between globalization as a contemporary political ideology and globalization as the increasing density of worldwide interaction networks relative to the density of national-level networks, which we call "structural globalization." Phil McMichael (1996) has studied the rise of "the globalization project"—the abandoning of Keynesian models of national development and a new emphasis on deregulation and opening national commodity and financial markets to foreign trade and investment. This is to point to the ideological aspects of the recent wave of international economic integration. The political term commonly used for this turn in political discourse is "neoliberalism."

The structural basis of the rise of the globalization project is the new level of integration reached by the global capitalist class. The internationalization of capital has long been an important part of the trend toward economic globalization. There have been many claims to represent the general interests of business before—indeed, every hegemon has made this claim—but the real integration of interests of the capitalists in each of the core states has reached a level greater than ever before in the latest round of structural globalization. This is the part of the model of a global stage of capitalism that must be taken seriously, though it can certainly be overdone. The world-system has now reached a point at which both the old interstate system based on separate national capitalist classes and new institutions representing the global interests of capitalists coexist and are powerful simultaneously. In this light, each country can be seen to have an important ruling-class fraction that is allied with the transnational capitalist class. This is an important development for the organizational prospects of a transnational popular opposition.

Neoliberalism began as the Reagan-Thatcher attack on the welfare state and on labor unions. It evolved into the structural adjustment policies of the International Monetary Fund and the triumphalism of global business after the demise of the Soviet Union. In U.S. foreign policy, it has found expression in a new emphasis on "democracy promotion" in the periphery and semiperiphery. Rather than propping up military dictatorships in Latin America, the emphasis has shifted toward coordinated action between the CIA and the U.S. National Endowment for Democracy to promote electoral institutions in Latin America and other semiperipheral and peripheral regions (Robinson 1996). Robinson points out that the kind of "low intensity democracy" that is being promoted is really best understood as "polyarchy," a regime form in which elites orchestrate a process of electoral competition and governance that legitimates state power. In so doing, it undercuts more radical political alternatives that might threaten the ability of national elites to maintain their wealth and power. Robinson convincingly argues that polyarchy and democracy-promotion are the political forms that are most congruent with a globalized and neoliberal world economy in which capital is given free rein to move to wherever profits are greatest.

World integration makes increasingly irrelevant any imperial authority that stands between the nation and the world market. This fuels independence movements as each ethnic group finds that its interests are increasingly difficult to represent domestically. Every nationality must have a sovereign state to operate at the global level. Military dominance by national minorities or neocolonists now pays fewer benefits as well. As a result, the geographic size of states is shrinking down to the size of nations. States ruling over multiple nations will continue to break up for the foreseeable future. New peripheral states now mimic the rules of what was the core world order of nation-states. There are as many as 3,000 ethnic nations with geographic identities. If only 20 percent achieve statehood, it would triple the number of states. The smaller and more specialized each nation-state, the greater the benefits to each of multistate government.

At the same time, world integration also fuels both regional economic integration and international political organization. Most noticeable are the three regional economic blocs of the European Common Market, NAFTA, and AFTA (Asian Free Trade Association). Older international political organizations, such as the UN, NATO, and the OAS (Organization of American States), are taking on new tasks and missions as they lose their Cold War definition. Meanwhile, the new WTO and numerous other IGOs are being formed with governance powers far greater than their predecessors. Of these, the EU comes the closest to being a multistate government. The biggest increase in global organization has been in global "civil society," as indicated by the geometric rise in the number of INGOs discussed earlier. The growth has mainly come in international versions of economic and professional organizations, but includes a rapid rise in sports, arts, entertainment, education, environmental, and women's organizations.

The rise of international organization follows a basic principle of contracting in markets. Any voluntary contract requires precontractual agreement on definitions and standards, and postcontractual enforcement or adjudication by a third party. This has been the function of the world order, to which core states have acceded peacefully for long periods only when a hegemon reinforced it. In the place of declining U.S. hegemony, a world polity is emerging from shared standards set by international organizations and shared norms of human rights and environmental protection set by global movements. Postmodern cultural relativity and national liberalism for citizens are giving way to a single global culture. As a global civil society, the phenomenal growth in INGOs largely serves the precontractual function, while the IGOs are haltingly being driven to become the "post" third-party enforcers. The greater the number of states and the decline of multinational states (empires), the greater the need for global and regional international authorities to adjudicate conflicts, guarantee standards, and otherwise regulate exchanges.

Multistate Hegemony and Global Governance

Three regional international economic blocs are emerging to dominate the world economy—the European Union, the North American Free Trade Association, and the Asian Free Trade Area.[9] As just these three regions will regulate the vast bulk of the world economy, a common standard among them would constitute an effective global standard. Yet none of the three is hegemonic over the other two. This creates an unprecedented opportunity for international and transnational social movements to have worldwide political effects (Pagnucco and Atwood 1994).

The long-term trend toward greater international political integration is likely to eventually result in the emergence of a world state (Chase-Dunn 1990a). The continued rise of global governance is most visible in the activities of the Group of Seven and the establishment of the World Trade Organization. Yet these institutions are still far from what would be a true world state. The question is how long the trend will take and what might happen to reverse it. Establishing a world state with sufficient security capability to prevent the recurrence of warfare among core states is clearly in the interest of all humanity. A new outbreak of warfare among core states, though it might begin on a "limited" basis using "conventional" weapons, could possibly degenerate into a war based on weapons of mass destruction if one side faces the choice of defeat versus using these weapons. Under these conditions, it is desirable, even necessary, for a true world state with sufficient political and military power to prevent warfare among core states to emerge.

How might such a world state come into existence?[10] We discussed the growth of international organizations that has been going on for at least 150 years and has accelerated wildly in the last twenty years (Boli and Thomas 1997). World-level governance, albeit not a world state, is becoming institutionalized. International capitalists have been the prime beneficiaries of global regulation, as is attested by the IMF and the WTO. Core states and capitalists do not want the massive economic and political upheavals that accompany collapse of the world monetary system, and so they support efforts to regulate "ruinous" competition and beggar-thy-neighbor politics. They also fear new wars and new holocausts, and so with reluctance may support strengthened global governance that can effectively adjudicate conflicts among nation-states.

In some ultimate sense, effective adjudication means the establishment of a global monopoly of legitimate violence. The process of state formation has a long history, based on the king's army being bigger than any combination of private armies that might be brought against him. While the idea of a world state may be a frightening specter to some, we are optimistic about it for several reasons. First, a world state is probably the most direct and stable way to prevent world war, a desideratum that must be at the top of everyone's list.[11] Secondly, the creation of a global state that can peacefully adjudicate disputes among nations will transform the existing interstate system. The interstate system is the political structure that stands behind the maneuverability of capital and its ability to escape organized workers and the social and environmental costs of profitable accumulation. While a world state may at first be largely controlled by capitalists, the very existence of such a state will provide a single focus for struggles to socially regulate investment decisions and to create the more balanced, egalitarian, and ecologically sound form of production and distribution discussed in the previous chapter. World revolutions take on a different meaning, and far more potency, when a world polity already exists to implement political demands from below.

In order to serve as an instrument for pacifying the next bout of hegemonic rivalry, a world state would need to emerge within the next few decades. This is time frame suggested by earlier cycles of warfare, hegemony, and the K-wave that we have outlined at the beginning of this chapter. If a K-wave upswing begins soon, or already has begun, it should be approaching its next peak in about 2015 or 2020. The period surrounding that peak is a window of vulnerability to another war among core states because past growth means that arms spending is not a heavy drag on the economy and because contending states will be anticipating a new period of increasing competition.

Although possible, we must admit that it is not probable that a true world government with the effective power to outlaw warfare among core states will emerge in the next few decades. Current events suggest that the probability is low even for a small UN force to accompany renewed national disarmament. In order to be a world government, the UN would need to democratically represent the peoples of the world and the realities of the world distribution of economic, political, and military power. At present, due to its construction after World War II, the United Nations Security Council does not even include Japan, Germany, or Italy. Further, the principle of the representation of states rather than people, a compromise intended to institutionalize the sovereign rights of nations, undermines the democratic legitimacy of the UN and obstructs its ability to intervene in favor of peoples whose human rights have been abused by member states. Reform of the United Nations has been discussed for decades but it is barely under way.

The International Monetary Fund and the new World Trade Organization are arguably important organs of the emerging world state that are supported by the most international fraction of the capitalist class. IMF dictates of draconian government policies as a prerequisite of loans, such as the recent U.S.-engineered bailout of Korea, must surely seem like world governance to national states desperate to restore the amity of global investors. Yet, as with the UN in the Gulf War, the full strength of the global economic governance still depends on U.S. leadership. As U.S. hegemony continues to decline, we should expect the United States to become more like other countries, with a high dissonance between its particular national interests and the general global interests, and between local and global segments of its population. The United States could undermine the WTO by continuing to pursue unilateral trade sanctions (most recently threatened against Japan) or undermine its leadership by trivializing it (through actions such as attempting to enforce the Helms-Burton Act against Cuba).

The great rush toward world government feared by patriotic (white) militiamen in the rural United States may appear to have stalled, at least in Weberian terms of monopolizing the military. The forces producing a long-term trend in international economic integration, however, are continuing to increase nonmilitary world governance. We fully expect continued proliferation of international organizations, both governmental and nongovernmental, although the pace of growth should slow as the absolute number has increased. World governance is here and we expect existing international organizations to take on ever greater importance, even if they never bear the name of a world government.

A further move toward world government (whether democratic or not) requires the initiative of a new world leader. If uneven development concentrates the leading economic sectors in one of the regional contenders for hegemony (EU, NAFTA, or AFTA), the leader would benefit most from a world government designed to enforce its version of "free" trade. The leader could then become hegemonic by institutionalizing its advantages in a world government. This creates the possibility of hegemonic rise without a global war, a historical first. It would be a major change in the nature of hegemony, but not necessarily a change in the cycle and would not by itself fundamentally alter the world-system. For fundamental change in the system, a world revolution would have to force the world government to become a democratic institution rather than a hegemonic instrument.

One chain of possible events proceeds from the democratization of states, to democratization of larger multistate polities (including the world leader), to global democracy. If the "two steps forward one step back" pattern of the past continues, a coalescence of global movements around democratizing international governance would be the first step, which could lead to the democratization of the multistate polities. A second world revolution might be necessary to institutionalize global democracy and initiate a socialist world bank, and so on. Subsequent world revolutions may not be necessary once electoral institutions for enacting global change are in place, although they cannot be ruled out. Nor can we rule out violent reactions against movements for global democracy. Violent actions initiated by global progressive movements, however, should be ruled out as a tactic or strategy in most cases. The experience of the last two world revolutions shows quite dramatically that movements that employ violent means against elected governments (and even against some communist ones) lose their popular support and can be crushed with impunity. Conversely, states that resort to extralegal violence against peaceful movements with wide support can trigger massive protests and international condemnation.

With modern media, even a single violent incident can become the subject of endless repetition and worldwide awareness. The extent of popular grief over celebrity tragedies (such as Princess Diana) or of horror over police brutality (such as Rodney King) is astounding. What particular event triggers a global response cannot be predicted. In fact, it must be unpredictable and unexpected by definition in order to capture media attention. What we can predict is that a world revolution is more likely to be triggered by some event during a world divide. We will also predict that a worldwide outpouring of protests, demonstrations, and concerted global actions that make up a world revolution will be necessary to change the conceptions and institutions of the world-system.

A new hegemon, whether it pushes for world government or not, is perhaps fifty years away, so speculation now about who the new hegemon might be is mostly a guessing game. Nevertheless, there are a few obvious possibilities: another round for the United States, this time with NAFTA; German-led European Union; Japan-led AFTA; or an alternative multistate in the form of Greater China. We contend that one of these has a greater propensity to support global democratization than the other three—the European Union. The European Union has the only institutional framework for multistate representative democracy. It also has the strongest and most organized working class to fight for global democracy. An institutional framework and an organized working class were the two key ingredients to democratization in the past. Europe also has the most extensive social-welfare system, and thus the most to lose from competition from highly exploited low-wage labor in authoritarian states. European workers, and their capitalists, would gain from the rise in wages and welfare elsewhere brought on by global democracy. Although most strongly supported by Europe, any movement for a democratic world government would still need to be coordinated transnationally by global movements.

Is the European Union the most likely next world leader? Many systemic theorists once pointed to Japan's concentration of leading economic sectors as making it best poised to contend for world leadership. If global war returns, as a homogeneous island country, Japan is also relatively insulated from conventional land war. Without a global war to decimate competitors, however, Japan would need to develop an international framework in order to lead. The EU's most important innovation is its regional federal framework, which places it in the best position to develop common world standards and expand interstate regulations

(Bornschier 1996). NAFTA is a poor copy, unable to include a multistate governance structure due to the previous sunk investment in U.S. hegemony and resistance to it. Although AFTA and other trade pacts exist in Asia, none compare to the EU or even NAFTA in regulating contracts.

Besides the three other contenders we identify, some look to Greater China, made up of China, Taiwan, Hong Kong, and overseas Chinese in Singapore and elsewhere, as perhaps an alternative type of hegemonic contender (Weede 1999). But, China also houses a huge impoverished peasantry that will consume the benefits of its high growth for decades before reaching European standards of living. Without Japan, China is not a contender, and vice versa. Japan is not part of Greater China, and the legacy of past antagonisms makes it unlikely that Japan and China could attain significant political integration.

It is the social innovation of multistate governance that gives Europe its potential lead, which others (NAFTA, AFTA) are following. Successful implementation of the euro currency will be the deciding factor in establishing its potential. Narrow focus on technical innovation obscures this advantage. Technical "backwardness," in that assembly-line production was less developed and craft traditions remain stronger than in the United States, may actually aid Europe in the transition to flexible production in some cases. Europe also has cultural advantages, and some disadvantages, with respect to its hegemonic competitors. Past European hegemony over other continents has produced shared languages and cultural institutions, but it has also produced a backlash against Eurocentrism. Both the United Kingdom and the United States benefit in present and future competition because the English language has become a global lingua franca. Both potential future leaders would seem to benefit from the assumed fact that the civilizational ideology and the institutional structures have a European origin. Indeed our own espousal of the values of democracy and equality could be interpreted as one more attempt to impose the ideas of the European Enlightenment on the peoples of the world. The critique of Eurocentrism in postcolonial thought is an important cultural element of resistance that the emergent movement for global democracy needs to take seriously. We have already pointed out that in our view Europeans did not dominate and exploit the rest of the world because of their work ethic or their ideology about rights and equality. Rather, it was the institutions of capitalism and imperialism that allowed Europeans to develop powerful military capabilities that were the main causes of European hegemony. In addition, we think that it is a massive mistake to attribute the values of egalitarianism and democracy exclusively to the European Enlightenment. These values were important in all human societies on Earth prior to the rise of institutionalized hierarchies. Thus, these values are part of the cultural heritages of all humans.

Ironically, the lack of imperialism beyond the East Asian region, along with different alphabets, means that linguistics is a limiting factor on the future global leadership potential of Japan and China. Bornschier (1996) contends that Japanese culture has little to offer in terms of a universalistic ideology that could potentially serve as the basis of a future hegemony. The recent experience of Europeans with multilingualism and multiculturalism places them in an excellent spot to champion these values on a global scale.

On the negative side of the ledger of potential future European leadership, we already mentioned that European companies have fared poorly in marketing technical innovations. Japan has done much better in this regard, although a long recession in the 1990s has reduced its prominence. The United States has had a huge advantage because of its much greater domestic-market size, although this comparative advantage is declining as European integration becomes more of a reality. The United States is still the world's policeman in terms of military power. Both Germany and Japan have constitutional amendments that greatly restrict their military capabilities. although trial balloons have risen in both about moving toward the rebuilding of military capability. These have been supported in some cases by the U.S. government under pressure to reduce its military expenditures. In most respects, the United States is still far ahead on economic indicators and, while still in a relative decline, equalization is still far off. But recall the discussion of U.S. hegemonic decline in Chapter 1 in which we pointed out that effective European economic integration will create a situation of global bipolarity of economic power, with the European Union and United States having nearly equal shares of the global product.

Modelski and Thompson (1996) predict a renewal of U.S. leadership in condominium with an alliance of core states constituted as global democracy. They contend that the new level of global economic integration and the enhanced potential for international communications due to information technologies make it likely that a new structure of global leadership can emerge without having to go through the trial of another world war. The pace of U.S. economic growth has fared better in the 1990s than the stodgy European pace or the Asian roller coaster. But we see big problems in store for the United States when the economy again slows down because of the extremely high internal inequality that has been created by decades of neoliberal streamlining and downsizing.

Europeans are now faced with the choice of either adopting the United States' lean and mean approach in order to combat unemployment or, as we advocate, pushing through world standards that raise the minimum for their competitors. So far, neoliberal streamlining appears to have the upper hand over the global project. Whether or not the EU is a strong contender for hegemony in the capitalist world-system, it has the most powerful institutions to support a world movement toward a global democracy. To be sure, global democracy is not something a hegemon or a capitalist-dominated world government will pursue itself. Instead, it will require transnational progressive organizing of such an unprecedented nature and scale that on looking back on these events we will have to say they achieved a world revolution.

The big picture and the long run also need to be kept in mind. Wagar's idea that global capitalism might self-destruct by means of war among core states is not without foundation in the dynamics of the system as presently constituted. Recall our scenario at the beginning of this chapter. A second sort of doom is also quite possible—that of a massive disruption of the global ecosystem. As Peter Taylor (1996) and many others have pointed out, the current development mode in which everyone is trying to consume as many resources and produce as much pollution as the Americans simply cannot continue. If the Chinese drive as many cars in the same ways as Americans now do, the biosphere will fry. Something new needs to happen regarding the plans for development. Taylor thinks that ecofascism, the rich building walls around their idyllic tree-filled parks to keep out the teeming poor, is a likely future. The current arguments about timetables for reducing pollution and the questionable justice of the rich North preaching to the poor South about sustainability while continuing to gobble up fossil fuels at an unprecedented rate (and at a historically low price), do not bode well for the possibility that these problems will be resolved without dire catastrophe.

Those of us who want to transform the system might take heart that "Doom One" (war) or "Doom Two" (environmental collapse), or some combination of the two, will produce a level of attention and readiness for change that patient organizing cannot. Wagar's deus ex machina is there in part because it is difficult to imagine that the ostrich will take its head out of the sand without a swift kick. But it is immoral to simply bide time waiting for massive disasters to occur so that we may take advantage of them. Instead, we must proceed as suggested above to organize a political force that can democratize the system and that will try to prevent these new holocausts from happening. But we should also be aware that these efforts may not succeed, and that it would also be wise to prepare a "Plan B" of the sort discussed by Wagar. These decisions that need not be made now, except for understanding and keeping in mind that reform and revolution required hard-fought conflict and that the past trend of progress was never inevitable.

The Link

Samir Amin (1990) contends that the agents of socialism and social progress are most heavily concentrated in the periphery. It is there that the capitalist world-system is most oppressive, and thus peripheral workers and peasants, the vast majority of the world proletariat, have the most to win and the least to lose. The presumption is that a string of revolutions in the periphery would brake global capital expansion, forcing core states and TNCs to either raise peripheral living standards or face global depression. If the latter were to occur, which is most likely, the resulting economic collapse would force core workers (especially immigrant and minority workers at the bottom) to join in the global movement to overthrow core states and TNCs.

The main problem with "Third Worldism" is not motivation, but opportunity. Where socialist movements have taken state power in the periphery, they are soon beset by powerful external forces that either overthrow or force them to abandon most of their socialist program. The example of Nicaragua is telling. Its stunning success at expanding literacy and health care reminds us of what socialist states can accomplish. Yet the Contra invasion, internal class polarization and economic collapse, and ultimate vote for capitulation in exchange for peace and aid, reasserted the limits of even popular democratic state action.

We have noted that antisystemic movements in the periphery have most usually been anti-imperialist class alliances, which succeeded in establishing at least the trappings of national sovereignty but not much in the way of social progress. Low levels of economic development make it simply harder to share power and wealth when there are very little of either. Socialists in the periphery must concentrate on economic development. To develop, the peripheral countries need capital and technology not locally available, and which must therefore be imported from core capitalist countries. National liberation, the biggest success of Third World socialism, is thus in constant tension with its central goal, economic development.

On the other hand, Marx and many contemporary Marxists have argued that socialism will be most effectively built by the action of industrial proletarians in the core of the world-system. Since core areas have already attained a high level of technological development, the establishment of socialized production and distribution should be easiest in the core. In addition, organized core workers have had the longest experience with industrial capitalism and the most opportunity to create socialist social relations. The presumption here has been that a string of revolutions would bring socialist governments throughout the core (perhaps through elections at least in part). A coalition of socialist states would then harness TNCs and set up global institutions for raising living standards in the periphery.

In contrast to the periphery, core workers may have experience and opportunity, but important sectors of core labor have lacked material interest and motivation. In the past, core industrial workers rarely competed directly with raw-material producers in the periphery, and they often benefited from the low cost of colonial imports. Their struggles were thus directed internally. High levels of development allowed core firms to pay wages and core states to incorporate labor in a way that averted radical political challenges to the power of capital. As we noted earlier, socialist movements by core industrial workers produced social-democratic welfare states, which in turn, reduced their exploitation and the threat of poverty. Capital paid key sectors of labor decent wages, resulting in a nonconfrontational relationship and relatively steady growth.

A large stratum of middle managers, professionals, and technical workers gained added leverage as agents of capital who directly controlled production. They were paid a loyalty bonus for their allegiance to employers in addition to their productivity. The existence of this "labor aristocracy" divided the working class in the core and undermined radical political challenges to capitalism. Nevertheless, it is true that even small victories in the core (e.g., further expansion of the welfare state, opposition to imperial policies, etc.) have important effects on peripheral and semiperipheral areas because of the relative power of core states.

We contend that both the "Third Worldist" and the core "workerist" positions have elements of truth in that both would be necessary in any thorough transformation of the system. The struggles over social standards, such as child labor and living wages, that are going on right now in the periphery will determine the direction of world labor-market competition, toward social-democratic competition over increasing human and social capital, or toward neoliberal competition toward the lowest wages and least-regulated investment. These are momentous consequences from thousands of small struggles that are never decided once, and never all in the same direction, but which can be pushed to trend in one direction or another. At the community and firm level where most of these struggles take place, transnational corporations and their subcontractors face a predominantly female labor force that is often desperate for paying jobs and heavily restrained legally and socially by patriarchy. Fought alone, the odds for a progressive result from these conflicts are not good.

In the core, labor and social movements that had been disorganized by international competition and declining efficacy of the welfare states (which we will discuss below), have begun to organize at the global and multistate level. As elsewhere, their struggles to improve their conditions are often organized along nationalist lines that could lead to protectionism and new forms of imperialist relations. Yet, the very same impetus is inspiring a solidarity strategy, one that pushes to raise the standards of competitors and to democratize global institutions.

Even as we recognize the necessity of both core and periphery movements, as well as the difference between them, we must also recognize that neither alone is a sufficient source of transformative global change. The link can be found in the zone of the world-system in which core and periphery intersect, the semiperiphery. To borrow a phrase, the semiperiphery is the weak link of the capitalist world economy.

Consider for a moment previous transformations between modes of production. In a comparative study of world-systems, Chase-Dunn and Hall (1997) studied the transition from kin-based modes of accumulation to state-based and capitalist modes over the last 12,000 years of social evolution. Their comparison of these transformations produced some tentative analogies about the possibility of a future transformation. They note that capitalists first came to state power in city-states located in semiperipheral areas of world-systems dominated by the tributary modes of accumulation. Semiperipheral societies were frequently the agents of those organizational and institutional changes that have produced social evolution and the transformation of modes of accumulation throughout recorded history. Chase-Dunn and Hall contend that semiperipheral locations are especially conducive to institutional innovations that have the potential to transform systemic logic. However, while sufficient to initiate global change, semiperipheral states were not sufficient to complete transformations. This required core states. It was not until capitalism came to control core states that the capitalist mode became predominant. Only after a long period in which market relations within and between states and empires had grown in importance were core states able to sustain a stable commitment to accumulation through commodity production for the world market. Thus, seen in a long-run comparative perspective, semiperipheral struggles and innovations have been crucial for fostering struggles and innovations within core states, and the latter have been crucial for eventual systemic transformation.

A new mode of accumulation builds by accretion in the interstices of an old one. A vivid contrast between the historical transition to capitalism and the potential transition to democratic socialism stems from differences in the logic of the two modes of accumulation. Capitalism can exist and thrive as a subsystem in the interstices of another mode of production, as it did for many centuries, gradually creating the institutional bases for its own eventual predominance. Its individualist and partial rationality thrives in a competitive and conflictive setting.

Democratic socialism, on the other hand, is a holistic mode of accumulation in which the whole arena of interaction needs to be organized on a collectively rational and democratic basis in which reciprocity and politically articulated redistribution play an important role. So efforts to build socialist relations (those that survive) tend to become reintegrated into the institutional logic of capitalism because they are exposed to the strong forces of the larger capitalist system.

Semiperipheral Socialism

The obstacles in the way of socialist movements in the periphery have been somewhat less daunting in the semiperiphery. Here we have had both motivation and opportunity. Semiperipheral areas are the terrain upon which the strongest efforts to establish socialism have been made in the past, and this is likely to be true of the future as well, even if names for it change. These states often have sufficient resources to be able to stave off core attempts at overthrow and to provide some protection to socialist institutions (such as national health care) if the political conditions for their emergence should arise. Semiperipheral revolutions and movements are not always socialist in character, as we have seen in Iran, but even these revolts set limits on core exploitation and provide alternative models for peripheral development. With the dissolution of the Soviet bloc, few revolutionaries can be unambiguously placed in a single category or camp in any case. Most, however, identify international capitalists as having enormous power over their destinies with little recourse, control, or consent. In general, semiperipheral regions have experienced more militant class-based movements because of their intermediate position in the core-periphery hierarchy (most notably in the NICs). While core exploitation of the periphery creates and sustains alliances among classes in both the core and the periphery, in the semiperiphery an intermediate world-system position undermines class alliances and provides a fruitful terrain for strong challenges to capitalism.

The Cuban Revolution in many ways confirms the hypothesis of semiperipheral revolutionary potential. For at least a century, Cuba had been semiperipheral with regard to its intermediate level of development and intermediary position between the United States and Latin America. The combined and uneven nature of Cuban society created a fertile terrain for revolution. But the peculiar geopolitical context in which the revolution took place during the Cold War acted to reproduce Cuba's dependence on sugar exports as a condition of its new dependency on the Soviet Union (Ekstein 1994). The relative recentness of the Cuban Revolution, along with accomplishments in the areas of education and health care, accounts for its greater resilience and resistance to recent changes in the larger world-system. Dissolution of the Soviet bloc threw Cuba into a deep depression, made worse by a tightening of the U.S. embargo. The lack of Cuban democracy prevents concerted international resistance to U.S. intervention, despite heavy investment and tourism from the rest of the Americas and Europe. Castro is using this investment and tourism to slowly rebuild a Cuban niche in the world economy with some surprising success, but also with the recognition that foreign investors and the world market hold far greater sway over people's livelihoods. Without supportive changes in the world-system, this type of niche may be the best that semiperipheral socialist states such as Cuba can accomplish. Though we support the democratization of the remaining socialist states and we hope they will support the movement toward global democracy, we expect that new revolutions in semiperipheral countries will be the strongest sources of such support (Chase-Dunn and Boswell 1999).

Once again, the core has developed new lead industries—computers and biotechnology—and much of large-scale heavy industry, the classical terrain of strong labor movements and socialist parties, has moved to the semiperiphery. This means that labor and socialist movements that bid for state power in the semiperiphery (e.g., South Africa, Brazil, Mexico, Korea) will be based more on an urbanized and organized proletariat in large-scale industry than were the earlier semiperipheral socialist revolutions in Russia and China. This should have positive consequences for the nature of these movements and for linking with similar movements in the core and periphery. The relationship between the city and the countryside should also be less antagonistic, and there should be far greater support for internal democracy, which will lessen the likelihood of core interference. The global expansion of communications has increased the salience of events in the semiperiphery for audiences in the core and this may serve to dampen core state intervention into the affairs of democratic semiperipheral states. With globalization, semiperipheral movements will have an unprecedented opportunity to initiate and coordinate a new approach to transnational firms that can link with core labor and social movements as well as national movements in the periphery. It is in this sense that the semiperiphery is the weak link of the capitalist world-system.

U.S. Socialism?

The European Union, we have argued, could be an important actor in generating multistate institutions that are democratic and that provide openings for progressive social movements. What does our world-system theory imply about progressive and socialist politics in the United States as we enter the new millennium? The United States is a declining hegemonic core state. This does not mean that the United States is in decline itself, but that its relative position in the system has changed. The processes of continental imperial expansion, economic mobility, and military success that have long undermined socialist and labor politics in the United States are less salient now. Further, a rise in inequality and decline in racial discrimination makes class distinctions more obvious, while a steady demographic shift toward a greater minority and female labor force increasingly lines up class with status distinctions. Structurally, there should be new openings for progressive movements and class politics in the long run.

This might seem unlikely given the current strength of global neoliberalism in terms of unrestrained world markets and, within the United States, the unusually strong and highly individualistic practice of national liberalism in terms of citizen-only rights. Yet, we have argued that global and national liberalism have come into contradiction and decline. Workers and other progressive groups within the United States will, we think, break out of the conceptual straitjacket of liberalism to try new ways to create equality and social democracy. That said, we see no possible scenario in which the United States might experience a radical socialist revolution in which a working-class party seizes state power and socializes the major means of production. Even if (when) an economic recession becomes a political crisis, a revolutionary situation requires a weak and undemocratic state, a weak and divided ruling class, a highly exploited but organized working class, and a strong and well-organized socialist party. These conditions are lacking and are not likely to emerge.

Social revolution, however, is not the only road to socialism. John Stephens (1980) has shown that important steps toward democratic socialism can be achieved by the route of the "democratic class struggle" within capitalist core states (see also, Korpi 1983; Przeworski 1985). In the United States, the eventual return of progressives to electoral power in a context in which the old liberal ideology has been exhausted may be fertile ground for the struggle for economic democracy. This prospect is enhanced by the demise of the "Soviet threat." The search for new bogeymen to legitimate the military-industrial complex is intense (e.g., Huntington 1996), but the openings for progressive politics are widening and will eventually be exploited by politicians who are willing to take the associated risks. Currently unable to see through or past the twin hegemony of liberalism, at some point the media circle of policymakers and commentators will suddenly and simultaneously discover its decline. Proposals for national investment planning, national health insurance, and even guaranteed jobs replacing welfare have not left the American political discourse and will return to its political forefront.

Investment politics, for instance, are currently being debated in terms of whether to invest the Social Security trust fund in the stock market. Much of this debate revolves around how to protect the stock market from state interference and how to protect the elderly from the stock market. While we are concerned more with the latter than the former, cronyism and pork-barrel politics are genuine concerns for market socialism (as China illustrates). Missing in this debate, however, is the potential for workers and others to exercise the type of control over capital now reserved only for the wealthiest 1 percent of the population. The government could offer coupons in a choice of mutual-fund plans, which could compete for investment on social and environmental grounds (with encouraging tax incentives) as well as on market returns. Couple this with a requirement that corporations must in part be owned by their employees, and we lay the foundation for a huge transfer of wealth, and the power of wealth, to the working and middle classes that would grow over time. Such reforms will not come easy, and even if successful will not in themselves constitute socialism or even social democracy in any coherent sense. They will not excite revolutionary passions and utopian dreams. Nevertheless, we should not underestimate the great potential contribution of such programs to social justice in the United States and abroad. Global changes will not occur without social changes in the core of the system.

These considerations lead us back to our discussion of socialist relations at the level of the whole world-system. The emergence of democratic collective rationality (socialism) at the world-system level is likely to be a slow process. The problem that we began with is that, left within its national borders, state socialism remained an authoritarian development project (as to a lesser extent has state-led capitalism in the NICs). The national results of these efforts have undoubtedly been important experiments within the logic of socialism, but they have left much to be desired. The tendency for authoritarian regimes to emerge in the communist states betrayed Marx's notion of a freely constituted association of direct producers, and the imperial control of Eastern Europe by the Russians was an insult to the idea of proletarian internationalism. The history of state socialism has increased our collective knowledge about how to build socialism despite these partial successes and obvious failures. It is important for all of us who want to build a more humane and peaceful world-system to understand the lessons of socialist movements in the semiperiphery, and the potential for future, more successful forms. As we have argued throughout, democracy within and between nations is a constituent element of the logic of socialism.

Some critics of the world-systems perspective have argued that emphasis on the structural importance of global relations necessarily leads to political "do-nothingism" while we wait for socialism to emerge at the world level. Agency seems elusive. We have tried to redress these criticisms. The world-systems perspective does indeed encourage us to examine global-level constraints and opportunities. In so doing, it allows one to allocate political energies in ways that will be most productive when these structural constraints are taken into account. Thus we find that a simple domino theory of the transformation to socialism is misleading and inadequate. Suppose that all firms or all nation-states adopted socialist relations internally but continued to relate to one another through competitive commodity production and political/military conflict. Such a hypothetical world-system would still be dominated by the logic of capitalism, and that logic would likely soon penetrate the internally "socialist" firms and states. This cautionary tale advises us to invest political resources in the construction of global organizations and in global organizing that forces existing organizations to become democratic.

Organizing Globally

That the emancipation of labour is neither a local nor a national, but a social problem, embracing all countries in which modern society exists, . . . this International Association and all societies and individuals adhering to it, will acknowledge truth, justice, and morality, as the basis of their conduct towards each other, and towards all men, without regard to color, creed, or nationality.
　　　　—From the "Inaugural Address and Provisional Rules of the
　　　　International Working Men's Association," Karl Marx, 1864

Over 135 years after the founding of the First International, the benefits of transnational organization are greater than ever, and increasing. Yet, the unity of political purpose and shared vision of a better world among workers and other progressive forces are perhaps at an all-time low. Why is this?

The full answer would require repeating most everything we have already said. Here we will focus on the question of social organizations organizing globally. Success for progressive movements has largely come from compelling states to enforce equal standards and to enact programs that raise standards within a national economy. Although most organizing takes place in the workplace or community, rather than in politics, labor requires a state that can fairly enforce contracts and spread benefits to the unorganized. The sovereign state, however, has lost efficacy with the increase in world integration and lost legitimacy as its programs have faltered. As the state's ability to manage its share of the world economy declines, movements that rely on state power suffer as well (Tilly 1995). Few who loathe government or think it incompetent will rally behind those dedicated to expanding state programs.

The statement above from the most prominent international labor organization of the nineteenth century embodies two different progressive agendas, "liberty" and "equality" (with "solidarity" being a source of both). Although the First International played but a small role, in the 135 years since its founding the spiraling trend of world revolutions has produced working-class success in both agendas. Liberation movements have produced juridical equality of individual citizens in the core and decolonization in the periphery. In a halting and still far from entirely complete fashion, slaves, ethnicities, races, and women became legally equal citizens at least in core states, roughly in that order. At times, both juridical and national forms of liberation have also meant loss of the dependent security of paternalism. Of greater importance to workers is that liberation lays the foundation for removing politically coercive sources of wage determination in the labor market and "superexploitation" of minorities and women in the workplace.

The other major labor success was in delivering the welfare state. Redistributive and protective welfare-state programs include poverty relief, old-age pensions, child-labor prohibitions, health insurance, occupational safety codes, environmental protection, and educational expansion. These now constitute a greater portion of core state budgets than does the military-judicial side that defines the state as the institution with a monopoly of legitimate violence. By setting a national floor on living standards, the welfare state shifted labor-market competition away from lower wages and toward greater productivity. This was a structural shift among core sates of tremendous value to average workers. Following World War II, rapidly increasing technological and human capital productivity in the core paid for both high wages for industrial workers and a slowly rising national floor. Unions led the creation of the welfare state, much more so than in increasing individual liberation, although success in one aided the other.

While far short of socialist or even liberal expectations, the combination of individual liberation and egalitarian welfare nevertheless dramatically improved the lives of working people in the core over the last hundred years. The extent of improvement is clear when compared, not to a utopian ideal of human relations, but to the rapacious "market despotism" that characterized the nineteenth century. Through state enforcement of welfare, the labor movement raised living standards for all workers, instead of just pursuing the select interests of union members. In fact, success has been sufficient to forestall revolutionary socialism in favor of reform wherever strong labor movements can make the state guarantee a class compromise (Przeworski 1985). The problem for the twenty-first century is that market despotism is making a rather impressive comeback.

The legitimacy of the state and of political action has declined correspondingly with the decline in state efficacy. Older generations lament noticeable losses of state-guaranteed benefits. Many among the younger generation have spurned youthful idealism for public cynicism and private nihilism. Globalization of cultural idioms further undermines the protection that national traditions and cultural diversity provided domestic markets from international competition. As such, decline of the state is seen as a crisis in national *values.*

It is no accident that every political leader in current times is disappointing at best. No head of state inspires confidence much less charts a path for other leaders to follow, as did the likes of Roosevelt and Churchill, or Lenin and Mao. Although vastly popular at times, neither left nor right respected and admired the ideological course set by Bush, Clinton, or Blair, no matter how far they tacked in one direction or the other. Lest Clinton's wobbly personality be blamed, his conservative contemporaries such as John Major and Boris Yeltsin failed so miserably that their popularity occasionally careened down toward single digits in approval ratings. Alain Juppé piloted France into a whirlpool of social protest. Even once-inspiring protest leaders such as Lech Walesa, Corazon Aquino, or Benazir Bhutto appeared adrift once they obtained state power. While political pundits endlessly sing the siren song of personal "character" and "values," they do so only because they have no faith that any policy, plan, or platform is obviously better than any other. Wily politicians respond by competing over who would be better at doing less. The problem, however, is not in the leaders, but rather, it is the sovereign state itself that has lost efficacy.

The decline of state efficacy has its main source in the rapid increase in the pace of globalization that has occurred over the last two decades. Increased economic and cultural interpenetration across state boundaries is obvious to most observers. When important parts of your breakfast have been jetted in from another hemisphere, you are living in a global system. States have always faced the trade-off in which raising domestic living standards through welfare programs or protective legislation reduces the ability of domestic firms to compete with those in less generous or less developed societies. What differs now is that world economic integration has risen to such a level, and continues to escalate so rapidly, that the trade-off has shifted markedly toward competition for ever lower labor costs. This is a shift in the global division of labor between core and periphery as well as a reorganization of industrial relations in the core. A much greater portion of core workers are now in direct competition with each other and with semiperipheral labor, a situation more similar perhaps to the period prior to the "second" industrial revolution at the end of the nineteenth century. Educated and professional workers still fare well, especially those in industries such as information technology that are rapidly growing. These valued employees increasingly differ from their more easily replaceable brethren and income inequality increases. Hardest hit have been low-skill industrial and service workers, especially less educated, immigrant, and dependent groups.

Economic interdependence and vastly increased power of transnational corporations have pitted competing states against one another to an extent not witnessed in the previous waves of globalization. But in addition to this, the states have been weakened by a massive ideological attack sponsored by a newly strengthened global fraction of the world capitalist class and supported by many citizens who felt they were not benefiting from the welfare institutions that had emerged after World War II. Robust growth during the 1990s tempered market despotism, which ironically aided in the erosion of support for traditional institutional safeguards against recessions. The welfare side of the progressive agenda has come under increasing attack and steady reversal. With globalization has come a neoliberal world order in which economic growth and state welfare are increasingly at odds.[12]

Explanations of stagnant wages, declining unions, increased child labor, corporate restructuring, government deficits, and shrinking welfare provision all point in varying degrees to increased world integration. Confronting declines in traditional unionized industries and declines in the efficacy of social action, labor unions have shrunk throughout the core. From 1980 to 1988, union density rates have declined by 1.4 percent in Canada to over 36 percent in France, with most countries showing continued decline or no change going into the 1990s. The decline began in the 1970s for many core countries, with the United States and Britain showing the largest overall losses. Only the Scandinavian countries appeared immune to decline in the 1980s, but unions have stagnated even there during the 1990s (Galenson 1994).

Global Governance and Labor Politics

Labor unions and politics have had a long history of internationalism, at least since the First International formed in 1864.[13] Many of the existing international labor organizations hail from the labor radicalization during the world revolution of 1968. As an organizing strategy to match the profusion of organized international capital, the attempt largely failed, mainly due to corporate resistance and to Cold War politics (Levinson 1972; Northrup and Rowan 1979).[14] The most powerful association, the International Federation of Free Trade Unions, opposed collaboration of its member unions with communist unions and international organizing floundered over the issue.

Since 1989–1992, the collapse of communism has made Cold War issues mute and globalization has brought new attention to international organizing and union collaboration.[15] For instance, in January 1998, AFL-CIO President John Sweeney made the first official visit to Mexico of someone in his office since Samuel Gompers toured the country in 1924 as president of the AFL.[16] After three-quarters of a century of neglect, the AFL-CIO's alarm over conditions in Mexico is only one cry in a chorus of demands for and debates over social policies to accompany deepening global and regional economic integration. These cries for action fall to a weakened labor movement that only since the formation of the EU and NAFTA has acquired a political locus for enforcing results of organizing that crosses state boundaries.

Multistate Polities and Labor Politics

We have discussed how the multistate institution created by the European Union, while not an advocate for global democracy itself, will create opportunities for labor and other progressive movements.[17] One source of opportunities is the Social Chapter of the 1993 Treaty on the European Union (Maastricht Treaty), which seeks to harmonize minimum labor and social polices across the EU and prevent undercutting competition over wages or working conditions. The Social Chapter, which began in 1989 as the Social Charter, does not enhance the power of labor organizations, but it does mandate desirable social standards for minimal working conditions and labor market mobility. To the extent that it is enforced,[18] applying a global version would be in the interest of EU workers and states, as well as the interests of semiperipheral workers. An EU-led world-system would thus be more vulnerable (or sensitive) to political pressure from the semiperiphery and links between it and core labor.

The strength of the Social Chapter is in its institutional procedures for binding enforcement in the European Court of Justice. While it does not give labor a voice commensurate with business in setting standards, labor and other progressive groups have indirect political representation in the European Parliament. To be sure, the Parliament is politically weak (although it should grow in importance) and there is the real possibility that the Social Chapter will be reversed, ignored, or tied up in procedure as happens in U.S. labor law. Neoliberal devolution of the EU industrial-relations system will not go uncontested, however. This was nowhere more evident than during the month of massive strikes by public workers in France in late 1995 (Cassen 1996; Ramonet 1996). The French state faced an EU requirement that it drop its deficit from 5 to 3 percent of GDP by 1997 in order to join the single currency union of the euro. France's conservative government at the time designed the cuts to come mainly from the constituency of its opposition, public workers. But such rapid deficit reduction would have caused significant pain throughout French society where unemployment was already in double digits, leading to widespread support for the strikers despite the personal inconveniences. Failure to adopt the euro, however, would mean a lost opportunity to discard costly and nonproductive currency and other transactions. France's economic growth is heavily entailed in continuing European integration, so that reversal would also cause severe economic dislocation. Despite a huge outpouring, the Conservative government's concessions were small and designed to give in only where it would not derail the overall goal.

A Socialist Party victory in the next election proved the inadequacy of any response the Conservatives could make. Jospin, the Socialist premier, has shifted some of the cost to the wealthy and has benefited from a more robust world economy in an apparently successful bid to reach the euro standards. Yet he too is making some welfare cuts, with little public resistance. The difference is an earned trust among the working classes that the benefits of the European Union will come their way. Whether the Socialists can maintain that trust depends in part on whether they can upgrade the Social Chapter, including pursuing a global version in the form of a "Global Charter."

An alternative model and bleak contrast is the situation of labor with respect to NAFTA and its sideshow, the North American Agreement on Labor Cooperation. The agreement's primary objective is to ensure that each country promotes compliance only with its own labor laws, and provides only symbolic means for cross-border enforcement (Stevis and Boswell 1999). The lack of much progress toward international labor cooperation among the unions of three proximate countries with only three major languages indicates that the road to real labor internationalism is a rocky one. Sweeney's visit highlighted labor's concerns over working conditions in Mexico and how they affect U.S. workers in the post-NAFTA era. More important than the publicity, however, is that President Sweeney made a point of publicly endorsing independent unions in Mexico. In defiance of its nominal counterpart in Mexico (the Mexican Workers' Federation), which had supported NAFTA, the AFL-CIO is supporting independent Mexican unions that target multinational corporations.[19] With declining state power and without a strong multistate apparatus to influence, organizing independent unions not connected to corporatist policies of an impotent state may be the best option at present. Besides being significant in their own terms, the EU and NAFTA policies are likely alternative models for future global and regional policies.

The labor provisions and social standards being attached to multistate agreements are arguably better than conditions at the global level, where the International Labor Organization is ineffectual and the WTO refuses to consider labor issues. We want to be careful not to overstate their importance or to romanticize the Social Chapter. The industrial-relations policies of several member countries are more progressive and there is a potential for these to regress to the EU mean. The regional blocs directly affect unions and provide them with new arenas for progressive contestation, but only as long as they are able to counter the divide-and-conquer strategy that capital has long employed. Successful organization in the EU and North America will enhance the global power of labor and will facilitate global coordination and collaboration. In this regard, labor-oriented INGOs can play a positive role, even without changing into a more federal or unitary type of organization. On the one hand, they can provide an overarching forum for the exchange of information and for communications among unions. Additionally, they can constitute the networks in which proposals for a global labor agenda can be aired, debated, and agreed upon (Keck and Sinkink 1998). On the other hand, they can be a means for helping to keep regional and sectoral efforts from degenerating into competition. Finally, the most progressive potential lies in the Social Chapter being an example for other multistate associations and the UN to adopt when faced with social conflict. A cluster of revolutionary events throughout the semiperiphery, for instance, could lead multistate associations, IGOs, and even frightened transnational corporations to search for new institutional arrangements that would guarantee a global charter of minimal standards.

Labor faces formidable tasks. The world economy has been moving in a neoliberal direction that diminishes domestic welfare, yet lacks democratic ways to establish international welfare institutions. The IGOs that could provide a forum for labor are weak and have marginalized labor's voice. Regional multistates in the core offer a stronger forum across borders, but have so far weakened the role of labor within states. Existing labor organizations are far from having common global or regional strategies. While the end of the Cold War offers opportunities for unity, labor organizations have to confront important challenges.

As labor's demise is entailed with the decline of the welfare state and rise of international governance, we would expect that deepening global integration will produce a resilient and compelling international labor presence in response. The bulk of core labor's predicament is due to the global competitive and technological transformations that we have outlined above, along with prohibitive state practices and resolute resistance by transnational corporations.[20] We should expect to and do find the most active and growing labor movements in the semiperiphery. To link these with core labor and social movements requires some form of international institutions, but we recognize that IGOs and INGOs are not inherently advantageous to workers and they should not be labor's only focus of action. Even if labor achieves greater global organizational and programmatic cohesion, there will still be immense obstacles to overcome. Labor rights do not have the fungibility of property rights, the enforceability of contractual agreements involving commodities, or the legitimacy of religious edicts and rituals. At present, patent violations stir a greater fury among global enforcers than do violations of child labor laws. No transnational legal or normative rules for workers match what is in place for capital, traders, states, or even churches. Nor do any of the shared principles that constitute the emerging world polity do so by directly empowering labor unions. The cognitive parameters of what exists will have to be changed.

World integration may benefit some skilled and educated core workers in the form of lower consumer prices and resulting economic expansion. But downsized skilled workers as well as unskilled and uneducated workers are increasingly competed down in the race toward the bottom in the name of global competitiveness. Numerous studies document how globalization produces core deindustrialization of mass production, with a consequent rise in inequality (Ross and Trachte, 1990; Braun 1997). Even among many skilled and educated workers, job shifts and benefit losses have created new possibilities for white-collar/blue-collar labor solidarity. Well-organized workers in countries that are winning in the competitive struggle gain increases in their incomes. This produces a labor politics of social democracy or of business unionism at the national level. But growing globalization of the economy undermines national unions and parties. Without a voice in the world polity, workers are unable to guarantee that the benefits of economic expansion will not be hoarded by capital.

Labor and the New Left:
Peace, Women's, and Environmental Movements

We have spoken in depth so far only of labor politics, and then only in terms of international unionization. This may surprise some, as labor unions and labor parties have been in decline of late in core countries, and the most international aspects of progressive politics are much more likely to be found in the "new" social movements. World market integration and transnational corporations are driving all organizations to face globalization. Among progressive movements, the peace, women's, environmental, and indigenous movements are at the forefront in building world politics. The global women's movement has made great strides in bringing together women from every continent to examine common interests and the issues that divide women of different classes, nations, and core-periphery status (Moghadam 1994). The cross-cultural nature of patriarchy makes for a proliferation of national women's movements, the international cooperation of which has logically followed. UN conferences have gone far in terms of organizing international cooperation into truly global concerns for women and environmentalists. The environmental movement, like the peace movement, has become globally organized because the problems of the biosphere are global in scope, as are the problems of peace. Greenpeace is perhaps the organization that is closest in character and action to Wagar's World Party.[21]

The relative disappointment of labor unions in matching the international organization of these movements, at least in popular perception, is in part a motivation for us to spend some of our effort on explaining the predicament of labor unions per se. Unions are critically important. They have long been the backbone of democracy and unionization is the single most important determinant in explaining the level of social welfare effort in core countries. More importantly, however, is that from a global perspective, the distinctions among these "old" and "new" movements begin to blur and their interests and goals begin to become intertwined. Once beyond national borders, progressive movements of all types increasingly take on goals and characteristics of the labor movement. While the class structure of the United States and other wealthy core countries is quite diverse, the vast bulk of the world population is made up of workers and peasants (with the latter almost entirely commodified and increasingly proletarianized in various forms). Further, where international politics is most relevant, the antagonists are most likely to be transnational corporations.

The critical unifying aspect from a long-term global perspective has been labor's political expression in the form of democratization itself. An impressive recent study by Rueschemeyer, Stephens, and Stephens (1992) demonstrates that the *working class* has been the central actor in democratization throughout the world (as opposed to earlier works that credited the bourgeoisie for democracy by considering "democratic" those republics that left the bulk of the population disenfranchised). Of fundamental importance is that democratic states can enforce the terms of a settlement between classes, guaranteeing labor gains without constant mobilization and ensuring labor social peace without resort to constant state repression (Przeworski 1985, 1991). Where it has been achieved, democracy has been labor's most significant gain, both as a way to limit the rapaciousness of the state and as a way to use the state to further progressive goals. This is a well-established relationship within states, which we will not belabor here. Let us instead briefly discuss how democratization is a critical unifier.

What of world peace movements? Although it is often not recognized as such, labor movements and peace movements are intertwined because both are efficacious to the extent that they foster democracy. This does not mean that labor movements always consciously support peace movements or even that they are natural allies. Peace and union organizations do frequently cooperate, and of course all workers have a general interest in peace. But interests sometimes conflict, as when unions represent workers in the defense industry. What connects them is democracy itself.

The most important factor in lowering the probability of war is *democracy*. Entrenched in the core since World War II, parliamentary democracy is becoming the norm among states in the semiperiphery and periphery. Historically, core democracies have rarely fought one another (Russett 1994). Electoral democracy deters war in the following eight ways: (1) restrains the autonomy and risk-taking of state leaders; (2) makes leaders justify wars in terms of popular self-interest (especially long ones); (3) gives voice to the victims of war; (4) creates an incentive to expand social spending (thus restraining military spending); (5) reduces the ability of capitalists to translate their particular interests into imperial-state interests; (6) makes democratic opponents difficult to demonize; (7) limits the time in power of leaders and governments; and (8) makes political commitments for peace, and for enforcing it, more credible when they have been debated and have found popular support. Of course democracies may deteriorate into dictatorships (i.e., Germany in the 1930s) or may suffer a majority tyranny (i.e., the former Yugoslavian states). The constraints are not absolute, but they have proven to be war's most powerful deterrent.

The importance of democracy, both state and global, should also be obvious for the efficacy of environmental and women's movements. No more telling is the dismal environmental experience in Eastern Europe. The lack of democratic rights permitted states and enterprises to engage in massive amounts of destructive pollution, often without the knowledge of the public and with little recourse when it was known. Environmental calamities were crucial in hastening the downfall of the communist states, Chernobyl rightly being the most famous. We should add that those typically most adversely affected by Chernobyl and other such disasters were the on-site workers and their families. There is an obvious labor constituency for environmental safety and even for much aesthetic protection. Where environmental and labor concerns differ most is over questions of economic development and growth. Given the massive poverty in most of the world, the debate is fruitful when it leads to devising methods for sustainable growth over the long term. Again, the communist-state experience hammers home the fact that eventually development is lost when the debate for alternatives to pollution is absent.

Perhaps less obvious, but more important, are the more direct labor aspects of women's movements at the global level. Central to most women's rights is the right to work itself, that is, eliminating the layers of patriarchy that prevent women from earning independent sources of income equal to males. Women's labor-force participation rates alone are important determinants of their overall social and physical well-being (and that of their children). With women's labor-force participation comes a greater return to, and desire for, education, starting with literacy in the poorest areas, along with greater urbanization. These in turn lead to smaller family sizes and better health access, which is the only desirable long-term remedy for overpopulation. Equally, women's limited rights in the semiperiphery are a prime source of their miserable wages and working conditions, which drag down all wages. Women workers on the global assembly line tend to be the world's most exploited (Ward 1990). While cultural heritages divide women on many issues, globally TNCs provide common ground on issues of work. Because of the large market and demographic effects, women's labor movements in the semiperiphery could be a vanguard movement for global change.

There are many other points that could be made, but these should be sufficient to clarify our position. At the global level, progressive movements are unified conceptually around political demands for national and global democracy. They also have their greatest commonality in demands for better living and working conditions for the working classes. This does not reduce all movements to labor movements, but it does logically put labor unions and parties at the center, where they have been historically. Vice versa, it means that the demands of women's and environmental movements that address working and living standards have the greatest global resonance.

While the core states are now all formally democratic, the larger multistate polities and the United Nations are only indirectly representative (the weak European Parliament notwithstanding) and few INGOs or IGOs are even broadly representative. International governmental organizations now serve as boards of directors for ruling states. For democratization to continue to restrain and utilize political power, social movements must *push for the extension of the consent of the governed to the global level.*

Global Democracy: Prospects and Strategies

The push to democratize world governance must come from "below," primarily from international labor unions, allied with other progressive movements. As in all previous world revolutions, a successful move to democratize a state is also likely to strengthen it. As such, movements to democratize international organizations are simultaneously movements to build a world state. Social and union movements need to become transnational actors to be efficacious globally. That is, global suffrage movements require a world party such as that proposed by Wagar (1996), which we discussed in the previous chapter, or some equivalent transnational organization, rather than an international collection of national parties. Vice versa, the world party or any other transnational social movement requires the construction of a world state to enforce a viable social contract.

Some critics of the idea of a world party contend that parties exist to contend for power in a state, and thus there can be no truly worldwide party until there is a world state. We would point out that there have been worldwide parties for centuries in the absence of a world state. For example, the Jesuits could be considered contenders for power within the European state system, and more recently, the Third International was such. Others seem to think that the idea of a formal party structure is outmoded in the information age and that a transnational network of the sort studied by Keck and Sinkink (1998) would be more appropriate. We support the idea of creating such networks for the purposes we have outlined, but we suppose that at some point the needs of group decisionmaking and institutional capability and continuity will require the formation of an actual party organization, or something like it. It will undoubtedly need to confront all the problems of democracy and oligarchic tendencies that progressive parties have faced in the past. But the alternative of leaving the future to itself is not really an option for those who understand the challenges that our species will face in the next century, or the opportunities lost through complacency.

Prospects

What are the prospects for a meaningful international labor politics? After fifty years of fruitless competition with its communist-dominated counterpart, the International Confederation of Free Trade Unions

(ICFTU) has emerged by default as the only viable international labor union. After some deliberation, the ICFTU has centered on globalization as its prime focus, emphasizing issues such as banning child labor. Heartening news, it must be tempered by the realization that the ICFTU is a federation of federations, with no direct authority or membership. It is mainly a representative of labor interests in the ILO and a conduit of information among members. No matter how successful in representing labor interests, the lack of any real enforcement power by the ILO limits success to symbolic victories. The regional situation is somewhat better with respect to the European Trade Union Confederation in the EU, but currently not very promising in North America. We have placed hope in militant labor movements in the semiperiphery, especially the NICs, and a new unionism is certainly evident.. These forces can play leading and catalytic roles. On the one hand, they can invent appropriate strategies for international labor politics. On the other hand, they can refocus the priorities of their own unions and federations. Such an impetus may not have to come from the top. Many locals, for instance, are well ahead of the parent unions and some unions pace their federations in internationalist tactics and strategies (Moody and McGinn 1992).

One problem is that many labor movements in the semiperiphery (and especially the periphery) are ideologically or programmatically nationalist. In our view, there is no a priori reason to believe that national radicalization will translate into global radicalization. In the absence of international mechanisms of collective action, even potentially internationalist labor movements will focus on national development and protection. Such a trend can be reinforced by various core union policies that reinforce nationalism or protectionism. The long-term solution is for core labor to support those developmental policies in the semiperiphery and periphery that will increase human productivity, such as primary education, and that emancipate workers from coercive conditions, such as increased women's rights. Increasing human productivity, rather than competing over who has the lowest wages, is the key to progressive global development. Standards that simply raise (semi)peripheral labor costs without raising productivity would cause capital flight from capital-poor areas.[22]

In this vein, we find "social movement unionism," whereby unions ally with or adopt the strategies of other social movements (Waterman 1993). Such alliances have historically been a source of expansion and innovation of the organizational and programmatic repertoire of labor. The next organizational and programmatic innovation necessary is for such alliances to become transnational and global movements. Global movement organizing also has great potential to affect the world polity directly (rather than mediated through states). Alliances will be strongest where the social-movement goals are work-related. There is no substitute for organizing people as workers as part of any alliance. Complementarily, unions cannot expect that all issues can be reduced to workplace concerns. The women's movement is an important example, as discussed above.

The prospects in the short run are only fair that labor movements will coalesce around a global program and will forge strong ties to women's, environmental, and peace movements. It is important to pick issues that can facilitate institution building of this sort. Among global labor issues, a requirement that TNCs and their subcontractors pay a global living wage is probably the single most important issue and would loom as the centerpiece of any global charter. A living wage is one that pays enough for a worker and one's family to have adequate food, clean water, elementary shelter, and other necessities according to the costs of the given community and country. It would be equivalent to the poverty level in the United States, which might seem an axiomatic minimum, but one which many exporters pay below by hiring mainly single women and/or drawing on labor from urban shantytowns that lack the above minimal conditions.

Another key issue is banning child labor, which would have the broadest appeal to forge movement links. Child labor may seem a major moral issue, but a rather small contributor to labor's global woes. This is true in the short run, and the immediate effect of an enforced ban would be increased hardship for many poor families. But from a longer-term perspective, there are ramifications of global significance. Banning child labor not only eliminates a source of cheap and highly exploitable labor, but it also stiffens the labor-supply elasticity of parents who must factor in greater child-care costs. The benefits to families of educating children also rise as the opportunity costs of lost work evaporate, as do the benefits to society of group supervision in schools of now idle children. Increased primary education, in turn, is a major source of higher productivity and growth in (semi)peripheral countries. All combined, these factors reduce fertility, which also has the long-term benefit of raising wages by restricting supply, and of increasing women's liberation.

The very strength of global capitalism and its present ideological and structural visibility present a new opportunity for organizing a counterhegemony on a global scale. The Washington Consensus on restructuring, deregulation, and privatization has caused such widespread grief that the world-system is becoming like a one-industry company town. Neoliberalism is a target that nearly all the popular movements can focus upon. In every country, there are political agents of the neoliberal "globalization project," usually the local sector of the global capitalist class and its allies. Cross-border organizing of resistance to these policies can be combined with support for strategies that are tailored to the specific conditions of each country. For example, in Guatemala the domestic neoliberals and their allies in the international financial organizations (the IMF and the World Bank) are relatively benign compared to the old landed oligarchy that wants to keep the peasants down on the farm. Cooperation and coordination between Guatemalan popular movements and progressives elsewhere requires that the specifics of the Guatemalan situation be taken into account (Chase-Dunn 1999).

Strategies

It is not possible to outline the specific strategies that global movements should follow. These can only be the result of the experiences of those engaged in progressive politics. We are willing to suggest a number of general challenges below that must be addressed before transnational movements can develop a consequential global politics.[23]

1. Transnational organizing may not be the best strategy in every case. International effects can also be achieved through coordinated action and social-movement alliance. Even when necessary, labor and other global movements must make informed judgment calls. The extent of integration is growing rapidly, but the degree and importance are highly uneven across the world economy.

2. International organizing will not be the mechanistic byproduct of world market integration. It will require more sharing of knowledge, more resources placed on transnational affairs, better education of members and, in general, concrete practical steps directed toward strategies of coordination and common action.

3. Weak federal organizations may be the easiest way to avoid national differences of interest, but they also tend to perpetuate labor's marginal role. While the appropriate organizations will have to take into account local conditions, they should reach some level of supranational authority with direct membership. The option of strong federations must be the long-term goal. Such federations could resemble the most democratic of the global environmental, human rights, or religious organizations.

4. The goals of international collaboration cannot be limited to coordinating existing unions. They must also include collective action and organizing of the unorganized workers and the unemployed, both in the core and the (semi)periphery.

5. Articulating transnational interests requires a new political discourse. The cognitive definitions of trade and rights will have to be changed to put labor rights on a par with patents and property. A global appeal to labor and social activists cannot be nationalist or narrowly self-serving; unions must embrace broader political and social agendas. A key step would be to promulgate a worldwide agenda, such as enunciating a "Global Charter." The center of the agenda would be a global living wage and a ban on child labor. Much of the practice of the agenda can start with global enforcement of existing laws and international standards.

6. Worldwide organizing is more likely to be closer in style to a social movement that is organized around a specific topic of broad appeal. Unions will benefit from strategic coordination with other progressive movements, such as women's and environmental organizations. A successful alliance for global action would offer the example and begin the training for other global organizing and for transforming existing IGOs. Specific campaigns could focus on planks of the Global Charter that have wide appeal. A good start would be worldwide abolition of child labor. Labor might draw solace from the example of the Abolitionist movement of the nineteenth century, whose broad-based but resource-poor international organizations drew on a collection of social, religious, and political allies to enact a nearly complete ban on slavery.

7. Global movements will need to deal with competition and conflict that may erupt between workers in different regional groupings, as well as between core and semiperipheral unions. A key question will be whose standards are adopted in trade, workplace, and other relationships that span state or regional boundaries.

8. Any global agenda must not be set at the expense of the unorganized workers in the core or the relatively poorer workers of the (semi)periphery. As such, a viable global living wage would be one that prevented wages from falling below subsistence level in each country, thus preventing degradation of human productivity and the subsidy of low wages with family subsistence labor. The living-wage level would rise with the level of development.

9. Global movements must contest the rules and organizations of international governance. While one should not limit strategies to only influencing IGOs or waste energy on purely symbolic fights, contract standards and market regulation are clearly shifting to the global level. There will surely be differences regarding both means and ends on this matter. To leave the rules of the new world order out of the agenda would, however, be folly.

10. A long-term strategy must address the issue of global democra-

cy. Continuing world economic integration will stimulate global political entities of growing relevance for determining the character of people's everyday lives. Labor, women's, environmental, and other progressive movements find themselves in an almost nineteenth-century situation of seeking global enfranchisement. We expect the movement for a voice in governmental institutions that span states to be for the twenty-first century what the movements to democratize national states were for the nineteenth and twentieth centuries.

Postscript: The First World Revolution Revisited?

Being world-system theorists, we find ourselves repeatedly drawn to theoretical analogies between historical periods centuries apart. Of past phases, the world-system now has some telling similarities with the early 1500s, when a previous world polity reigned over Europe. Enforcement of the then Catholic polity was taken up by the largest economic and military actor, then the Hapsburgs/Spain, now the United States. But the world leader in terms of innovation was Portugal, which was too small and tied to the old Catholic polity to become hegemonic—a fate perhaps now held by Japan. Leadership shifted to the Netherlands, whose organizational and technical innovations led the way to world hegemony when Spain was finally defeated.

   Dutch hegemony required a world revolution coming at the end of a global war. This was the key turning point in securing the transition to a capitalist world-system. We have cast the European Union in the role of the United Netherlands. Of all the current contenders, it has the greatest possibility of leading the world through another transition, this time to global democracy. To do so, the EU or any other world leader would have to provide a long-term and integrating rationale for democratizing global governance.

   We have argued that the potential for coordinated union and social action is better within the EU than any of the other emerging superblocs. This is not surprising given the political forum for coordination and the greater resources of European unions than elsewhere. What is important from a world-system perspective is that the EU offers a prime training ground for how to coordinate among diverse nations and serves as an institutional model to other potential blocs (including NAFTA). This has proven to be to its advantage in global forums where the EU is supplanting the United States as the initiator of global standardization in many technical and commercial fields (Loya and Boli 1999). If political integration is successful, then the EU could offer a real alternative to U.S. hegemony, although that contest probably remains at least a generation away. In the meantime, there is the potential for labor-

and social-movement success within the EU to cascade throughout the world economy. Such a spillover, however, will not take place unless an alliance of global movements—labor, environmental, and women's— and revolutionary states in the semiperiphery actively engage the challenge of internationalism. A cluster of revolts in the semiperiphery, when matched with demands from core social movements and peripheral states, could suddenly make debated issues of global standards an obvious solution. This would in retrospect appear to be a world revolution, one that would initiate new movements for global change. No world leader, not even a benign multistate hegemon, will move toward global democracy unless pushed by the disenfranchised. The force of the push depends on the extent that we can organize globally. While the probability of such a development in the next fifty years may not be high, it is more than just possible. It is a history we can choose to make.

Notes

1. Here is another point on which we differ from Wagar. He has the world war occurring in 2044 during the next K-wave downturn. Many assume that wars are most likely to occur during B-phases because they remember World War II. But research by Goldstein (1988) and Boswell and Sweat (1991) show that world wars are more likely to occur late in a K-wave upswing.

2. The assumption here and in step 6 is that there can be a future major war among core powers with modern weapons of mass destruction that does not destroy or radically disrupt the whole system.

3. In two other instances a world leader reached step 5 but failed to consolidate leadership into hegemony (Modelski and Thompson 1996; Boswell 1995).

4. Consecutive British and U.S. hegemonies have made English the premier lingua franca of the world-system, but developments in communications technology are radically lowering the costs of translation so that multilingual communication is much more feasible than ever before.

5. Recent deregulation of agriculture has been a major cause of antigovernment movements in core countries, including the United States (McMichael 1996).

6. Silver's (1995, pp. 158–169) research shows that the biggest outbreaks of labor unrest at the global level have occurred just following both World War I and World War II.

7. Jonathan Friedman (1994) contends that the multiplication of nationalist and indigenous identities that is legitimated by postmodern philosophy is a typical feature that emerges during hegemonic and imperial declines in all earlier civilizational systems as well.

8. One major result of heightened integration is that mass-production technology is increasingly commonplace. Firms using low-skill labor more easily move investment to the (semi)periphery where workers are less expensive and more oppressed, especially women workers. Core labor experienced "deindustrialization" (Bluestone and Harrison 1982), while newly industrialized countries

rose into the semiperiphery. Core production cannot compete with the (semi)periphery simply in terms of labor costs.

9. A fourth trade bloc, Mercosur, has emerged in the Southern Cone of Latin America.

10. Chase-Dunn (1990a) examined the problem of world-state formation in the context of how the capitalist mode of production has altered the long-run cycle of empire formation and disintegration that was typical of earlier world-systems in which tributary modes were dominant.

11. Despite all the recent progress toward disarmament, it is necessary to remember that warfare continues to be a legitimate way of resolving conflicts as long as there is an interstate system.

12. For an excellent overview of this particular issue, see Cox (1987, especially chapter 8).

13. For background and case studies, see Lorwin (1929, 1953).

14. Opposition to transnational organizing at that time also came from national unions, including the AFL-CIO (Ross 1973), and the largest German union, IG-Metal (Olle and Scholler 1977/1987, p. 40). Both feared communist entanglement.

15. See various articles in *Labor Research Review,* nos. 21 (1993) and 23 (1995); also see Boswell and Stevis (1997).

16. "U.S. Labor Leader Seeks Union Support in Mexico," *New York Times International,* January 23, 1998, p. A3.

17. The European Trade Union Confederation, formed in 1972, is the main umbrella organization. It has coordinated union action to influence the EU.

18. So far, enforcement has focused only on those standards that lessen the competitive advantages of the more underdeveloped member countries (Silvia 1991; Hall 1992; Rhodes 1995).

19. The AFL-CIO has also given support to workers elsewhere, such as in Guatemala (Armbruster 1998).

20. We cannot here deal with all the IGOs and labor organizations that are prominent in international labor politics. However, Boswell and Stevis's 1997 examination of the existing global and regional labor organizations inevitably points a second finger at factors internal to labor movements.

21. See, for instance, the Amsden-Rothstein debate in Rothstein (1995).

22. Similarly, indigenous movements have long organized globally to bring their issues before the League of Nations and the United Nations (Wilmer 1993). The resurgence of indigenous peoples in recent decades challenges the existing structure of sovereignties, the histories of conquest, and our ability to construct a just world in which cultural heritages and minority rights are respected.

23. This section and the preceding discussion draw on Boswell and Stevis (1997). We wish to acknowledge and thank the contribution of Dimitris Stevis, a political scientist at Colorado State University, who specializes in international labor and environmental issues.

References

Abonyi, Arpad. 1982. "Eastern Europe's Reintegration," pp. 181–203 in C. Chase-Dunn, ed., *Socialist States in the World System.* Beverly Hills: Sage.

Agee, Phillip. 1975. *Inside the Company: CIA Diary.* New York: Stonehill.

Amin, Samir. 1990. *Delinking: Towards a Polycentric World.* London: Zed Press.

———. 1992. *Empire of Chaos.* New York: Monthly Review Press.

Amsden, Alice H. 1995. "Hype or Help?" *The Boston Review* XX, no. 6 (December/January): 3–6.

Andors, Steven. 1977. *China's Industrial Revolution: Politics, Planning and Management, 1949 to the Present.* New York: Pantheon Books.

Armbruster, Ralph. 1998. "Cross-Border Labor Organizing in the Garment and Automobile Industries: The Phillips Van-Heusen and Ford Cuautitlan Cases." *Journal of World-Systems Research* 4: 20–41. http://www.csf.colorado.edu/wsystems/jwsr.html.

Arrighi, Giovanni. 1994. *The Long Twentieth Century: Money, Power and the Origins of Our Times.* New York: Verso.

Arrighi, Giovanni, Terence K. Hopkins, and Immanuel Wallerstein. 1989a. *Antisystemic Movements.* London and New York: Verso.

———. 1989b. "1968: The Great Rehearsal," pp. 19–33 in T. Boswell, ed., *Revolution in the World-System.* New York: Greenwood Press.

———. 1992. "1989, the Continuation of 1968." *Review* 15, no. 2 (spring): 221–242.

Arrighi, Giovanni, and Beverly Silver. 1999. *Chaos and Governance in the Modern World-System: Comparing Hegemonic Transitions.* Minneapolis: University of Minnesota Press.

Ash, Timothy G. 1983. *The Polish Revolution, 1980–82.* London: Johnathan Cape.

Babeuf, Gracchus. [1797] 1964. "Excerpts from the Trial of Babeuf," pp. 56–71 in F. Albert and R. Sanders, eds., *Socialist Thought: A Documentary History.* Garden City, NY: Anchor.

———. [1797] 1967. *The Defense of Gracchus Babeuf Before the High Court of Vendôme.* Edited & translated by John Anthony Scott. Amherst, MA: University of Massachusetts Press.

Bairoch, Paul. 1993. *Economics and World History: Myths and Paradoxes.* Chicago: University of Chicago Press.

———. 1996. "Globalization Myths and Realities: One Century of External Trade and Foreign Investment," pp. 173–192 in Robert Boyer and Daniel Drache, eds., *States Against Markets: The Limits of Globalization*. London and New York: Routledge.

Bardhan, Pranab K. 1993. "On Tackling the Soft Budget Constraint in Market Socialism," pp. 145–155 in P.K. Bardham and J.E. Roemer, eds., *Market Socialism: The Current Debate*. New York: Oxford University Press.

Bardhan, Pranab K., and John E. Roemer, eds. 1993a. *Market Socialism: The Current Debate*. New York: Oxford University Press.

———. 1993b. "Introduction," pp. 3–17 in P.K. Bardhan and J.E. Roemer, eds., *Market Socialism: The Current Debate*. New York: Oxford University Press.

Barr, Kenneth. 1979. "Long Waves: A Selective Annotated Bibliography." *Review* 2, no. 4: 675–718.

Bellamy, Edward. 1888. *Looking Backward 2000–1887*. Boston: Ticknor.

Bergesen, Albert. 1995. "Postmodernism and the World-System." *Protosoziologie* 7: 54–59.

Bergesen, Albert, and Roberto Fernandez. 1999. "Who Has the Most Fortune 500 Firms?: A Network Analysis of Global Economic Competition, 1956–1989," pp. 151–173 in Volker Bornschier and Christopher Chase-Dunn, eds., *The Future of Global Conflict*. London: Sage.

Bergesen, Albert, and Ronald Schoenberg. 1980. "Long Waves of Colonial Expansion and Contraction, 1415–1969," pp. 231–278 in Albert J. Bergesen, ed., *Studies of the Modern World-System*. New York: Academic Press.

Bernstein, Eduard. 1965. *Evolutionary Socialism: A Criticism and Affirmation*. New York: Schocken Books.

Bielasiak, Jack. 1982. "Party Leadership and Mass Participation in Developed Socialism," pp. 121–153 in J. Seroka and M.D. Simon, eds., *Developed Socialism in the Soviet Bloc: Political Theory and Political Reality*. Boulder: Westview Press.

Bierce, Ambrose. 1911. *The Devil's Dictionary*. London: Cornwall Press.

Block, Fred L. 1977. *The Origins of International Economic Disorder: A Study of United States International Monetary Policy from World War II to the Present*. Berkeley: University of California Press.

———. 1987. *The Mean Season: The Attack on the Welfare State*. New York: Pantheon Books.

Bluestone, Barry, and Bennett Harrison. 1982. *The Deindustrialization of America: Plant Closings, Community Abandonment, and the Dismantling of Basic Industry*. New York: Basic Books.

Boli, John, and George M. Thomas. 1997. "World Culture in the World Polity." *American Sociological Review* 62, no. 2: 171–190.

Boli-Bennet, John. 1980. "Global Integration and the Universal Increase of State Dominance, 1910–1970," pp. 77–108 in Albert J. Bergesen, ed., *Studies of the Modern World-System*. New York: Academic Press.

Bollen, Kenneth A., and Pamela M. Paxton. 1997. "Democracy Before Athens," pp. 13–44 in Manus Midlarsky, ed., *Inequality, Democracy and Economic Development*. Cambridge: Cambridge University Press.

Bonacich, Edna. 1972. "A Theory of Ethnic Antagonism: The Split Labor Market," *American Sociological Review* XXXVII, no. 5: 547–549.

Bonacich, Edna, Lucie Cheng, Norma Chinchilla, Nora Hamilton, and Paul Ong. 1994. *Global Production: The Apparel Industry in the Pacific Rim*. Philadelphia: Temple University Press.

Bornschier, Volker. 1996. *Western Society in Transition.* New Brunswick, NJ: Transaction Press.
———. 1999. "Hegemonic Decline, West European Unification and the Future Structure of the Core," pp. 77–98 in V. Bornschier and C. Chase-Dunn, eds., *The Future of Global Conflict.* London: Sage.
Bornschier, Volker, and Christopher Chase-Dunn. 1985. *Transnational Corporations and Underdevelopment.* New York: Praeger.
———, eds. 1999. *The Future of Global Conflict.* London: Sage.
Borocz, Jozsef. 1992. "Dual Dependency and Property Vacuum: Social Change on the State Socialist Semiperiphery." *Theory and Society* 21: 77–104.
———. 1993. "Simulating the Great Transformation: Property Change Under Prolonged Informality in Hungary." *Archives Europennes de Sociologie* 34, no. 1: 81–107.
———. 1999. "From Comprador State to Auctioneer State: Property Change, Realignment, and Peripheralization in Post-State-Socialist Central and Eastern Europe," pp. 193–209 in D.A. Smith, D.J. Solinger, and S.C. Topik, eds., *States and Sovereignty in the Global Economy.* London: Routledge.
Borocz, Jozsef, and David Smith. 1995. "Introduction: Late Twentieth Century Challenges for World-System Analysis," pp. 1–16 in David A. Smith and Jozsef Borocz, eds., *A New World Order? Global Transformation in the Late Twentieth Century.* New York: Praeger.
Boswell, Terry. 1987. "Accumulation Innovations in the American Economy: The Affinity for Japanese Solutions to the Current Crisis," pp. 95–126 in T. Boswell and A. Bergesen, eds., *America's Changing Role in the World-System.* New York: Praeger.
———, ed. 1989. *Revolution in the World-System.* New York: Greenwood Press.
———. 1989a. "Colonial Empires and the Capitalist World-System: A Time Series Analysis of Colonization, 1640–1960." *American Sociological Review* 54, no. 2: 180–196.
———. 1989b. "World Revolution and Revolution in the World-System," pp. 1–17 in T. Boswell, ed., *Revolution in the World-System.* New York: Greenwood Press.
———. 1995. "Hegemony and Bifurcation Points in World History." *Journal of World-System Research* 1, no. 15.
———. 1998. "Revolutions in the Core of the World-System," paper presented at the International Studies Convention, Minneapolis.
———. 1999. "Hegemony and Bifurcation Points in World History," pp. 263–284 in V. Bornschier and C. Chase-Dunn, eds., *The Future of Global Conflict,* London: Sage.
Boswell, Terry, and Christopher Chase-Dunn. 1996. "The Future of the World-System." *International Journal of Sociology and Social Policy* 16, nos. 7-8: 148–179.
Boswell, Terry, and William Dixon. 1990. "Dependency and Rebellion: A Cross-National Analysis." *American Sociological Review* 55, no. 4: 540–559.
———. 1993. "Marx's Theory of Rebellion: A Cross-National Analysis of Class Exploitation, Economic Development, and Violent Revolt." *American Sociological Review* 58, no. 5: 681–702.
Boswell, Terry, and David Jorjani. 1988. "Uneven Development and the Origins of Split Labor Market Discrimination: A Comparison of Black, Chinese and Mexican Immigrant Minorities in the United States," pp. 169–186 in J.

Smith et al., eds., *Racism and Sexism in the World-Economy*. Westport, CT: Greenwood.

Boswell, Terry, and Kristin Marsh. 1998. "Revolutions in the Core of the World System, 1492–1992." Presented at the annual meeting of the International Studies Association, Milwaukee, WI.

Boswell, Terry, and Ralph Peters. 1990. "State Socialism and the Industrial Divide in the World Economy: A Comparative Essay on the Rebellions in Poland and China." *Critical Sociology* 17, no. 1: 3–35.

Boswell, Terry, and Dimitris Stevis. 1997. "Globalization and International Labor Organizing: A World-System Perspective." *Work and Occupation* 24, no. 3: 288–308.

Boswell, Terry, and Mike Sweat. 1991. "Hegemony, Long Waves and Major Wars: A Time Series Analysis of Systemic Dynamics, 1496–1967." *International Studies Quarterly* 35, no. 2: 123–150.

Bowles, Samuel, and Herbert Gintis. 1990. "Contested Exchange: New Microfoundations for the Political Economy of Capitalism." *Politics and Society* 18, no. 2: 165–222.

Bowles, Samuel, David M. Gordon, and Thomas E. Weisskopf. 1983. *Beyond the Waste Land: A Democratic Alternative to Economic Decline*. Garden City, NY: Anchor Press/Doubleday.

Braudel, Fernand. 1984. *The Perspective of the World*. New York: Harper and Row.

Braun, Denny. 1997. *The Rich Get Richer*. 2nd ed. Chicago: Nelson-Hall.

Braverman, Harry. 1974. *Labor and Monopoly Capital*. New York: Monthly Review Press.

Brenner, Aaron. 1999. "International Rank-and-File Solidarity: Labor's Democratic Response to Globalization." Paper presented at the annual meeting of the International Studies Association, Washington DC, February 20, 1999.

Brucan, Silviu. 1989. *Pluralism and Social Conflict: A Social Analysis of the Communist World*. New York: Praeger.

Bukharin, Nikolai. [1917] 1973. *Imperialism and World Economy*. New York: Monthly Review Press.

Bunce, Valerie. 1985. "The Empire Strikes Back: The Evolution of the Eastern Bloc from a Soviet Asset to a Soviet Liability." *International Organization* 39: 1–46.

———. 1989. "The Polish Crisis of 1980–1981 and Theories of Revolution," pp. 167–189 in T. Boswell, ed., *Revolution in the World-System*. New York: Greenwood.

Burawoy, Michael. 1979. *Manufacturing Consent*. University of Chicago Press.

———. 1985. *The Politics of Production: Factory Regimes Under Capitalism and Socialism*. London: Verso.

Burns, John P., and Stanley Rosen, eds. 1986. *Policy Conflicts in Post-Mao China*. Armonk, NY: M.E. Sharpe.

Camus, Albert. 1991. *The Myth of Sisyphus, and Other Essays*. Translated by Justin O'Brien. New York: Vintage Books.

Cassen, Bernand. 1996. "Quand la societe dit 'non.'" *Le monde diplomatique*, no. 502 (January): 1, 8–9.

Cereseto, Shirley, and Howard Waitzkin. 1986. "Capitalism, Socialism and the Physical Quality of Life." *International Journal of Health Services* 16, no. 4: 643–658.

Chandler, Alfred. P., Jr. 1977. *The Visible Hand: The Managerial Revolution in American Business.* Cambridge: Harvard University Press.

Chase-Dunn, Christopher, ed. 1982. *Socialist States in the World-System.* Beverly Hills: Sage Publications.

————. 1990a. "World State Formation: Historical Processes and Emergent Necessity." *Political Geography Quarterly* 9, no. 2: 108–130.

————. 1990b. "Resistance to Imperialism: Semiperipheral Actors." *Review* 13, no. 1 (winter): 1–32.

————. 1992. "The Spiral of Capitalism and Socialism," pp. 165–187 in Louis F. Kreisberg, ed., *Research in Social Movements, Conflict and Change,* vol. 14. Greenwich, CT: Jai Press.

————. 1995. "World-Systems: Similarities and Differences," pp. 246–259 in Sing C. Chew and Robert A. Denemark, eds., *The Underdevelopment of Development: Essays in Honor of Andre Gunder Frank.* Thousand Oaks, CA: Sage.

————. 1998. *Global Formation: Structures of the World-Economy.* 2nd ed. Lanham, MD: Rowman and Littlefield.

————. 1999. "Guatemala in the Global System." *Journal of Interamerican Studies and World Affairs.* Special Issue on Guatemalan Development and Democracy.

Chase-Dunn, Christopher, and Terry Boswell. 1999. "Postcommunism and the Global Commonwealth." *Humboldt Journal of Social Relations* 24, no. 1/2: 195–219.

Chase-Dunn, Christopher, and Thomas D. Hall. 1997. *Rise and Demise: Comparing World-Systems.* Boulder, CO: Westview.

Chase-Dunn, Christopher, and Bruce Podobnik. 1999. "The Next World War: World-System Cycles and Trends," pp. 40–65 in V. Bornschier and C. Chase-Dunn, eds., *The Future of Global Conflict.* London: Sage.

Chase-Dunn, Christopher, and Richard Rubinson. 1977. "Toward a Structural Perspective on the World-System." *Politics and Society* 7, no. 4: 453–476.

Chase-Dunn, Christopher, Yukio Kawano, and Benjamin Brewer. 2000. "Trade Globalization Since 1795: Waves of Integration in the World-System." *American Sociological Review.* Millennial Symposium.

Chirot, Daniel, ed. 1991. *The Crisis of Leninism and the Decline of the Left.* Seattle: University of Washington Press.

Collins, Randall, and David Waller. 1992. "What Theories Predicted the State Breakdown and Revolution of the Soviet Bloc?" pp. 31–47 in Louis Kreisberg and David Segal, eds., *Research in Social Movements, Conflict and Change,* vol. 14. Greenwich, CT: JAI Press.

Comisso, Ellen. 1986. "State Structures and Political Processes Outside the CMEA: A Comparison," pp. 401–422 in Ellen Comisso and Laura D. Tyson, eds., *Power, Purpose and Collective Choice: Economic Strategy in Socialist States.* Ithaca, NY: Cornell University Press.

Comisso, Ellen, and Laura D. Tyson, eds. 1986. *Power, Purpose and Collective Choice: Economic Strategy in Socialist States.* Ithaca, NY: Cornell University Press.

Cox, Robert. 1987. *Production, Power and World Order: Social Forces in the Making of History.* New York: Columbia University Press.

Cumings, Bruce. 1987. "The Origins and Development of the Northeast Asian Political Economy: Industrial Sectors, Product Cycles and Political Consequences," pp. 44–83 in Fred Deyo, ed., *The Political Economy of New Asian Industrialism.* Ithaca: NY: Cornell University Press.

————. 1991. "Illusion, Critique, and Responsibility: The 'Revolution of '89' in West and East," pp. 100–128 in Daniel Chirot, ed., *The Crisis of Leninism and the Decline of the Left.* Seattle: University of Washington Press.

Curtis, Michael. 1986. *Totalitarianism.* New Brunswick: Transaction.

Dassbach, Carl, Nurhan Davutyan, Jianping Dong, and Barry Fay. 1995. "Long Waves Prior to 1790." *Review* 18, no. 2 (spring): 305–325.

Davies, James C. 1962. "Toward a Theory of Revolution." *American Sociological Review* 27: 5–19.

Deutscher, Isaac. 1949. *Stalin: A Political Biography.* Oxford: Oxford University Press.

Dixon, Bill, and Terry Boswell. 1996a. "Dependency, Disarticulation, and Denominator Effects: Another Look at Foreign Capital Penetration." *American Journal of Sociology* 102, no. 2: 543–563.

————. 1996b. "Differential Productivity, Negative Externalities, and Foreign Capital Penetration: Reply to Firebaugh." *American Journal of Sociology* 102, no. 2: 576–584.

Drainville, Andre C. 1995. "Left Internationalism and the Politics of Resistance in the New World Order," pp. 217–238 in David A. Smith and Jozsef Borocz, eds., *A New World Order? Global Transformations in the Late Twentieth Century.* New York: Praeger.

Drass, Kriss A., and Edgar Kiser. 1988. "Structural Roots of Visions of the Future: World System Crisis and Stability and the Production of Utopian Literature in the United States, 1883–1975." *International Studies Quarterly* 32: 421–438.

Eckstein, Susan. 1994. *Back from the Future: Cuba Under Castro.* Princeton, NJ: Princeton University Press.

Economic Report of the President. 1985. Washington, DC: U.S. Government Printing Office.

Economic Report of the President. 1989. Washington, DC: U.S. Government Printing Office.

Edwards, Richard. 1979. *Contested Terrain: The Transformation of the Workplace in the Twentieth Century.* New York: Basic Books.

Elster, Jon. 1978. "Exploring Exploitation." *Journal of Peace Research* 15: 3–17.

Engels, Frederick. 1935 [1882]. *Socialism: Utopian and Scientific.* New York: International Publishers.

Evans, Peter. 1995. *Embedded Autonomy: States and Industrial Transformation.* Princeton, NJ: Princeton University Press.

Fernandez-Kelly, Patricia. 1994. "Broadening the Scope: Gender and the Study of International Development," in A.D. Kincaid and A. Portes, eds., *Comparative National Development.* Chapel Hill: University of North Carolina Press.

Fisher, Louis. 1964. *The Life of Lenin.* New York: Harper and Row.

Folbre, Nancy. 1994. "Roemer's Market Socialism: A Feminist Critique." *Politics and Society* 22, no. 4: 595–606.

Frank, Andre Gunder. 1980. "Long Live Transideological Enterprise: The Socialist Economies in the Capitalist International Division of Labor and West-East-South Political Economic Relations," chapter 4 in A.G. Frank, ed., *Crisis: In the World Economy.* New York: Holmes and Meier.

————. 1989. "Liberty, Equality and Fraternity/Solidarity: From Transitory Revolution to Transformatory Social Movements," pp. 33–42 in T. Boswell, ed., *Revolution in the World-System.* New York: Greenwood.

———. 1998. *Reorient: Global Economy in the Asian Age.* Berkeley: University of California Press.

Friedman, David. 1988. "Beyond the Age of Ford: Features of Flexible-System Production," pp. 254–265 in F. Hearn, ed., *The Transformation of Industrial Organization.* Belmont: Wadsworth.

Friedman, Jonathan. 1994. *Cultural Identity and Global Process.* London: Sage.

Fukuyama, Francis. 1992. *The End of History and the Last Man.* New York: Free Press.

Galenson, W. 1994. *Trade Union Growth and Decline: An International Study.* New York: Praeger.

Gereffi, Gary, and Miguel Korzeniewicz, eds. 1994. *Commodity Chains and Global Capitalism.* New York: Praeger.

Gille, Zsuzsa. (forthcoming). "State Socialism's Wasted Legacies: The Rise and Fall of Industrial Ecology in Hungary." *World Development.*

Gills, Barry K. 1997. "Globalisation and the Politics of Resistance." *New Political Economy* 2, no. 1: 11–15.

Gilpin, Robert. 1981. *War and Change in World Politics.* Cambridge: Cambridge University Press.

Gitlin, Todd. 1987. *The Sixties.* New York: Bantam.

Goldfrank, Walter L. 1982. "The Soviet Trajectory," pp. 147–156 in C. Chase-Dunn, ed., *Socialist States in the World-System.* Beverly Hills, CA: Sage.

———. 1983. "The Limits of Analogy: Hegemonic Decline in Great Britain and the United States," pp. 143–154 in A. Bergesen, ed., *Crises in the World-System.* Beverly Hills: Sage.

———. 1989. "Harvesting Counterrevolution: Agricultural Exports in Pinochet's Chile," pp. 89–98 in T. Boswell, ed., *Revolution in the World-System.* Westport, CT: Greenwood.

———. 1999. "Beyond Cycles of Hegemony: Economic, Social and Military Factors," pp. 66–76 in V. Bornschier and C. Chase-Dunn, eds., *The Future of Global Conflict.* London: Sage.

Goldstein, Joshua. 1988. *Long Cycles: Prosperity and War in the Modern Age.* New Haven, CT: Yale University Press.

Goldstone, Jack A. 1991. *Revolution and Rebellion in the Early Modern World.* Berkeley: University of California Press.

Goodwin, Jeff. 1989. "Colonialism and Revolution in Southeast Asia: A Comparative Analysis," pp. 59–80 in T. Boswell, ed., *Revolution in the World-System.* New York: Greenwood.

Gorbachev, Mikhail S. 1987. *Perestroika: New Thinking for Our Country and the World.* New York: Harper and Row.

———. 1990 [1991]. "Address to the Soviet Communist Party," pp. 436–456 in Brinton and Rinzler, eds., *Without Force or Lies.* San Francisco: Mercury House.

Gordon, David. 1980. "Stages of Accumulation and Long Economic Cycles," in T.K. Hopkins and I. Wallerstein, eds., *Processes of the World-System.* Beverly Hills: Sage.

———. 1988. "The Global Economy: New Edifice or Crumbling Foundation?" *New Left Review* 168: 24–64.

Gordon, David, Richard Edwards, and Michael Reich. 1982. *Segmented Work, Divided Workers.* Cambridge: Cambridge University Press.

Gramsci, Antonio. 1971. *Prison Notebooks.* New York: International Publishers.

Greenwald, John. 1989. "Too Much All in the Family." *Time* (June 5) 133, no. 23: 23.

Greskovits, Bela. 1997. "Social Responses to Neoliberal Reforms in Eastern Europe," pp. 269–289 in Manus Midlarsky, ed., *Inequality, Democracy and Economic Development*. Cambridge: Cambridge University Press.

Grimes, Peter. 1996. "Economic Cycles and Mobility." Ph.D. dissertation, Johns Hopkins University, Department of Sociology, Baltimore.

———. 1999. "The Horsemen and the Killing Fields," pp. 13–42 in Walter Goldfrank and Andrew Szasz, eds., *Ecology and Capitalism*. Westport, CT: Greenwood Press.

Hall, Mark. 1992. "Legislating for Employee Participation: A Case Study of the European Works Councils Directive." *Warwick Papers in Industrial Relations*, no. 39.

Hall, Thomas D., ed. 1999. *A World-Systems Reader: New Perspectives on Gender, Urbanism, Cultures, Indigenous Peoples, and Ecology*. Lanham, MD: Rowman & Littlefield.

Harvey, David. 1989. *The Condition of Postmodernity*. Cambridge, MA: Blackwell.

———. 1995. "Globalization in Question." *Rethinking Marxism* 8, no. 4 (winter): 1–17.

Hearn, Frank, ed. 1988. *The Transformation of Industrial Organization*. Belmont: Wadsworth.

Hegel, Georg W.F. 1956. *The Philosophy of History*. New York: Dover.

Henige, David P. 1970. *Colonial Governors from the Fifteenth Century to the Present*. Madison: University of Wisconsin Press.

Hicks, Alexander. 1988. "National Collective Action and Economic Performance: A Review Article." *International Studies Quarterly* 32, no. 2: 131–154.

Hill, Christopher. 1958. *Puritanism and Revolution*. London: Secker and Warburg.

Hinton, William. 1990. *The Great Reversal: The Privatization of China, 1978–1989*. New York: Monthly Review Press.

Hirst, Paul, and Grahame Thompson. 1996. *Globalization in Question: The International Economy and the Possibilities of Governance*. Cambridge: Polity Press.

Hobsbawm, Eric. 1994. *The Age of Extremes: A History of the World, 1914–1991*. New York: Pantheon.

Hoerr, John. 1989. "The Payoff from Teamwork." *Business Week* (July 10) 3114: 56–62.

Holsti, Kalevi. 1991. *Peace and War: Armed Conflict and International Order, 1648–1989*. Cambridge: Cambridge University Press.

Hopkins, Terence K., and Immanuel Wallerstein. 1979. "Cyclical Rhythms and Secular Trends in the Capitalist World-Economy." *Review* 2: 483–500.

Huntington, Samuel P. 1996. *The Clash of Civilizations and the Remaking of World Order*. New York: Simon and Schuster.

James, C.L.R. 1963. *The Black Jacobins: Toussaint L'Ouverture and the San Domingo Revolution*. New York: Vintage.

Jameson, Fredric. 1991. *Postmodernism, or the Cultural Logic of Late Capitalism*. Durham, NC: Duke University Press.

Jonas, Susanne. 1991. *The Battle for Guatemala: Rebels, Death Squads and U.S. Power*. Boulder, CO: Westview.

Jones, T. Anthony. 1983. "Models of Socialist Development." *International Journal of Comparative Sociology* 24: 186–199.

Junne, Gerd. 1999. "Global Cooperation or Rival Trade Blocs?" pp. 99–118 in Volker Bornschier and Christopher Chase-Dunn, eds., *The Future of Global Conflict.* London: Sage.

Ju Zhongyi. [1980] 1986. "'New Economic Group' versus 'Petroleum Group,'" pp. 192–197 in J.P. Burns and S. Rosen, eds., *Policy Conflicts in Post-Mao China.* Armonk, NY: M.E. Sharpe.

Keck, Margaret, and Kathryn Sikkink. 1998. *Activists Beyond Borders: Advocacy Networks in International Politics.* Ithaca, NY: Cornell University Press.

Keister, Lisa A. 1998. "Engineering Growth: Business Group Structure and Firm Performance in China's Transition Economy." *American Journal of Sociology* 104, no. 2 (September): 404–440.

Kennedy, Paul. 1987. *The Rise and Fall of the Great Powers.* New York: Vintage.

Kentor, Jeffrey. 1998. "The Long-Term Effects of Foreign Capital Penetration on Economic Growth." *American Journal of Sociology* 103, no. 4 (January): 1024–1046.

Keohane, Robert. 1984. *After Hegemony.* Princeton, NJ: Princeton University Press.

Kincaid, A. Douglas, and Alejandro Portes, eds. 1994. *Comparative National Development.* Chapel Hill: University of North Carolina Press.

Kiser, Edgar. 1985. "Utopian Literature and the Ideology of Monopoly Capitalism: The Case of Edward Bellamy's *Looking Backward,*" pp. 1–26 in R. Braungart, ed., *Research in Political Sociology,* Vol. 1. Greenwich, CT: JAI Press.

Kiser, Edgar, and Kriss A. Drass. 1987. "Changes in the Core of the World-System and the Production of Utopian Literature in Great Britain and the United States, 1883–1975." *American Sociological Review* 52 (April): 286–293.

Kolko, Joyce. 1988. "On the Centrally Planned Economies." *Monthly Review* (April): 22–44.

Kondratieff, N.D. 1926 [1979]. "The Long Waves in Economic Life." *Review* 2, no. 4: 519–562.

Kornai, Janos. 1989. "The Hungarian Reform Process: Visions, Hopes, and Reality," pp. 32–94 in Victor Nee and David Stark, eds., *Remaking the Economic Institutions of Socialism.* Palo Alto, CA: Stanford University Press.

Korpi, Walter. 1983. *The Democratic Class Struggle.* London: Routledge.

Korzeneiwicz, Roberto P., and Timothy P. Moran. 1997. "World Economic Trends in the Distribution of Income, 1965–1992." *American Journal of Sociology* 102: 1000–1039.

Kowalewski, David. 1991. "Core Intervention and Periphery Revolution, 1821–1985." *American Journal of Sociology* 97, no. 1 (July): 70–95.

———. 1991. "Periphery Revolutions in World-System Perspective, 1821–1985." *Comparative Political Studies* 24, no. 1 (April): 76–99.

Krasner, Steven. 1985. *Structural Conflict: The Third World Against Global Liberalism.* Berkeley: University of California Press.

Kremple, Lothar, and Thomas Pluemper. 1999. "International Division of Labor and Global Economic Processes: An Analysis of the International Trade of Cars with World Trade Data," http://www.mpi-fg-koeln.mpg.de/~lk/netvis/globale/.

Kumar, Krishan. 1992. "The Revolutions of 1989: Socialism, Capitalism, and Democracy." *Theory and Society* 21, no. 3 (June): 309–356.

Kundera, Milan. [1978] 1981. *The Book of Laughter and Forgetting.* New York: Penquin.

Labor Research Review, no 21. 1993. "No More Business as Usual: Labor's Corporate Campaigns."

Labor Research Review, no 23. 1995. "Confronting Global Power: Union Strategies for the World Economy."

Laibman, David. 1995. "An Argument for Comprehensive Socialism." *Socialism and Democracy* 9, no. 2: 83–93.

Lange, Oskar. 1938. *On the Economic Theory of Socialism.* Minneapolis: University of Minnesota Press.

Larrabee, F. Stephen. 1989. "Perestroika Shakes Eastern Europe." *Bulletin of the Atomic Scientists* (March).

Lepak, Keith John. 1988. *Prelude to Solidarity: Poland and the Politics of the Gierek Regime.* New York: Columbia University Press.

Lenin, V. I. 1967. *On the United States of America.* Moscow: Progress Publishers.

———. 1970. *The State and Revolution.* Peking: Foreign Language Press.

Levinson, C. 1972. *International Unionism.* London: Allen and Unwin.

Levy, Jack. S. 1983. *War in the Modern Great Power System, 1495–1975.* Lexington: University Press of Kentucky.

———. 1985. "Theories of General War." *World Politics* 37: 344–374.

Lipietz, Alain. 1987. *Mirages and Miracles: The Crisis of Global Fordism.* London: Verso.

Lipset, Seymour Martin. 1991. "No Third Way: A Comparative Perspective on the Left," pp. 183–232 in Daniel Chirot, ed., *The Crisis of Leninism and the Decline of the Left: The Revolutions of 1989.* Seattle: University of Washington Press.

Lorwin, Lewis. 1929. *Labor and Internationalism.* New York: Macmillan Company.

———. 1953. *The International Labor Movement: History, Policies, Outlook.* New York: Harpers and Brothers Publishers.

Loya, Thomas A., and John Boli. 1999. "Standardization in the World Polity: Technical Rationalization over Power," pp. 169–197 in J. Boli and G.M. Thomas, eds., *Constructing World Culture: International Nongovernmental Organizations Since 1875.* Stanford: Stanford University Press.

Maddison, Angus. 1995. *Monitoring the World Economy, 1820–1992.* Paris: OECD

Mandel, Ernest. 1975. *Late Capitalism.* London: New Left Books.

———. 1980. *Long Waves of Capitalist Development.* Cambridge: Cambridge University Press.

Mander, Jerry, and Edward Goldsmith, eds. 1996. *The Case Against the Global Economy: And for a Turn Toward the Local.* San Francisco: Sierra Club Books.

Mann, Michael. 1993. *The Sources of Social Power,* Vol. 3, *The Rise of Classes and Nation-States, 1760–1914.* Cambridge: Cambridge University Press.

Marcuse, Herbert. 1964. *One Dimensional Man.* Boston: Beacon Press.

Marer, Paul, Janos Arvay, John O'Connor, and Dan Swenson. 1991. "Historically Planned Economies: A Guide to the Data." I.B.R.D. (World Bank), Socioeconomic Data Division and Socialist Economies Reform Unit.

Markoff, John. 1996. *Waves of Democracy: Social Movements and Political Change.* Thousand Oaks, CA: Pine Forge Press.

————. 1999. "From Center to Periphery and Back Again: Reflections on the Geography of Democratic Innovation," pp. 229–246 in Michael Hanagan and Charles Tilly, eds., *Extending Citizenship, Reconfiguring States.* Lanham, MD: Rowman and Littlefield.

Marx, Karl. [1846] 1983. "The German Ideology," pp. 162–196 in E. Kamenka, ed., *Portable Karl Marx.* New York: Penguin Books.

————. [1867] 1967. *Capital,* Vol. 1. New York: International Publishers.

Marx, Karl, and Fredrick Engels. [1848] 1983. "The Communist Manifesto," pp. 203–241 in E. Kamenka, ed., *The Portable Karl Marx.* New York: Penguin Books.

Mayer, Tom. 1994. *Analytical Marxism.* Thousand Oaks, CA: Sage.

McCormick, Thomas J. 1989. *America's Half Century: United States Foreign Policy in the Cold War.* Baltimore: Johns Hopkins University Press.

McMichael, Philip. 1996. *Development and Social Change: A Global Perspective.* Thousand Oaks, CA: Pine Forge Press.

McNally, David. 1990. "Beyond Nationalism, Beyond Protectionism: Labor and the Canada-U.S. Free Trade Agreement." *Review of Radical Political Economics* 22, no. 1: 179–194.

Mensch, Gerhard. 1978. *Stalemate in Technology.* Cambridge, MA: Ballenger.

Meyer, John W. 1987. "The World Polity and the Authority of the Nation-State," pp. 41–70 in G. Thomas, ed., *Institutional Structure: Constituting State, Society and the Individual.* Beverly Hills: Sage.

————. 1989. "Conceptions of Christendom: Notes on the Distinctiveness of the West," pp. 395–413 in Melvin L. Kohn, ed., *Cross-National Research in Sociology.* Newbury Park, CA: Sage.

————. 1999. "The Changing Cultural Content of the Nation-State: A World Society Perspective," pp. 123–143 in G. Steinmetz, ed., *State/Culture: State-Formation After the Cultural Turn.* Ithaca, NY: Cornell University Press.

Meyer, John W., John Boli, George M. Thomas, and Francisco Ramirez. 1997. "World Society and the Nation-State." *American Journal of Sociology* 103: 144–181.

Meyer, John W., John Boli-Bennett, and Christopher Chase-Dunn. 1975. "Convergence and Divergence in Development." *Annual Review of Sociology* 1: 223–246.

Michnik, Adam. 1990. "The Moral and Spiritual Origins of Solidarity," pp. 239–253 in W. Brinton and A. Rinzler, eds., *Without Force or Lies.* San Francisco: Mercury House.

Mies, Maria. 1986. *Patriarchy and Accumulation on a World Scale.* London: Zed Books.

Misra, Joya, and Terry Boswell. 1997. "Dutch Hegemony During the Age of Mercantilism." *Acta Politica: International Journal of Political Science* 32, no. 2: 174–209.

Mitchell, B.R. 1992. *International Historical Statistics: Europe 1750–1988.* 3rd ed. New York: Stockton.

————. 1993. *International Historical Statistics: The Americas 1750–1988.* 2nd ed. New York: Stockton.

————. 1995. *International Historical Statistics: Africa, Asia, & Oceania 1750–1988.* 2nd ed. New York: Stockton.

Mittelman, James H., ed. 1996. *Globalization: Critical Reflections.* Boulder, CO: Lynne Rienner.

Modelski, George, and William R. Thompson. 1988. *Seapower in Global Politics, 1494–1993.* Seattle: University of Washington Press.

———. 1996. *Leading Sectors and World Powers: The Co-Evolution of Global Economics and Politics.* Columbia: University of South Carolina Press.

Moene, Karl Ove, and Michael Wallerstein. 1993. "What's Wrong with Social Democracy," pp. 219–235 in P.K. Bardhan. and J.E. Roemer, eds., *Market Socialism: The Current Debate.* New York: Oxford University Press.

Moghadam, Valentine M. 1989. "Populist Revolution and the Islamic State in Iran," pp. 147–166 in T. Boswell, ed., *Revolution in the World-System.* New York: Greenwood.

———. 1994. "Women and Identity Politics in Theoretical and Comparative Perspective," pp. 3–26 in V. M. Moghadam, ed., *Identity Politics and Women: Cultural Reassertions and Feminisms in International Perspective.* Boulder, CO: Westview Press.

———. 1997. *Women, Work and Economic Reform in the Middle East and North Africa.* Boulder, CO: Lynne Rienner.

Moody, Kim, and Mary McGinn. 1992. *Unions and Free Trade: Solidarity vs. Competition.* Detroit: Labor Notes.

Muller, Edward N. 1986. "Income Inequality and Political Violence: The Effect of Influential Cases." *American Sociological Review* 51: 441–445.

———. 1988. "Inequality, Repression, and Violence: Issues of Theory and Research Design (Reply to Hartman and Hsiao)." *American Sociological Review* 53, no. 5 (October): 800–806.

———. 1989. "Democracy, Economic Development, and Income Inequality." *American Sociological Review* 53: 50–68.

Muller, Edward N., and Michell A. Seligson. 1987. "Inequality and Insurgency." *American Political Science Review* 81, no. 2: 425–449.

Murphy, Craig. 1994. *International Organization and Industrial Change: Global Governance Since 1850.* New York: Oxford.

———. 1999. "Egalitarian Social Movements and New World Orders." Presented at the annual meeting of the Eastern Sociological Society, Boston, March 4.

Navarro, Vicente. 1998. "Neoliberalism, 'Globalization,' Unemployment, Inequalities, and the Welfare State." *International Journal of Health Services* 28, no. 4: 607–682.

Nee, Victor. 1989. "Peasant Entrepreneurship and the Politics of Regulation in China," pp. 169–207 in V. Nee and D. Stark, eds., *Remaking the Economic Institutions of Socialism: China and Eastern Europe.* Stanford: Stanford University Press.

Nee, Victor, and Raymond V. Liedka. 1997. "Markets and Inequality in the Transition from State Socialism," pp. 202–226 in Manus Midlarsky, ed., *Inequality, Democracy and Economic Development.* Cambridge: Cambridge University Press.

Nee, Victor, and David Stark. 1989. *Remaking the Economic Institutions of Socialism: China and Eastern Europe.* Stanford: Stanford University Press.

Northrup, H.R., and R. Rowan. 1979. *Multinational Collective Bargaining Attempts: The Record, the Cases and the Prospects.* Multinational Industrial Relations Series, no. 6. Philadelphia: Industrial Research Unit, The Wharton School, University of Pennsylvania.

Offe, Claus. 1991. "Capitalism by Democratic Design?" *Social Research* 58, no. 4 (winter): 865–892.

Olle, W., and W. Scholler. [1977] 1987. "World Market Competition and Restrictions Upon International Trade Union Policies," pp. 26–47 in R.E. Boyd, R. Cohen, and C.W. Gutkind, eds., *International Labour and the Third World: The Making of a New Working Class.* Aldershot, UK: Avebury.

Ollman, Bertell, ed. 1998. *Market Socialism: The Debate Among Socialists.* London: Routledge.

Pagnucco, Ronald, and David Atwood. 1994. "Global Strategies for Peace and Justice." *Peace Review* 6, no. 4: 411–418. Special Issue on Transnational Social Movements.

Paige, Jeffery M. 1975. *Agrarian Revolution: Social Movements and Export Agriculture in the Underdeveloped World.* New York: Free Press.

Palmer, R.R. 1954. "The World Revolution of the West: 1763–1801." *Political Science Quarterly* 69, no. 1: 1–14.

People's Daily. [1981] 1986. "Heavy Industry Must Readjust Its Service Orientation," in J.P. Burns and S. Rosen, eds., *Policy Conflicts in Post-Mao China.* Armonk, NY: M.E. Sharpe.

Piore, M.J., and C.F. Sabel. 1984. *The Second Industrial Divide: Possibilities for Prosperity.* New York: Basic Books.

Polanyi, Karl. 1944. *The Great Transformation.* Boston: Beacon Press.

Poulantzas, Nicos. 1973. *Political Power and Social Classes.* London: New Left Books.

Przeworski, Adam. 1980. "Material Bases of Consent: Economics and Politics in a Hegemonic System." *Political Power and Social Theory* 1: 21–66.

———. 1985. *Capitalism and Social Democracy.* Cambridge: Cambridge University Press.

Putterman, Louis. 1991. *Democracy and the Market: Political and Economic Reforms in Eastern Europe and Latin America.* Cambridge: Cambridge University Press.

———. 1994. "Comments on A Future for Socialism." *Politics and Society* 22, no. 4: 489–505.

Pye, Lucian W. 1988. *The Mandarin and the Cadre: China's Political Culture.* Ann Arbor: University of Michigan.

Rady, Martyn. 1995. "1989 and All That." *Slavonic and East European Review* 73, no. 1 (January): 111–116.

Ramirez, Francisco O., Yasemin Soysal, and Suzanne Shanahan. 1997. "Cross-National Acquisition of Women's Suffrage Rights." *American Sociological Review* 62, no. 5: 735–745.

Ramonet, Ignacio. 1996. "L'espoir." *Le monde diplomatique,* no 502 (January): 1.

Rasler, Karen, and William R. Thompson. 1994. *The Great Powers and Global Struggle, 1490–1990.* Lexington: University of Kentucky Press.

Reich, Robert. 1992. *The Work of Nations.* New York: Vintage.

Rhodes, M. 1995. "A Regulatory Conundrum: Industrial Relations and the Social Dimension," pp. 78–112 in S. Leibfried and P. Pierson, eds., *European Social Policy: Between Fragmentation and Integration.* Washington, DC: Brookings Institution.

Robinson, William I. 1996. *Promoting Polyarchy: Globalization, U.S. Intervention, and Hegemony.* New York: Cambridge University Press.

———. 1997. "A Case Study of Globalization Processes in the Third World: A Transnational Agenda in Nicaragua." *Global Society* 2, no. 1: 61–91.

Roemer, John E. 1982. *A General Theory of Exploitation and Class.* Cambridge, MA: Harvard University Press.

———. 1988. *Free to Lose.* Cambridge, MA: Harvard University Press.

———. 1993. "Can There Be Socialism After Communism?" pp. 89–107 in P.K. Bardhan and J.E. Roemer, eds., *Market Socialism: The Current Debate.* New York: Oxford University Press.

———. 1994a. *A Future for Socialism.* Cambridge, MA: Harvard University Press.

———. 1994b. "A Future for Socialism." *Politics and Society* 22, no. 4: 447–478.

Roemer, John E., and Joaquim Silvestre. 1993. "Investment Policy and Market Socialism," pp. 108–119 in P.K. Bardhan and J.E. Roemer, eds., *Market Socialism: The Current Debate.* New York: Oxford University Press.

Ross, Irwin. 1973. "Labor's Big Push for Protectionism." *Fortune* 88, no. 3 (March): 92–97, 170, 172, 174.

Ross, Robert J.S. 1999. "Hot Under the Collar: Contradictions, Development and New Theory in the Anti-Sweatshop Movement." Presented at the annual meeting of the Eastern Sociological Society, Boston, March 4.

Ross, Robert J.S., and Kent C. Trachte. 1990. *Global Capitalism: The New Leviathan.* Albany: SUNY Press.

Rostow, Walt W. 1978. *The World Economy: History and Prospect.* Austin: University of Texas Press.

Rothenstein, Richard. 1995. "The Case for Labor Standards." *Boston Review* XX, no. 6 (December/January): 7–11.

Rothschilde-Whitt, Joyce. 1979. "The Collectivist Organization: An Alternative to Rational Bureaucratic Models." *American Sociological Review* 44: 509–527.

Rueschemeyer, Dietrich, Evelyne H. Stephens, and John D. Stephens. 1992. *Capitalist Development and Democracy.* Chicago: University of Chicago Press.

Ruggie, John G. 1998. *Constructing the World Polity.* London: Routledge.

Russett, Bruce. 1994. "The Democratic Peace," pp. 21–43 in Volker Bornschier and Peter Lengyel, eds., *Conflicts and New Departures in World Society.* World Society Studies, vol. 3. New Brunswick, NJ: Transaction Press.

Sakarov, Andrei. 1968 [1991]. "Thoughts on Progress, Peaceful Coexistence, and Intellectual Freedom" pp. 3–42 in W. Brinton and A. Rinzler, eds., *Without Force or Lies.* San Francisco: Mercury House.

Sampson, Steven L. 1989. "Romania: House of Cards." *Telos* 79: 217–224.

Sanderson, Stephen. 1994. *Social Transformations: A General Theory of Historical Development.* Cambridge, MA: Blackwell.

Schumpeter, Joseph. 1939. *Business Cycles.* New York: McGraw-Hill.

Schweickart, David. 1996. *Against Capitalism.* Boulder, CO: Westview.

———. 1998. "Market Socialism: A Defense," p. 723 in Bertell Ollman, ed., *Market Socialism: The Debate Among Socialists.* London: Routledge.

Scott, Catherine V., and Gus B. Cochrane. 1989. "Revolution in the Periphery: Angola, Cuba, Mozambique and Nicaragua," pp. 43–58 in T. Boswell, ed., *Revolution in the World-System.* Westport, CT: Greenwood.

Selden, Mark. 1988. *The Political Economy of Chinese Socialism.* New York: Sharpe.

Sewell, William. H. 1980. *Work and Revolution in France.* Cambridge: Cambridge University Press.

————. 1985. "Ideological and Social Revolutions: Reflections on the French Case." *Journal of Modern History* 57: 57–85.

Shannon, Richard Thomas. 1996. *An Introduction to the World-Systems Perspective.* Boulder, CO: Westview.

Shirk, Susan. 1989. "The Political Economy of Chinese Industrial Reform," pp. 328–364 in V. Nee and D. Stark, eds., *Remaking the Economic Institutions of Socialism: China and Eastern Europe.* Stanford: Stanford University Press.

Silver, Beverly. 1995. "World Scale Patterns of Labor-Capital Conflict: Labor Unrest, Long Waves and Cycles of Hegemony." *Review* 18, no. 1: 155–192.

————. 1996. "The Decline of Labor Militancy: A Core-Centric Myth?" A paper presented at the American Sociological Association meetings, New York, August 16–20.

Silver, Beverly, and Eric Slater. 1999. "The Social Origins of World Hegemonies," pp. 151–216 in Giovanni Arrighi and Beverly Silver, eds., *Chaos and Governance in the Modern World-System: Comparing Hegemonic Transitions.* Minneapolis: University of Minnesota Press.

Silvia, Stephen J. 1991. "The Social Charter of the European Community: A Defeat for European Labor." *Industrial and Labor Relations Review* 44, no. 4 (July): 626–643.

Simon, Maurice D. 1982. "Developed Socialism and the Polish Crisis," pp. 99–117 in J. Seroka and M.D. Simon, eds., *Developed Socialism in the Soviet Bloc: Political Theory and Political Reality.* Boulder: Westview.

Sklair, Leslie. 1991. *Sociology of the Global System.* Baltimore: Johns Hopkins University Press.

Skocpol, Theda. 1979. *States and Social Revolutions.* New York: Cambridge University Press.

Skvorecky, Josef. 1990. "Czech Writers: Politicians in Spite of Themselves," pp. 253–264 in W. Brinton and A. Rinzler, eds., *Without Force or Lies.* San Francisco: Mercury House.

Smart, Berry. 1994. "Sociology, Globalization and Postmodernity: Comments on the 'Sociology for One World' Thesis." *International Sociology* 9, no. 2: 149–160.

Smith, David A. 1996. *Third World Cities in Global Perspective: The Political Economy of Uneven Urbanization.* Boulder, CO: Westview.

Smith, David A., and Douglas White. 1992. "Structure and Dynamics of the Global Economy: Network Analysis of International Trade, 1965–1980." *Social Forces* 70, no. 4: 857–893.

So, Alvin Y., and Stephen W.K. Chiu. 1995. *East Asia and the World Economy.* Thousand Oaks, CA: Sage.

Sokolovski, Joan. 1982. "States, Classes and the Chinese Socialist Transition," pp. 157–180 in C. Chase-Dunn, ed., *Socialist States in the World-System.* Beverly Hills, CA: Sage.

Soros, George. 1998. *The Crisis of Global Capitalism.* New York: Pantheon.

Stark, David. 1996. "Recombinant Property in Eastern European Capitalism." *American Journal of Sociology* 101: 993–1027.

Stavis, Benedict. 1974. *Making Green Revolution: The Politics of Agricultural Development in China.* Ithaca, NY: Rural Development Committee.

Stephens, John. 1980. *The Transition from Capitalism to Socialism.* Atlantic Highlands, NJ: Humanities Press.

Stevis, Dimitris. 1998. "International Labor Organizations, 1864–1997: The Weight of History and the Challenges of the Present." *Journal of World-Systems Research* 4: 52–75. http://csf.colorado.edu/wsystems/jwsr.html

Stevis, Dimitris, and Terry Boswell. 1999. *Procedure and Substance in International Labor Policies: The North American Agreement for Labor Cooperation and the Social Chapter of the European Union*, unpublished manuscript.

Stinchcombe, Arthur L. 1994. "Class Conflict and Diplomacy: Haitian Isolation in the 19th-Century World System." *Sociological Perspectives* 37, no. 1 (spring): 1–23.

Strang, David. 1990. "From Dependency to Sovereignty: An Event History Analysis of Decolonization 1870–1987." *American Sociological Review* 55, no. 6: 846–860.

Su, Tieting. 1995. "Changes in World Trade Networks: 1938, 1960, 1990." *Review* 18, no. 3 (summer): 431–459.

Suter, Christian. 1992. *Debt Cycles in the World-Economy: Foreign Loans, Financial Crises and Debt Settlements, 1820–1990*. Boulder, CO: Westview.

Szelenyi, Ivan. 1989. "Eastern Europe in an Epoch of Transition: Toward a Socialist Mixed Economy," pp. 208–232 in Victor Nee and David Stark, eds., *Remaking the Economic Institutions of Socialism*. Palo Alto: Stanford University Press.

Tarrow, Sidney. 1994. *Power in Movement: Social Movements, Collective Action and Politics*. Cambridge: Cambridge University Press.

Taylor, Peter J. 1996. *The Way the Modern World Works: World Hegemony to World Impasse*. New York: John Wiley.

Terlouw, Cornelis P. 1992. *The Regional Geography of the World-System*. Utrecht, Netherlands: Rijksuniversiteit Utrecht.

Terrill, Ross. 1989. "China After Deng." *World Monitor* 2, no. 7: 28–37.

Therborn, Goran. 1980. *The Power of Ideology and the Ideology of Power*. London: Verso.

Thomas, George M., et al. 1987. *Institutional Structure: Constituting State, Society and the Individual*. Beverly Hills: Sage.

Thompson, William R. 1990. "Long Waves, Technological Innovation and Relative Decline." *International Organization* 44: 201–233.

Thurow, Lester. 1996. *The Future of Capitalism*. New York: William Morrow.

Ticktin, Hillel. 1998. "The Problem Is Market Socialism," pp. 55–81 in Bertell Ollman, ed., *Market Socialism: The Debate Among Socialists*. London: Routledge.

Tilly, Charles. 1985. "War Making and State Making as Organized Crime," pp. 169–191 in Peter Evans, Dietrich Rueschemeyer, and Theda Skocpol, eds., *Bringing the State Back In*. Cambridge: Cambridge University Press.

———. 1978. *From Mobilization to Revolution*. Reading, MA: Addison-Wesley.

———. 1993. *European Revolutions, 1492–1992*. Oxford: Blackwell.

———. 1995. "Globalization Threatens Labor's Rights." *International Labor and Working-Class History*, no. 47 (spring): 1–23.

Timberlake, Michael, ed. 1985. *Urbanization in the World-Economy*. New York: Academic.

Tobin, James. 1996. *Essays in Economics, National and International*. Cambridge, MA: MIT Press.

Trotsky, Leon. 1931. *The Permanent Revolution*. New York: Pioneer Publishers.

———. 1937. *The Revolution Betrayed*. New York: Merit Publishers.

United Nations. 1983–1984. *Statistical Yearbook.* New York: United Nations.

———. 1994. *World Investment Report 1994: Transnational Corporations, Employment and the Workplace.* New York: United Nations.

———. 1995. *The World's Women 1995: Trends and Statistics.* New York: United Nations.

Vogel, David. 1995. *Trading Up: Consumer and Environmental Regulation in a Global Economy.* Cambridge, MA: Harvard University Press.

Wagar, W. Warren. 1992. *A Short History of the Future.* 2nd ed. Chicago: University of Chicago Press.

———. 1996. "Toward a Praxis of World Integration." *Journal of World-Systems Research* 2, no. 2. http://csf.colorado.edu/wsystems/jwsr.html.

Wallerstein, Immanuel. 1974. *The Modern World-System.* Vol. I. New York: Academic Press.

———. 1980. *The Modern World-System.* Vol. II. New York: Academic Press.

———. 1984a. "The Three Instances of Hegemony in History of the Capitalist World-Economy." *International Journal of Comparative Sociology* 24: 100–108.

———. 1984b. *The Politics of the World-Economy: The States, the Movements and the Civilizations.* Cambridge: Cambridge University Press.

———. 1989. *The Modern World-System.* Vol. III. New York: Academic Press.

———. 1995. *After Liberalism.* New York: New Press.

———. 1997. "Liberalism and Democracy." *Acta Politica: International Journal of Political Science* 32, no. 2: 113–127.

———. 1998. *Utopistics.* New York: New Press.

Walton, John. 1984. *Reluctant Rebels.* New York: Columbia University Press.

Walton, John, and David Seddon. 1994. *Free Markets and Food Riots: The Politics of Global Adjustment.* Oxford: Blackwell.

Ward, Kathryn B. 1984. *Women in the World-System.* New York: Praeger.

Ward, Kathryn B., ed. 1990. *Women Workers and Global Restructuring.* Ithaca, NY: ILR Press, School of Industrial and Labor Relations, Cornell University.

Waterman, Peter. 1993. "Social-Movement Unionism: A New Union Model for a New World Order?" *Review* 16, no. 3 (summer): 245–278.

Weber, Max. 1946. "Class, Status and Party," pp. 180–195 in H. Gerth and C.W. Mills, eds., *From Max Weber.* New York: Oxford University Press.

———. 1978. *Economy and Society,* Vol. 1. Edited by Gunther Roth and Claus Wittich. Berkeley: University of California Press.

Weber, Robert Phillip. 1983. "Cyclical Theories of Crises in the World-System," pp. 37–55 in A. Bergesen, ed., *Crises in the World-System.* Beverly Hills: Sage.

Weede, Erich. 1981. "Income Inequality. Average Income and Domestic Violence." *Journal of Conflict Resolution* 25: 639–654.

———. 1999. "Future Hegemonic Rivalry Between China and the West?" in Volker Bornschier and Christopher Chase-Dunn, eds., *The Future of Global Conflict.* London: Sage.

Weisskopf, Thomas E. 1993. "A Democratic Enterprise-Based Market Socialism," pp. 120–141 in P.K. Bardhan and J.E. Roemer, eds., *Market Socialism: The Current Debate.* New York: Oxford University Press.

Weitzman, Martin L. 1984. *The Share Economy.* Cambridge, MA: Harvard University Press.

Wickham-Crowley, Timothy. 1991. *Guerillas and Revolution in Latin America.* Princeton, NJ: Princeton University Press.

Williamson, Oliver E. 1975. *Markets and Hierarchies*. New York: Free Press.
———. 1985. *The Economic Institutions of Capitalism*. New York: Free Press.
Wilmer, Franke. 1993. *The Indigenous Voice in World Politics*. Newbury Park, CA: Sage.
Wilson, William. 1996. *When Work Disappears*. New York: Vintage.
World Bank (I.B.R.D.). 1980. *World Tables*. 2nd ed. Baltimore: Johns Hopkins University Press.
———. 1983. *World Tables*, vol. 2. Baltimore: Johns Hopkins University Press.
———. 1998. *World Development Indicators*. http://www.worldbank.org/html/extpb/wdi98.htm.
Wright, Erik Olin. 1975. "Alternative Perspectives in the Marxist Theory of Accumulation and Crisis." *The Insurgent Sociologist* VI, no. 1 (fall): 5–40.
———. 1985. *Classes*. London: Verso.
Wright, Quincy. 1942. *A Study of War*. Chicago: University of Chicago Press.
Yang, Dori Jones, Bill Javetski, and William J. Holstein. 1989. "The Outside World Puts China on Hold." *Business Week* 3114 (July 10): 40–41.
Zilversmit, Arthur. 1967. *The First Emancipation: The Abolition of Slavery in the North*. Chicago: University of Chicago Press.

Index

vision of a better, 208–210; hegemonic stability, great power imperialism *vs.*, 108–109; inequality
reduced, political sources of, 91;
liberation movements, national,
81, 88; periphery brought into the
interstate system as formally sovereign states, 24; periphery brought
into the interstate system by, 45;
waves of, 59–60
Deindustrialization, 102, 105, 235
Democracy: core global zone, 203;
low intensity, 212; peace, international, 152; periphery global
zone, 152, 203; progress, the ideology of, 238; revolutions of 1989,
155; rights necessary for,
civil/individual human, 5–6; semiperiphery global zone, 152, 153,
203; social contracts, 153; social
movements on the global level,
239; war, democracy lowering
probability of, 237; workers partic-
ipating in struggles for, 132; working class, 155, 236–237. *See also*
Global democracy; Social democracy
Dependency, 26, 146, 192
Depressions, economic, 81, 92
Deregulation, 137, 211
Developing countries. *See* Third
World countries
Development strategy for rapid
industrialization by a semiperiph-
eral state, 85
Disruption of the global ecosystem,
220
Divides, world, 48, 98–106, 127–128.
See also Revolutions of 1989
Dominican Republic, 89
Domino theory of the transition to
world socialism, 4, 135
Drainville, Andre, 194
Dual dependency, structure of, 146
Dubcek, Alexander, 155
Dulles, Allen, 2
Dutch Revolution, 26, 60, 73, 87–88

East Timor, 173
Ecofascism, 220
Economic issues and system volatility: Asia, 28, 102, 143; austerity
regimes, 131, 137; capital intensification, 33; Chicago-school economic policies, 145, 149; China,
39; cycles of recession and stagnation, 10–11; debt, 103, 105, 112,
126, 142; democracy, economic, 6;
depressions, economic, 81, 92;
divides and national revolutions,
world, 100–106; efficiency, market, 137, 147; equality and growth,
tradeoff between, 150; Europe,
Eastern, 11–12; France, 233; globalization, economic, 33–34;
growth, economic, 100–104, 112,
150, 219, 231; inflation, 103, 124,
125; interdependence, economic,
231; interest rates, 189–190; labor
employing capital, 148–150;
loans, 121, 142, 190; market-based
solutions, 137; markets perceived
as evil, 147; nationalism, economic, 12; New Economic Policy
(NEP), 106–107; Poland,
115–116, 122; redistribution of
wealth, 190–191; revolutions,
world, 52, 71; revolutions of 1989,
99; Roemer's proposal, 180–184;
Russian Revolution of 1917, 71;
soft-budget constraints, 177; state
socialism, 11, 101, 136, 137, 139,
140; transnational corporate
investment, 27–28, 185, 188–190,
193, 238; United States, 219; wel-
fare state and economic growth at
odds, 231. *See also* Capital;
Capitalism; Kondratieff long wave
(K-wave)
Education, 139, 194, 224–225
Efficacy, decline in state, 230
Efficiency, market, 137, 147
Egalitarianism, 183, 194, 218–219
Elected government, 6
Electoral democracy, 237
Electrical energy, 139
El Salvador, 89, 145
Employee ownership, 188. *See also*
Labor
End of Racism, The, 172
Energy consumption, 140, 141
Engels, Friedrich, 76

About the Book

At the core of this book is the argument that, though the word "social-ism" is widely held in disdain in the current discourse about the world's past and its future, the idea of socialism as collective rationality and popular democracy is far from dead.

Boswell and Chase-Dunn describe a spiral of capitalism and social-ism—of economic expansion and social progress—that creates repeated opportunities for positive transformation at the global level. They con-tend that social democracy is both desirable and possible at the level of the world-system. And they present a straightforward, compelling case in support of that contention.

The book begins with an explanation of the structural dynamics of the world-system and goes on to explore the great failures, and the limit-ed successes, that were the outcome of efforts to build a state-socialist "second world." A final section addresses the possible futures of the world-system and, especially, how to move realistically toward global democracy.

Terry Boswell is professor and chair of sociology at Emory University. He is author of *America's Changing Role in the World-System* and *Revolution in the World-System*. **Christopher Chase-Dunn** is professor of sociology at Johns Hopkins University. His recent publications include *Rise and Demise: Comparing World-Systems* and *The Future of Global Conflict*.